THE PHILIPPINE
ISLANDS, 1493-1898

EMMA HELEN BLAIR

THE PHILIPPINE ISLANDS, 1493-1898

VOLUME I, 1493-1529

explorations by early navigators, descriptions of the islands and their peoples, their history and records of the catholic missions, as related in contemporaneous books and manuscripts, showing the political, economic, commercial and religious conditions of those islands from their earliest relations with European nations to the beginning of the nineteenth century

with historical introduction and additional notes by
Edward Gaylord Bourne.

BIBLIOBAZAAR

THE PHILIPPINE
ISLANDS, 1493-1898

CONTENTS

Papal Bulls of 1493: Inter cætera (May 3), Eximiæ (May
3), Inter cætera (May 4), Extension de la concesion
(September 25). Alexander VI; Rome, 1493

Treaty of Tordesillas. Fernando V and Isabel of Castile,
and João II of Portugal; Tordesillas, June 7, 1494

[Note on correspondence of Jaime Ferrer regarding the
Line of Demarcation—1493-95.]

Compact between the Catholic Sovereigns and the King of
Portugal. Fernando V and Isabel of Castile, and João II
of Portugal; Madrid, April 15, 1495.

Papal Bull, Præcelsæ Leo X; Rome, November 3, 1514.

Instructions from the King of Spain to his ambassadors.
Cárlos I of Spain; Valladolid, February 4, 1523.

Letter to Juan de Zúñiga. Cárlos I of Spain; Pamplona,
December 18, 1523.

Treaty of Vitoria. Cárlos I of Spain, and João III of
Portugal; Vitoria, February 19, 1524 Junta of Badajoz:
extract from the records in the possession and
ownership of the Moluccas. Badajoz; April 14-May 13,
1524

Opinions concerning the ownership of the Moluccas.
Hernando Colon, Fray Tomás Duran, Sebastian
Caboto, and Juan Vespucci; Badajoz April 13-15,
1524 Letters to the Spanish delegates at the Junta of

GENERAL PREFACE

The entrance of the United States of America into the arena of world-politics, the introduction of American influence into Oriental affairs, and the establishment of American authority in the Philippine archipelago, all render the history of those islands and their, numerous peoples a topic of engrossing interest and importance to the reading public, and especially to scholars, historians, and statesmen. The present work—its material carefully selected and arranged from a vast mass of printed works and unpublished manuscripts—is offered to the public with the intention and hope of casting light on the great problems which confront the American people in the Philippines; and of furnishing authentic and trustworthy material for a thorough and scholarly history of the islands. For this purpose, the Editors reproduce (mainly in English translation) contemporaneous documents which constitute the best original sources of Philippine history. Beginning with Pope Alexander VI's line of demarcation between the Spanish and the Portuguese dominions in the New World (1493), the course of history in the archipelago is thus traced through a period of more than three centuries, comprising the greater part of the Spanish régime.

In the selection of material, the Editors have sought to make the scope of the work commensurate with the breadth of the field, and to allot to each subject space proportioned to its interest; not only the political relations, but the social and religious, economic and commercial conditions of the Philippines have received due attention and care. All classes of writers are here represented— early navigators, officials civil and military, ecclesiastical dignitaries, and priests belonging to the various religious orders who conducted the missions among the Filipino peoples. To the letters, reports, and narratives furnished by these men are added numerous royal decrees, papal bulls and briefs, and other valuable documents. Most of this material is now for the first time made accessible to English-speaking readers; and the great libraries and archives of Spain, Italy, France, England, Mexico, and the United States have generously contributed to furnish it.

In the presentation of these documents, the Editors assume an entirely impartial attitude, free from any personal bias, whether political or sectarian. They aim to secure historical accuracy, especially in that aspect which requires the sympathetic interpretation of each author's thought and intention; and to depict faithfully the various aspects of the life of the Filipinos, their relations with other peoples (especially those of Europe), and the gradual ascent of many tribes from barbarism. They invite the reader's especial attention to the Introduction furnished for this series by Professor Edward Gaylord Bourne, of Yale University—valuable alike for its breadth of view and for its scholarly thoroughness. The Bibliographical Data at the end of each volume will supply necessary information as to sources and location of the documents published therein; fuller details, and of broader scope, will be given in the volume devoted to Philippine bibliography, at the end of the series.

In preparing this work, the Editors have received most friendly interest and aid from scholars, historians, archivists, librarians, and State officials; and from prominent ecclesiastics of the Roman Catholic church, and members of its religious orders. Especial thanks are due to the following persons: Hon. John Hay, Secretary of State, Washington; Sr. D. Juan Riaño, secretary of the Spanish Legation, Washington; Hon. Bellamy Storer, late U.S. Minister to Spain; Hon. Robert Stanton Sickles, secretary of U.S. Legation, Madrid; Dr. Thomas Cooke Middleton, O.S.A., Villanova College, Penn.; Rev. Thomas E. Sherman, S.J., St. Ignatius College, Chicago; Rev. John J. Wynne, S.J., Apostleship of Prayer, New York; Rev. Ubaldus Pandolfi, O.S.F., Boston; Bishop Ignatius F. Horstmann, Cleveland; Bishop Sebastian G. Messmer, Green Bay, Wis.; Fray Eduardo Navarro Ordóñez, O.S.A., Colegio de Agustinos, Valladolid, Spain; Rev. Pablo Pastells, S.J., Sarría, Barcelona, Spain; Charles Franklin Thwing, LL.D., President of Western Reserve University; Frederick J. Turner, Director of the School of History, University of Wisconsin; Richard T. Ely (director) and Paul S. Reinsch, of the School of Economics and Political Science,

University of Wisconsin; Edward G. Bourne, Professor of History, Yale University; Herbert Putnam (librarian), Worthington C. Ford, P. Lee Phillips, A.P.C. Griffin, James C. Hanson, and other officials, Library of Congress, Washington, D. C.; Wilberforce Eames (librarian) and Victor H. Paltsits, Lenox Library, New York; William I. Fletcher, librarian of Amherst College; Reuben G. Thwaites and Isaac S. Bradley, State Historical Society of Wisconsin; William C. Lane (librarian) and T.J. Kiernan, Library of Harvard University; John D. Fitzgerald, Columbia University, New York; Henry Vignaud, chief secretary of U.S. Legation, Paris; Sr. D. Duque del Almodovar del Rio, Minister of State, Madrid, Spain; Sr. Francisco Giner de los Rios, of University of Madrid, and Director of Institución Libre de Enseñanza; Sr. Ricardo Velasquez Bosco, Madrid; Sr. D. Cesáreo Fernández Duro, of Real Academia de la Historia, Madrid; Sr. D. Eduardo de Hinojosa, Madrid; Sr. D. Pedro Torres Lanzas, Director of Archivo General de Indias, Seville; Sr. D. Julian Paz, Director of Archivo General, Simancas; Sr. D. Francisco de P. Cousiño y Vazquez, Librarian of Museo-Biblioteca de Ultramar, Madrid.

Favors from the following are also acknowledged. Benj. P. Bourland, Professor of Romance Languages, Western Reserve University; Professor C.H. Grandgent, Department of Romance Languages, Harvard University; John Thomson, Free Library of Philadelphia; George Parker Winship, Carter-Brown Library, Providence, R.I.; Addison Van Name, Librarian of Yale University; Otto H. Tittmann, U.S. Coast and Geodetic Survey, and Dr. Otis T. Mason, Curator U.S. National Museum, Washington, D. C.; Rev. Laurence J. Kenny, S.J., St. Louis University; Rev. Henry J. Shandelle, S.J., Georgetown University, Washington; Rev. Thomas Hughes, S.J., and Rev. Rudolf J. Meyer, S.J., Rome, Italy; Dr. N. Murakami, Imperial University, Tokyo, Japan; Sr. D. Vicente Vignau y Balester, Director of Archivo Histórico-Nacional, Madrid; Sr. D. Conde de Ramonones, Minister of Public Instruction, Madrid; Sr. D.W.E. Retana, Civil Governor of province of Huesca, Spain; Sr. D. Clemente Miralles de Imperial (director) and Sr. D. J. Sanchez Garrigós (librarian), of Compañia General de Tabacos de Filipinas, Barcelona; Rev. Julius Alarcon, S.J., Rev. Joaquin Sancho, S.J., Rev. J.M. de Mendia, S.J., and the late Rev. José María Vélez, S.J., Madrid; Rev. T. M. Obeso, S.J., Bilbao; Rev. José Algué, S.J., Director of Observatory, Manila, Luzon; Fray Tirso Lopez, O.S.A., and Fray

Antonio Blanco, O.S.A., Colegio de Agustinos, Valladolid; Sr. Antonio Rodriguez Villa, Biblioteca de la Real Académia de la Historia, Madrid; Sr. Roman Murillo y Ollo, Librarian, Real Académia Española, Madrid; and officials of Biblioteca Nacional, Madrid; Sr. Gabriel Pereira, Director of Bibliotheca Nacional, Lisbon; Sr. P.A. d'Azevedo, Director of Archivo Nacional (Torre do Tombo), Lisbon; Sr. José Duarte Ramalho Ortigão (director) and Sr. Jordão A. de Freitas (official), Bibliotheca Real da Ajuda, Lisbon; officials of Academia Real das Sciencias, Lisbon; and officials of U.S. Legations, Lisbon and Madrid.

Emma Helen Blair
James Alexander Robertson

HISTORICAL INTRODUCTION

by Edward Gaylord Bourne

The American people are confronted with two race problems, one within their own confines and long familiar but still baffling solution; the other, new, remote, unknown, and even more imperatively demanding intelligent and unremitting effort for its mastery.

In the first case there are some eight millions of people ultimately derived from various savage tribes in Africa but long since acclimatized, disciplined to labor, raised to civilized life, Christianized, and by the acquisition of the English language brought within a world of ideas inaccessible to their ancestors. Emancipated by the fortune of war they are now living intermingled with a ruling race, in it, but not of it, in an unsettled social status, oppressed by the stigma of color and harassed and fettered by race prejudice.

In the other case there are six or seven millions of Malays whose ancestors were raised from barbarism, taught the forms and manners of civilized life, Christianized, and trained to labor by Catholic missionaries three centuries ago. A common religion and a common government have effaced in large measure earlier tribal differences and constituted them a people; yet in the fullest sense of the word a peculiar people. They stand unique as the only large mass of Asiatics converted to Christianity in modern times. They have not, like the African, been brought within the Christian pale by being torn from their natural environment and schooled through slavery; but, in their own home and protected from general contact with Europeans until recent times, they have been moulded through the patient teaching, parental discipline, and self-sacrificing devotion of the missionaries into a whole unlike any similar body elsewhere in the world. They, too, by the fortunes of war have lost their old rulers and guides and against their will submit their future to alien hands. To govern them or to train them to govern themselves are tasks almost equally perplexing, nor is the problem made easier or clearer by the clash of contradictory estimates of their culture and capacity which form the ammunition of party warfare.

What is needed is as thorough and intelligent a knowledge of their political and social evolution as a people as can be gained from a study of their history. In the case of the Negro problem the historical sources are abundant and accessible and the slavery question is accorded, preeminent attention in the study of American history. In the Philippine question, however, although the sources are no less abundant and instructive they are and have been highly inaccessible owing, on the one hand, to the absolute rarity of the publications containing them, and, on the other, to their being in a language hitherto comparatively little studied in the United States. To collect these sources, scattered and inaccessible as they are, to reproduce them and interpret them in the English language, and to make it possible for university and public libraries and the leaders in thought and policy to have at hand the complete and authentic records of the culture and life of the millions in the Far East whom we must understand in order to do them justice, is an enterprise large in its possibilities for the public good.

In accordance with the idea that underlies this collection this Introduction will not discuss the Philippine question of today nor Philippine life during the last half century, nor will it give a short history of the Islands since the conquest. For all these the reader may be referred to recent publications like those of Foreman, Sawyer, or Worcester, or earlier ones like those of Bowring and Mallat, or to the works republished in the series. The aim of the Introduction is rather to give the discovery and conquest of the Philippines their setting in the history of geographical discovery, to review the unparalleled achievements of the early conquerors and missionaries, to depict the government and commerce of the islands before the revolutionary changes of the last century, and to give such a survey, even though fragmentary, of Philippine life and culture under the old régime as will bring into relief their peculiar features and, if possible, to show that although the annals of the Philippines may be dry reading, the history of the Philippine people is a subject of deep and singular interest.

The Philippine Islands in situation and inhabitants belong to the Asiatic world, but, for the first three centuries of their recorded history, they were in a sense a dependency of America, and now the whirligig of time has restored them in their political relations to the Western Hemisphere. As a dependency of New Spain they constituted the extreme western verge of the Spanish dominions and were commonly known as the Western Islands[2] *(Las Islas del Poniente)*. Their discovery and conquest rounded out an empire which in geographical extent far surpassed anything the world had then seen. When the sun rose in Madrid, it was still early afternoon of the preceding day in Manila, and Philip II was the first monarch who could boast that the sun never set upon his dominions.[3]

In one generation, 1486-1522, the two little powers of the Iberian Peninsula had extended their sway over the seas until they embraced the globe. The way had been prepared for this unparalleled achievement by the courage and devotion of the Portuguese Prince Henry the Navigator, who gave his life to the advancement of geographical discovery and of Portuguese commerce. The exploration of the west coast of Africa was the school of the navigators who sailed to the East and the West Indies, and out of the administration of the trade with Africa grew the colonial systems of later days.

In the last quarter of the fifteenth century the increasing obstructions in Egypt and by the Turks to the trade with the East Indies held out a great prize to the discoverer of an all-sea route to the Spice Islands. Bartholomew Diaz and Vasco da Gama solved this problem for Portugal, but the solution offered to Spain by Columbus and accepted in 1492 revealed a New World, the Indies of the West.

The King of Portugal, zealous to retain his monopoly of African and eastern exploration, and the pious sovereigns of Spain, desirous to build their colonial empire on solid and unquestioned foundations, alike appealed to the Pope for a definition of their rights and a confirmation of their claims. The world seemed big enough and with a spacious liberality Pope Alexander VI granted Ferdinand and Isabella the right to explore and to take possession of all the hitherto unknown and heathen parts of the world west of a certain line drawn north and south in the Atlantic Ocean. East of that line the rights of Portugal, resting on their explorations and the grants of earlier popes, were confirmed.

The documentary history of the Philippines begins with the Demarcation Bulls and the treaty of Tordesillas, for out of them grew Magellan's voyage and the discovery of the islands; and without them the Philippines would no doubt have been occupied by Portugal and later have fallen a prey to the Dutch as did the Moluccas.

King John of Portugal was dissatisfied with the provisions of the Demarcation Bulls. He held that the treaty between Spain and Portugal in 1479 had resigned to Portugal the field of oceanic discovery, Spain retaining only the Canaries; and he felt that a boundary line only a hundred leagues west of the Azores not only was an infringement on his rights but would be a practical embarrassment in that it would not allow his sailors adequate sea room for their African voyages.

His first contention was hardly valid; the second, however, was reasonable and, as Columbus had estimated the distance from the Canaries to the new islands at over nine hundred leagues, the Catholic sovereigns were disposed to make concessions. By the treaty of Tordesillas, June 7, 1494, it was agreed that the Demarcation Line should be drawn three hundred and seventy leagues west of the Cape Verde Islands.[4] This treaty accepted the principle of the Papal arbitration but shifted the boundary to a position supposed to be half-way between the Cape Verde Islands and the newly discovered islands of Cipangu and Antilia.[5]

Neither in the Papal Bulls nor in the Treaty of Tordesillas was there any specific reference to an extension of the Line around the globe or to a division of the world. The arrangement seems to have contemplated a free field for the exploration and conquest of the unknown parts of the world, to the eastward for Portugal, and to the westward for Spain. If they should cross each other's tracks priority of discovery would determine the ownership.[6]

The suggestion of the extension of the line around the globe and of the idea that Spain was entitled to what might be within the hemisphere set off by the Demarcation Line and its extension to the antipodes does not appear until the time of Magellan, and it is then that we first meet the notion that the Pope had divided the world between Spain and Portugal like an orange.[7]

The Portuguese reached India in 1498. Thirteen years later Albuquerque made conquest of Malacca of the Malay Peninsula, the great entrepôt of the spice trade; but even then the real goal, the islands where the spices grow, had not been attained. The command of the straits, however, promised a near realization of so many years of labor, and, as soon as practicable, in December 1511, Albuquerque despatched Antonio d'Abreu in search of the precious islands. A Spanish historian of the next century affirms that Magellan accompanied d'Abreu in command of one of the ships, but this can hardly be true.[8] Francisco Serrão, however, one of the Portuguese captains, was a friend of Magellan's and during his sojourn of several years in the Moluccas wrote to him of a world larger and richer than that discovered by Vasco da Gama. It is probable, as the historian Barros, who saw some of this correspondence, sugguests, that Serrão somewhat exaggerated the distance from Malacca to the Moluccas, and so planted the seed which bore such fruit in Magellan's mind.[9]

The year after the Portuguese actually attained the Spice Islands, Vasco Nuñez de Balboa, first of Europeans (1513), set eyes upon the great South Sea. It soon became only too certain that the Portuguese had won in the race for the land of cloves, pepper, and nutmegs. But, in the absence of knowledge of the true dimensions of the earth and with an underestimate of its size generally prevailing, the information that the Spice Islands lay far to the east of India revived in the mind of Magellan the original project of Columbus to seek the land of spices by the westward route. That he laid this plan before the King of Portugal, there seems good reason to believe, but when he saw no prospect for its realization, like Columbus, he left Portugal for Spain. It is now that the idea is evolved that, as the Moluccas lie so far east of India, they are probably in the Spanish half of the world, and, if approached from the west, may be won after all for the Catholic king. No appeal for patronage and support could be more effective, and how much reliance Magellan and his financial backer Christopher Haro placed upon it in their petition to King Charles appears clearly in the account by Maximilianus Transylvanus of Magellan's presentation of his project: "They both showed Caesar that though it was not yet quite sure whether Malacca was within the confines of the Spaniards or the Portuguese, because, as yet, nothing of the longitude had been clearly proved, yet, it was quite plain that the Great Gulf and the people of Sinae lay within the Spanish boundary. This too was held to be most certain, that the islands which they call the Moluccas, in which all spices are produced, and are thence exported to Malacca, lay within the Spanish western division, and that it was possible to sail there; and that spices could be brought thence to Spain more easily, and at less expense and cheaper, as they come direct from their native place."[10]

Equally explicit was the contract which Magellan entered into with King Charles: "Inasmuch as you bind yourself to discover in the dominions which belong to us and are ours in the Ocean Sea within the limits of our demarcation, islands and mainlands and rich spiceries, etc." This is followed by an injunction "not to discover or do anything within the demarcation and limits of the most serene King of Portugal."[11]

Las Casas, the historian of the Indies, was present in Valladolid when Magellan came thither to present his plan to the King. "Magellan," he writes, "had a well painted globe in which the whole world was depicted, and on it he indicated the route he proposed to take, saving that the strait was left purposely blank so that no one should anticipate him. And on that day and at that hour I was in the office of the High Chancellor when the Bishop [of Burgos, Fonseca] brought it [i.e. the globe] and showed the High Chancellor the voyage which was proposed; and, speaking with Magellan, I asked him what way he planned to take, and he answered that he intended to go by Cape Saint Mary, which we call the Rio de la Plata and from thence to follow the coast up until he hit upon the strait. But suppose you do not find any strait by which you can go into the other sea. He replied that if he did not find any strait that he would go the way the Portuguese took.—This Fernando de Magalhaens must have been a man of courage and valiant in his thoughts and for undertaking great things, although he was not of imposing presence because he was small in stature and did not appear in himself to be much."[12]

Such were the steps by which the Papal Demarcation Line led to the first circumnavigation of the globe, the greatest single human achievement on the sea.[13] The memorable expedition set out from Seville September 20, 1519. A year elapsed before the entrance to the strait named for the great explorer was discovered. Threading its sinuous intricacies consumed thirty-eight days and then followed a terrible voyage of ninety-eight days across a truly pathless sea. The first land seen was the little group of islands called Ladrones from the thievishness of the inhabitants, and a short stay was made at Guam. About two weeks later, the middle of March, the little fleet reached the group of islands which we know as the Philippines but which Magellan named the islands of St. Lazarus, from the saint whose day and feast were celebrated early in his stay among them.[14]

The calculations of the longitude showed that these islands were well within the Spanish half of the world and the success with which a Malay slave of Magellan, brought from Sumatra, made himself understood[15] indicated clearly enough that they were not far from the Moluccas and that the object of the expedition, to discover a westward route to the Spice Islands, and to prove them to be within the Spanish demarcation, was about to be realized. But Magellan, like Moses, was vouchsafed only a glimpse of the Promised Land. That the heroic and steadfast navigator should have met his death in a skirmish with a few naked savages when in sight of his goal, is one of the most pathetic tragedies in history.[16]

The difficulties, however, of approaching the Moluccas by the western route through the straits of Magellan (that Cape Horn could be rounded was not discovered till 1616), the stubborn and defiant attitude of the King of Portugal in upholding his claims, the impossibility of a scientific and exact determination of the Demarcation Line in the absence of accurate means for measuring longitude,—all these, reinforced by the pressure of financial stringency led King Charles in 1529 to relinquish all claims to or rights to trade with the Moluccas for three hundred and fifty thousand ducats.[17] In the antipodes a Demarcation Line was to be drawn from pole to pole seventeen degrees on the equator, or two hundred and ninety-seven leagues east of the Moluccas, and it was agreed that the subjects of the King of Castile should neither sail or trade beyond that line, or carry anything to the islands or lands within it.[18] If a later scientific and accurate determination should substantiate the original claims of either party the money should be returned[19] and the contract be dissolved. Although the archipelago of St. Lazarus was not mentioned in this treaty it was a plain renunciation of any rights over the Philippines for they lie somewhat to the west of the Moluccas.

The King of Spain, however, chose to ignore this fact and tacitly assumed the right to conquer the Philippines. It was, however, thirteen years before another attempt was made in this direction. By this time the conquest and development of the kingdom of New Spain made one of its ports on the Pacific the natural starting point. This expedition commanded by Rui Lopez de Villalobos was despatched in 1542 and ended disastrously. The Portuguese Captain-general in the Moluccas made several vigorous protests against the intrusion, asserting that Mindanao fell within the Portuguese Demarcation and that they had made some progress in introducing Christianity.[20]

Villalobos left no permanent mark upon the islands beyond giving the name "Felipinas" to some of them, in honor of "our fortunate Prince."[21]

Nearly twenty years elapsed before another expedition was undertaken, but this was more carefully organized than any of its predecessors, and four or five years were absorbed in the preparations. King Philip II, while respecting the contract with Portugal in regard to the Moluccas, proposed to ignore its provisions in regard to other islands included within the Demarcation Line of 1529. In his first despatch relative to this expedition in 1559 he enjoins that it shall not enter the Moluccas but go "to other islands that are in the same region as are the Philippines and others that were outside the said contract, but within our demarcation, that are said to produce spices."[22]

Friar Andrés de Urdaneta, who had gone to the Moluccas with Loaisa in 1525, while a layman and a sailor, explained to the king that as *la isla Filipina* was farther west than the Moluccas the treaty of Zaragoza was just as binding in the case of these islands as in that of the Moluccas, and that to avoid trouble some "legitimate or pious reason for the expedition should be assigned such as the rescue of sailors who had been lost on the islands in previous expeditions or the determination of the longitude of the Demarcation Line"[23]

It is clear from the sequel that King Philip intended, as has been said, to shut his eyes to the application of the Treaty of Zaragoza to the Philippines. As they did not produce spices the Portuguese had not occupied them and they now made no effectual resistance to the Spanish conquest of the islands.[24] The union of Portugal to the crown of Spain in 1580 subsequently removed every obstacle, and when the Portuguese crown resumed its independence in 1640 the Portuguese had been driven from the Spice Islands by the Dutch.

This is not the place to narrate in detail the history of the great expedition of Legaspi. It established the power of Spain in the Philippines and laid the foundations of their permanent organization. In a sense it was an American enterprise. The ships were built in America and for the most part equipped here. It was commanded and guided by men who lived in the New World. The work of Legaspi during the next seven years entitles him to a place among the greatest of colonial pioneers. In fact he has no rival. Starting with four ships and four hundred men, accompanied by five Augustinian monks, reinforced in 1567 by two hundred soldiers, and from time to time by similar small contingents of troops and monks, by a combination of tact, resourcefulness, and courage he won over the natives, repelled the Portuguese and laid such foundations that the changes of the next thirty years constitute one of the most surprising revolutions in the annals of colonization. A most brilliant exploit was that of Legaspi's grandson, Juan de Salcedo, a youth of twenty-two who with forty-five men explored northern Luzon, covering the present provinces of Zambales, Pangasinán, La Union, Ilocos, and the coast of Cagayán, and secured submission of the people to Spanish rule.[25] Well might his associates hold him "unlucky because fortune had placed him where oblivion must needs bury the most valiant deeds that a knight ever wrought."[26] Nor less deserving of distinction than Legaspi and his heroic grandson was Friar Andrés de Urdaneta the veteran navigator whose natural abilities and extensive knowledge of the eastern seas stood his commander in good stead at every point and most effectively contributed to the success of the expedition. Nor should the work of the Friars be ignored. Inspired by apostolic zeal, reinforced by the glowing enthusiasm of the Catholic Reaction, gifted and tireless, they labored in harmony with Legaspi, won converts, and checked the slowly-advancing tide of Mohammedanism. The ablest of the Brothers, Martin de Rada, was preaching in Visayan within five months.

The work of conversion opened auspiciously in Cebu, where Legaspi began his work, with a niece of Tupas, an influential native, who was baptized with great solemnity. Next came the conversion of the Moor [Moslem] "who had served as interpreter and who had great influence throughout all that country." In 1568 the turning point came with the baptism of Tupas and of his son. This opened the door to general conversion, for the example of Tupas had great weight.[27]

It is a singular coincidence that within the span of one human life the Spaniard should have finished the secular labor of breaking the power of the Moslem in Spain and have checked his advance in the islands of the antipodes. The religion of the prophet had penetrated to Malacca in 1276, had reached the Moluccas in 1465, and thence was spreading steadily northward to Borneo and the Philippines. Iolo (Sulu) and Mindanao succumbed in the sixteenth century and when Legaspi began the conquest of Luzon in 1571 he found many Mohammedans whose settlement or conversion had grown out of the trade relations with Borneo. As the old Augustinian chronicler Grijalva remarks, and his words are echoed by Morga and by the modern historian Montero y Vidal:[28] "So well rooted was the cancer that had the arrival of the Spaniards been delayed all the people would have become Moors, as are all the islanders who have not come under the government of the Philippines."[29]

It is one of the unhappy legacies of the religious revolution of the sixteenth century that it has fixed a great gulf between the Teutonic and the Latin mind, which proves impassable for the average intellect. The deadly rivalries of Catholic and Protestant, of Englishman and Spaniard, have left indelible traces upon their descendants which intensify race prejudice and misunderstanding. The Englishman or American looks with a contempt upon the economic blindness or incapacity of the Spaniard that veils his eyes to their real aims and achievements.

The tragedies and blunders of English colonization in America are often forgotten and only the tragedies and blunders of Spanish colonization are remembered. In the period which elapsed between the formulation of the Spanish and of the English colonial policies religious ideals were displaced by the commercial, and in the exaltation of the commercial ideal England took the lead. Colonies, from being primarily fields for the propagation of Christianity and incidentally for the production of wealth, became the field primarily for industrial and commercial development and incidentally for Christian work. The change no doubt has contributed vastly to the wealth of the world and to progress, but it has been fatal to the native populations. The Spanish policy aimed to preserve and civilize the native races, not to establish a new home for Spaniards, and the colonial legislation provided elaborate safeguards for the protection of the Indians. Many of these were a mere dead letter but the preservation and civilization of the native stock in Mexico, Central and South America, and above all in the Philippines stand out in marked contrast, after all allowances and qualifications have been made, with the fate, past and prospective, of the aborigines in North America, the Sandwich Islands, New Zealand, and Australia, and clearly differentiate in their respective tendencies and results the Spanish and English systems. The contrast between the effects of the Spanish conquest in the West Indies, Mexico, and the Philippines reflects the development of the humane policy of the government. The ravages of the first conquistadores, it should be remembered, took place before the crown had time to develop a colonial policy.

It is customary, too, for Protestant writers to speak with contempt of Catholic missions, but it must not be forgotten that France and England were converted to Christianity by similar methods. The Protestant ridicules the wholesale baptisms and conversions and a Christianity not even skin-deep, but that was the way in which Christianity was once propagated in what are the ruling Christian nations of today. The Catholic, on the other hand, might ask for some evidence that the early Germans, or the Anglo-Saxons would ever have been converted to Christianity by the methods employed by Protestants.

The wholesale baptisms have their real significance in the frame of mind receptive for the patient Christian nurture that follows. Christianity has made its real conquests and is kept alive by Christian training, and its progress is the improvement which one generation makes upon another in the observance of its precepts. One who has read the old Penitential books and observed the evidences they afford of the vitality of heathen practices and rites among the people in England in the early Middle Ages will not be too harsh in characterizing the still imperfect fruits of the Catholic missions of the last three centuries.

In the light, then, of impartial history raised above race prejudice and religious prepossessions, after a comparison with the early years of the Spanish conquest in America or with the first generation or two of the English settlements, the conversion and civilization of the Philippines in the forty years following Legaspi's arrival must be pronounced an achievement without a parallel in history. An examination of what was accomplished at the very ends of the earth with a few soldiers and a small band of missionaries will it is believed reveal the reasons for this verdict. We are fortunate in possessing for this purpose, among other materials, a truly classic survey of the condition of the islands at the opening of the seventeenth century written by a man of scholarly training and philosophic mind, Dr. Antonio de Morga, who lived in the islands eight years in the government service.[30]

The Spaniards found in the population of the islands two sharply contrasted types which still survive—the Malay and the Negrito. After the introduction of Christianity the natives were commonly classified according to their religion as Indians (Christian natives), Moors[31] (Mohammedan natives), and Heathen (Gentiles) or Infidels. The religious beliefs of the Malays were not held with any great tenacity and easily yielded to the efforts of the missionaries. The native taste for the spectacular was impressed and gratified by the picturesque and imposing ceremonials of the church.

Their political and social organization was deficient in cohesion. There were no well established native states but rather a congeries of small groups something like clans. The headship of these groups or *barangays* was hereditary and the authority of the chief of the *barangay* was despotic.[32] This social disintegration immensely facilitated the conquest; and by tact and conciliation, effectively supported by arms, but with very little actual bloodshed, Spanish sovereignty was superimposed upon these relatively detached groups, whose essential features were preserved as a part of the colonial administrative machinery. This in turn was a natural adaptation of that developed in New Spain. Building upon the available institutions of the *barangay* as a unit the Spaniards aimed to familiarize and accustom the Indians to settled village life and to moderate labor. Only under these conditions could religious training and systematic religious oversight be provided. These villages were commonly called *pueblos* or *reducciones*, and Indians who ran away to escape the restraints of civilized life were said to "take to the hills" *(remontar)*.

As a sign of their allegiance and to meet the expenses of government every Indian family was assessed a tribute of eight reals, about one dollar, and for the purpose of assessment the people were set off in special groups something like feudal holdings *(encomiendas)*. The tribute from some of the *encomiendas* went to the king. Others had been granted to the Spanish army officers or to the officials.[33] The "Report of the *Encomiendas* in the Islands in 1591" just twenty years after the conquest of Luzon reveals a wonderful progress in the work of civilization. In the city of Manila there was a cathedral and the bishop's palace, monasteries for the Austin, Dominican, and Franciscan Friars, and a house for the Jesuits. The king maintained a hospital for Spaniards; there was also a hospital for Indians in the charge of two Franciscan lay brothers. The garrison was composed of two hundred soldiers. The Chinese quarter or *Parián* contained some two hundred shops and a population of about two thousand. In the suburb of Tondo there was a convent of Franciscans and another of Dominicans who provided Christian teaching for some forty converted Sangleyes (Chinese merchants). In Manila and the adjacent region nine thousand four hundred and ten tributes were collected, indicating a total of some thirty thousand six hundred and forty souls under the religious instruction of thirteen missionaries *(ministros de doctrina)*, besides the friars in the monasteries. In the old province of La Pampanga the estimated population was 74,700 with twenty-eight missionaries; in Pangasinán 2,400 souls with eight missionaries; in Ilocos 78,520 with twenty missionaries; in Cagayán and the Babuyan islands 96,000 souls but no missionaries; in La Laguna 48,400 souls with twenty-seven missionaries; in Vicol and Camarines with the island of Catanduanes 86,640 souls with fifteen missionaries, etc., making a total for the islands of 166,903 tributes or 667,612 souls under one hundred and forty missionaries, of which seventy-nine were Augustinians, nine Dominicans, forty-two Franciscans. The King's *encomiendas* numbered thirty-one and the private ones two hundred and thirty-six.[34]

Friar Martin Ignacio in his *Itinerario*, the earliest printed description of the islands (1585), says: "According unto the common opinion at this day there is converted and baptised more than foure hundred thousand soules."[35]

This system of *encomiendas* had been productive of much hardship and oppression in Spanish America, nor was it altogether divested of these evils in the Philippines. The payment of tributes, too, was irksome to the natives and in the earlier days the Indians were frequently drafted for forced labor, but during this transition period, and later, the clergy were the constant advocates of humane treatment and stood between the natives and the military authorities. This solicitude of the missionaries for their spiritual children and the wrongs from which they sought to protect them are clearly displayed in the *Relacion de las Cosas de las Filipinas* of Domingo de Salazar, the first bishop, who has been styled the "Las Casas of the Philippines."[36]

That it was the spirit of kindness, Christian love, and brotherly helpfulness of the missionaries that effected the real conquest of the islands is abundantly testified by qualified observers of various nationalities and periods,[37] but the most convincing demonstration is the ridiculously small military force that was required to support the prestige of the Catholic king. The standing army organized in 1590 for the defense of the country numbered four hundred men![38] No wonder an old viceroy of New Spain was wont to say: *"En cada fraile tenía el rey en Filipinas un capitan general y un ejercito entero"*—"In each friar in the Philippines the King had a captain general and a whole army."[39] The efforts of the missionaries were by no means restricted to religious teaching, but were also directed to promote the social and economic advancement of the islands. They cultivated the innate taste for music of the natives and taught the children Spanish.[40] They introduced improvements in rice culture, brought Indian corn and cacao from America and developed the cultivation of indigo and coffee, and sugar cane. Tobacco alone of the economic plants brought to the islands by the Spaniards owes its introduction to government agency.[41]

The young capital of the island kingdom of New Castile, as it was denominated by Philip II, in 1603 when it was described by Morga invites some comparison with Boston, New York, or Philadelphia in the seventeenth century. The city was surrounded by a wall of hewn stone some three miles in circuit. There were two forts and a bastion, each with a garrison of a few soldiers. The government residence and office buildings were of hewn stone and spacious and airy. The municipal buildings, the cathedral, and the monasteries of the three orders were of the same material. The Jesuits, besides providing special courses of study for members of their order, conducted a college for the education of Spanish youth. The establishment of this college had been ordered by Philip II in 1585 but it was 1601 before it was actually opened.[42] Earlier than this in 1593 there had been established a convent school for girls,[43] the college of Saint Potenciana. In provisions for the sick and helpless, Manila at the opening of the seventeenth century was far in advance of any city in the English colonies for more than a century and a half to come.[44] There was first the royal hospital for Spaniards with its medical attendants and nurses; the Franciscan hospital for the Indians administered by three priests and by four lay brothers who were physicians and apothecaries and whose skill had wrought surprising cures in medicine and surgery; the House of Mercy, which took in sick slaves, gave lodgings to poor women, portioned orphan girls, and relieved other distresses; and lastly, the hospital for Sangleyes or Chinese shopkeepers in the Chinese quarter.[45] Within the walls the houses, mainly of stone and inhabited by Spaniards, numbered about six hundred. The substantial buildings, the gaily-dressed people, the abundance of provisions and other necessaries of human life made Manila, as Morga says, "one of the towns most praised by the strangers who flock to it of any in the world."[46] There were three other cities in the islands, Segovia and Cazeres in Luzon, and the city of the "most holy name of Jesus" in Cebú, the oldest Spanish settlement in the archipelago. In the first and third the Spanish inhabitants numbered about two hundred and in Cazeres about one hundred. In *Santisimo nombre de Jesús* there was a Jesuit college.

Although the Indians possessed an alphabet before the arrival of the Spaniards and the knowledge of reading and writing was fairly general they had no written literature of any kind.[47] A Jesuit priest who had lived in the islands eighteen years, writing not far from 1640, tells us that by that time the Tagals had learned to write their language from left to right instead of perpendicularly as was their former custom, but they used writing merely for correspondence.

The only books thus far in the Indian languages were those written by the missionaries on religion.[48]

In regard to the religious life of the converted Indians the Friars and Morga speak on the whole with no little satisfaction. Friar Martin Ignacio in 1584 writes: "Such as are baptised, doo receive the fayth with great firmenesse, and are good Christians, and would be better, if that they were holpen with good ensamples."[49] Naturally the Spanish soldiers left something to be desired as examples of Christianity and Friar Martin relates the story of the return from the dead of a principal native—"a strange case, the which royally did passe of a trueth in one of these ilandes,"—who told his former countrymen of the "benefites and delights" of heaven, which "was the occasion that some of them forthwith received the baptisme, and that others did delay it, saying, that because there were Spaniard souldiers in glory, they would not go thither, because they would not be in their company."[50]

Morga writing in 1603 says: "In strictest truth the affairs of the faith have taken a good footing, as the people have a good disposition and genius, and they have seen the errors of their paganism and the truths of the Christian religion; they have got good churches and monasteries of wood, well constructed, with shrines and brilliant ornaments, and all the things required for the service, crosses, candlesticks, chalices of gold and silver, many brotherhoods and religious acts, assiduity in the sacraments and being present at divine service, and care in maintaining and supplying their monks, with great obedience and respect; they also give for the prayers and burials of their dead, and perform this with all punctuality and liberality."[51] A generation later the report of the Religious is not quite so sanguine: "They receive our religion easily and their lack of intellectual penetration saves them from sounding the difficulties of its mysteries. They are too careless of fulfilling the duties of the Christianity which they profess and must needs be constrained by fear of chastisement and be ruled like school children. Drunkenness and usury are the two vices to which they are most given and these have not been entirely eradicated by the efforts of our monks."[52] That these efforts were subsequently crowned with a large measure of success is shown by the almost universal testimony to the temperate habits of the Filipinos.

This first period of Philippine history has been called its Golden Age. Certainly no succeeding generation saw such changes and advancement. It was the age of Spain's greatest power and the slow decline and subsequent decrepitude that soon afflicted the parent state could not fail to react upon the colony. This decline was in no small degree the consequence of the tremendous strain to which the country was subjected in the effort to retain and solidify its power in Europe while meeting the burden of new establishments in America and the Philippines. That in the very years when Spaniards were accomplishing the unique work of redeeming an oriental people from barbarism and heathenism to Christianity and civilized life, the whole might of the mother-country should have been massed in a tremendous conflict in Europe which brought ruin and desolation to the most prosperous provinces under her dominion, and sapped her own powers of growth, is one of the strangest coincidences in history.

Bending every energy for years to stay the tide of change and progress, suppressing freedom of thought with relentless vigor, and quarantining herself and her dependencies against new ideas, conservatism grew to be her settled habit and the organs of government became ossified. Policies of commercial restriction which were justifiable or at least rationally explicable in the sixteenth century lasted on, proof against innovation or improvement, until the eighteenth century and later. Consequently from the middle of the seventeenth century at the period of the rapid rise of colonial powers of France, Holland, and England, the Spanish colonies find themselves under a commercial regime which increasingly hampers their prosperity and effectually blocks their advancement.

The contrast between the Spanish possessions and those of the other maritime powers became more marked as time went on. The insuperable conservatism of the home government gave little opportunity for the development of a class of energetic and progressive colonial officials, and financial corruption honeycombed the whole colonial civil service.

Such conditions: the absence of the spirit of progress, hostility to new ideas, failure to develop resources, and the prevalence of bribery and corruption in the civil service, insure abundant and emphatic condemnation at the present day for the Spanish colonial system. But in any survey of this system we must not lose sight of the terrible costs of progress in the tropical colonies of Holland, France, and England; nor fail to compare the *pueblos* of the Philippines in the eighteenth century with the plantations of San Domingo, or Jamaica, or Java, or with those of Cuba in the early nineteenth century when the spirit of progress invaded the island.

To facilitate the understanding of the historical materials which will be collected in this series and to lay the foundation for a just and appreciative comparison of the institutions of the Philippines with those of other European dependencies in the tropics, it will be my aim now to bring into relief the distinctive features of the work wrought in the islands which raised a congeries of Malay tribes to Christian civilization, and secured for them as happy and peaceful an existence on as high a plane as has yet been attained by any people of color anywhere in the world, or by any orientals for any such length of time.

Such a survey of Philippine life may well begin with a brief account of the government of the islands. This will be followed by a description of the commercial system and of the state of the arts and of education, religion, and some features of social life during the eighteenth century and in the first years of the nineteenth before the entrance of the various and distracting currents of modern life and thought. In some cases significant details will be taken from the works of competent witnesses whose observations were made somewhat earlier or later. This procedure is unobjectionable in describing a social condition on the whole so stationary as was that of the Philippines before the last half century.

From the beginning the Spanish establishments in the Philippines were a mission and not in the proper sense of the term a colony. They were founded and administered in the interests of religion rather than of commerce or industry. They were an advanced outpost of Christianity whence the missionary forces could be deployed through the great empires of China and Japan, and hardly had the natives of the islands begun to yield to the labors of the friars when some of the latter pressed on adventurously into China and found martyrs' deaths in Japan. In examining the political administration of the Philippines, then, we must be prepared to find it a sort of outer garment under which the living body is ecclesiastical. Against this subjection to the influence and interests of the Church energetic governors rebelled, and the history of the

Spanish domination is checkered with struggles between the civil and religious powers which reproduce on a small scale the mediæval contests of Popes and Emperors.

Colonial governments are of necessity adaptations of familiar domestic institutions to new functions. The government of Spain in the sixteenth century was not that of a modern centralized monarchy but rather of a group of kingdoms only partially welded together by the possession of the same sovereign, the same language, and the same religion. The King of Spain was also the ruler of other kingdoms outside of the peninsula. Consequently when the New World was given a political organization it was subdivided for convenience into kingdoms and captaincies general in each of which the administrative machinery was an adaptation of the administrative machinery of Spain. In accordance with this procedure the Philippine islands were constituted a kingdom and placed under the charge of a governor and captain general, whose powers were truly royal and limited only by the check imposed by the Supreme Court (the *Audiencia*) and by the ordeal of the *residencia* at the expiration of his term of office. Among his extensive prerogatives was his appointing power which embraced all branches of the civil service in the islands. He also was *ex officio* the President of the *Audiencia*.[53] His salary was $8,000[54] a year, but his income might be largely augmented by gifts or bribes.[55] The limitations upon the power of the Governor imposed by the *Audiencia*, in the opinion of the French astronomer Le Gentil, were the only safeguard against an arbitrary despotism, yet Zúñiga, a generation later pronounced its efforts in this direction generally ineffectual.[56] The *residencia* to which reference has been made was an institution peculiar in modern times to the Spanish colonial system, it was designed to provide a method by which officials could be held to strict accountability for all acts during their term of office. Today reliance is placed upon the force of public opinion inspired and formulated by the press and, in self-governing communities, upon the holding of frequent elections. The strength of modern party cohesion both infuses vigor into these agencies and neutralizes their effectiveness as the case may be. But in the days of the formation of the Spanish Empire beyond the sea there were neither free elections, nor public press, and the criticism of the government was sedition. To allow a contest in the courts involving the governor's powers during his term of office would be subversive of his authority. He was then to be kept within bounds by realizing that a day of judgment was impending, when everyone, even the poorest Indian, might in perfect security bring forward his accusation.[57] In the Philippines the *residencia* for a governor lasted six months and was conducted by his successor and all the charges made were forwarded to Spain.[58] The Italian traveler Gemelli Careri who visited Manila in 1696 characterizes the governor's *residencia* as a "dreadful Trial," the strain of which would sometimes "break their hearts."[59]

On the other hand, an acute observer of Spanish-American institutions of the olden time intimates that the severities of the *residencia* could be mitigated and no doubt such was the case in the Philippines.[60] By the end of the eighteenth century the *residencia* seems to have lost its efficacy.[61] The governorship was certainly a difficult post to fill and the remoteness from Europe, the isolation, and the vexations of the *residencia* made it no easy task to get good men for the place. An official of thirty years experience, lay and ecclesiastical, assures us in the early seventeenth century that he had known of only one governor really fitted for the position, Gomez Perez Dasmariñas. He had done more for the happiness of the natives in three years than all his predecessors or successors. Some governors had been without previous political experience while others were deficient in the qualities required in a successful colonial ruler.[62]

The supreme court or *Audiencia* was composed of four judges *(oidores,* auditors) an attorney-general *(fiscal)* a constable, etc. The governor who acted as president had no vote.[63] Besides the functions of this body as the highest court of appeal for criminal and civil cases it served as has been said as a check upon the governor. Down to 1715 the *Audiencia* took charge of the civil administration in the interim between the death of a governor and the arrival of his successor, and the senior auditor assumed the military command.[64] Attached to the court were advocates for the accused, a defender of the Indians, and other minor officials. In affairs of public importance the *Audiencia* was to be consulted by the governor for the opinions of the auditors.[65]

For the purposes of local administration the islands were subdivided into or constituted Provinces under *alcaldes mayores* who exercised both executive and judicial functions, and superintended the collection of tribute.[66] The *alcaldes mayores* were allowed to engage in trade on their own account which resulted too frequently in enlisting their interest chiefly in money making and in fleecing the Indians.[67]

The provincial court consisted of the *alcalde mayor,* an assessor who was a lawyer, and a notary. The favoritism and corruption that honeycombed the civil service of Spain in the colonies in the days of her decline often placed utterly unfit persons in these positions of responsibility. A most competent observer, Tomás de Comyn, many years the factor of the Philippine Commercial Company, has depicted in dark colors, and perhaps somewhat overdrawn the evils of the system.[68]

The subdivision of the provinces was into *pueblos* each under its petty governor or *gobernadorcillo*. The *gobernadorcillo* was an Indian and was elected annually. In Morga's time the right of suffrage seems to have been enjoyed by all married Indians,[69] but in the last century it was restricted to thirteen electors.[70] The *gobernadorcillo* was commonly called the "captain." Within the *pueblos* the people formed little groups of from forty to fifty tributes called *barangays* under the supervision of *cabezas de barangay*. These heads of *barangay* represent the survival of the earlier clan organization and were held responsible for the tributes of their groups. Originally the office of *cabeza de barangay* was no doubt hereditary, but it became generally elective.[71] The electors of the *gobernadorcillo* were made up of those, who were or had been *cabezas de barangay* and they after three years of service became eligible to the office of petty governor.

In the few Spanish towns in the islands the local government was similar to that which prevailed in America, which in turn was derived from Spain. That of Manila may be taken as an example. The corporation, *El Cabildo* (chapter) consisted of two ordinary *alcaldes*, eight *regidores*, a registrar, and a constable. The *alcaldes* were justices, and were elected annually from the householders by the corporation. The *regidores* were aldermen and with the registrar and constable held office permanently as a proprietary right. These permanent positions in the *cabildo* could be bought and sold or inherited.[72]

Turning now to the ecclesiastical administration, we find there the real vital organs of the Philippine governmental system. To the modern eye the islands would have seemed, as they did to the French scientist Le Gentil, priest-ridden. Yet it was only through the Friars that Spain retained her hold at all.[73] A corrupt civil service and a futile and decrepit commercial system were through their efforts rendered relatively harmless, because circumscribed in their effects. The continuous fatherly interest of the clergy more than counterbalanced the burden of the tribute.[74] They supervised the tilling of the soil, as well as the religious life of the people; and it was through them that the works of education and charity were administered.[75]

The head of the ecclesiastical system was the Archbishop of Manila, who in a certain sense was the Patriarch of the Indies.[76] The other high ecclesiastical digntaries were the three bishops of Cebú, of Segovia in Cagayán, and of Cazeres in Camarines; and the provincials of the four great orders of friars, the Dominicans, Augustinians, the Franciscans, the barefooted Augustinians, and the Jesuits.[77] In the earlier days the regular clergy (members of the orders) greatly outnumbered the seculars, and refused to acknowledge that they were subject to the visitation of bishop or archbishop. This contention gave rise, at times, to violent struggles. During the eighteenth and nineteenth centuries the proportionate number of seculars increased. In 1750 the total number of parishes was 569, of which 142, embracing 147,269 persons, were under secular priests. The numbers in charge of the orders were as follows:

	Villages.	Souls.
Augustinians,	115	252,963
Franciscans,	63	141,193
Jesuits,	93	209,527
Dominicans,	51	99,780
Recollects,	105	53,384

making a total of 569 parishes and 904,116 souls.[78]

These proportions, however, fail to give a correct idea of the enormous preponderance of the religious orders; for the secular priests were mostly Indians and could exercise nothing like the influence of the Friars upon their cures.[79]

In these hundreds of villages the friars bore sway with the mild despotism of the shepherd of the flock. Spanish officials entered these precincts only on occasion. Soldiers were not to be seen save to suppress disorders. Spaniards were not allowed to live in these communities, and visitors were carefully watched.[80] As Spanish was little known in the provinces, the curate was the natural intermediary in all communications between the natives and the officials or outsiders. In some provinces there were no white persons besides the *alcalde mayor* and the friars. Without soldiers the *alcalde mayor* must needs rely upon the influence of the friars to enable him to execute his duties as provincial governor. In contemplating their services for civilization and good order Tomas de Comyn rises to enthusiasm. "Let us visit," he writes, "the Philippine Islands, and with astonishment shall we there behold extended ranges, studded with temples and spacious convents, the Divine worship celebrated with pomp and splendour; regularity in the streets, and even luxury in the houses and dress; schools of the first rudiments in all the towns, and the inhabitants well versed in the art of writing. We shall see there causeways raised, bridges of good architecture built, and, in short, all the measures of good government and police, in the greatest part of the country, carried into effect; yet the whole is due to the exertions, apostolic labours, and pure patriotism of the ministers of religion. Let us travel over the provinces, and we shall see towns of 5, 10, and 20,000 Indians, peacefully governed by one weak old man, who, with his doors open at all hours, sleeps quiet and secure in his dwelling, without any other magic, or any other guards, than the love and respect with which he has known how to inspire his flock."[81]

If this seems too rosy a picture, it still must not be forgotten that at this time the ratio of whites to Indians in the islands was only about one to sixteen hundred,[82] that most of these lived in Manila, and that the entire military force was not more than two thousand regular troops.[83] As has been intimated this condition lasted down until a comparatively recent period. As late as 1864 the total number of Spaniards amounted to but 4,050 of whom 3,280 were government officials, etc., 500 clergy, 200 landed proprietors, and 70 merchants; and in the provinces the same conditions prevailed that are described by Comyn.[84] In more than half of the twelve hundred villages in the islands "there was no other Spaniard, no other national authority, nor any other force to maintain public order save only the friars."[85]

Recurring for a moment to the higher ecclesiastical organization, the judicial functions of the church were represented by the archbishop's court and the commissioner of the Inquisition. The Episcopal court, which was made up of the archbishop, the vicar-general, and a notary, tried cases coming under the canon law, such as those relating to matrimony and all cases involving the clergy. Idolatry on the part of the Indians or Chinese might be punished by this court.[86] The Holy Inquisition transplanted to New Spain in 1569 stretched its long arm across the great ocean to the Philippines, in the person of a commissioner, for the preservation of the true faith. The Indians and Chinese were exempted from its jurisdiction. Its processes were roundabout, and must have given a considerable proportion of its accused a chance to die a natural death. The Commissioner must first report the offense to the Court in New Spain; if a trial was ordered, the accused must be sent to Mexico, and, if convicted, must be returned to the Philippines to receive punishment.[87]

The most peculiar feature of the old regime in the Philippines is to be found in the regulations of the commerce of the islands. In the *Recopilacion de leyes de los reinos de las Indias*, the code of Spanish colonial legislation, a whole title comprising seventy-nine laws is devoted to this subject. For thirty years after the conquest the commerce of the islands was unrestricted and their prosperity advanced with great rapidity.[88] Then came a system of restrictions, demanded by the protectionists in Spain, which limited the commerce of the islands with America to a fixed annual amount, and effectively checked their economic development. All the old travelers marvel at the possibilities of the islands and at the blindness of Spain, but the policy absurd as it may seem was but a logical application of the protective system not essentially different from the forms which it assumes today in our own relations to Porto Rico, Cuba, and the Philippines.

The Seville merchants through whose hands the Spanish export trade to the New World passed looked with apprehension upon the importation of Chinese fabrics into America and the exportation of American silver to pay for them. The silks of China undersold those of Spain in Mexico and Peru, and the larger the export of silver to the East the smaller to Spain. Consequently to protect Spanish industry and to preserve to Spanish producers the American market,[89] the shipment of Chinese cloths from Mexico to Peru was prohibited in 1587. In 1591 came the prohibition of all direct trade between Peru or other parts of South America and China or the Philippines,[90] and in 1593 a decree—not rigorously enforced till 1604—which absolutely limited the trade between Mexico and the Philippines to $250,000 annually for the exports to Mexico, and to $500,000 for the imports from Mexico, to be carried in two ships not to exceed three hundred tons burden.[91] No Spanish subject was allowed to trade in or with China, and the Chinese trade was restricted to the merchants of that nation.[92]

All Chinese goods shipped to New Spain must be consumed there and the shipping of Chinese cloths to Peru in any amount whatever even for a gift, charitable endowment, or for use in divine worship was absolutely prohibited.[93] As these regulations were evaded, in 1636 all commerce was interdicted between New Spain and Peru.[94] A commerce naturally so lucrative as that between the Philippines and New Spain when confined within such narrow limits yielded monopoly profits. It was like a lottery in which every ticket drew a prize. In these great profits every Spaniard was entitled to share in proportion to his capital or standing in the community.[95] The assurance of this largess, from the beginnings of the system, discouraged individual industry and enterprise, and retarded the growth of Spanish population.[96] Le Gentil and Zúñiga give detailed descriptions of the method of conducting this state enterprise[97] after the limits had been raised to $500,000 and $1,000,000 respectively for the outgoing and return voyage. The capacity of the vessel was measured taking as a unit a bale about two and one-half feet long, sixteen inches broad and two feet high. If then the vessel could carry four thousand of these bales, each bale might be packed with goods up to a value of one hundred and twenty-five dollars. The right to ship was known as a *boleta* or ticket. The distribution of these tickets was determined at the town hall by a board made up of the governor, attorney-general, the dean of the *audiencia*, one *alcalde*, one *regidor* and eight citizens.[98]

To facilitate the allotment and the sale of tickets they were divided into sixths. Tickets were ordinarily worth in the later eighteenth century in times of peace eighty dollars to one hundred dollars, and in war time they rose to upwards of three hundred dollars.[99] Le Gentil tells us that in 1766 they sold for two hundred dollars and more, and that the galleon that year went loaded beyond the limit.[100] Each official as the perquisite of his office had tickets. The regidores and alcaldes had eight.

The small holders who did not care to take a venture in the voyage disposed of their tickets to merchants or speculators, who borrowed money, usually of the religious corporations, at twenty-five to thirty per cent per annum to buy them up and who sometimes bought as many as two or three hundred.[101] The command of the Acapulco galleon was the fattest office within the gift of the Governor, who bestowed it upon "whomsoever he desired to make happy for the commission," and was equivalent to a gift of from $50,000 to $100,000.[102] This was made up from commissions, part of the passage-money of passengers, from the sale of his freight tickets, and from the gifts of the merchants. Captain Arguelles told Careri in 1696 that his commissions would amount to $25,000 or $30,000, and that in all he would make $40,000; that the pilot would clear $20,000 and the mates $9,000 each.[103] The pay of the sailors was three hundred and fifty dollars, of which seventy-five dollars was advanced before the start. The merchants expected to clear one hundred and fifty to two hundred per cent. The passenger fare at the end of the eighteenth century was $1,000 for the voyage to Acapulco, which was the hardest, and $500 for the return.[104] Careri's voyage to Acapulco lasted two hundred and four days. The ordinary time for the voyage to Manila was seventy-five to ninety days.[105] Careri's description of his voyage is a vivid picture of the hardships of early ocean travel, when cabin passengers fared infinitely worse than cattle today. It was a voyage "which is enough to destroy a man, or make him unfit for anything as long as he lives;" yet there were those who "ventured through it, four, six and some ten times."[106]

Acapulco in New Spain had little reason for existence, save for the annual fair at the time of the arrival of the Manila ship, and the silver fleet from Peru. That event transformed what might more properly be called "a poor village of fishermen" into "a populous city," for the space of about two weeks.[107]

The commerce between the Philippines and Mexico was conducted in this manner from 1604 to 1718, when the silk manufacturers of Spain secured the prohibition of the importation of Chinese silk goods into New Spain on account of the decline of their industry. A prolonged struggle before the Council of the Indies ensued, and in 1734 the prohibition was revoked and the east and west cargoes fixed at $500,000 and $1,000,000 respectively.[108] The last *nao*, as the Manila-Acapulco galleon was called, sailed from Manila in 1811, and the final return voyage was made in 1815. After that the commerce fell into private hands, the annual exports were limited to $750,000 and the ports of San Blas (Mexico), Guayaquil (Ecuador), and Callao (Peru) were opened to it.

Other changes were the establishment of direct communication with Spain and trade with Europe by a national vessel in 1766.[109] These expeditions lasted till 1783 and their place was taken in 1785 by the Royal Philippine Company, organized with a capital of $8,000,000, and granted the monopoly of the trade between Spain and the islands.[110] The Manila merchants resented the invasion of their monopoly of the export trade, and embarrassed the operations of the company as much as they could.[111] It ceased to exist in 1830.

By this system for two centuries the South American market for manufactures was reserved exclusively for Spain, but the protection did not prevent Spanish industry from decay and did retard the well-being and progress of South America. Between Mexico and the Philippines a limited trade was allowed, the profits of which were the perquisites of the Spaniards living in the Philippines and contributed to the religious endowments. But this monopoly was of no permanent advantage to the Spanish residents. It was too much like stock-jobbing, and sapped all spirit of industry. Zúñiga says that the commerce made a few rich in a short time and with little labor, but they were very few; that there were hardly five Spaniards in Manila worth $100,000, nor a hundred worth $40,000, the rest either lived on the King's pay or in poverty.[112] "Every morning one could see in the streets of Manila, in the greatest poverty and asking alms, the sons of men who had made a fine show and left much money, which their sons had squandered because they had not been well trained in youth."[113] The great possibilities of Manila as an entrepot of the Asiatic trade were unrealized; for although the city enjoyed open trade with the Chinese, Japanese, and other orientals,[114] it was denied to Europeans and the growth of that conducted by the Chinese and others was always obstructed by the lack of return cargoes owing to the limitations placed upon the trade with America and to the disinclination of the Filipinos to work to produce more than was enough to insure them a comfortable living and pay their tributes. That the system was detrimental to the economic progress of the islands was always obvious and its evils were repeatedly demonstrated by Spanish officials. Further it was not only detrimental to the prosperity of the islands but it obstructed the development of Mexico.

Grau y Monfalcon in 1637 reported that there were fourteen thousand people employed in Mexico in manufacturing the raw silk imported from China. This industry might be promoted by the relaxation of the restrictions on trade. It would also be for the advantage of the Indians of Peru to be able to buy for five pence a yard linen from the Philippines, rather than to be compelled to purchase that of Rouen at ten times the price.[115] But such reasoning was received then as it often is now, and no great change was made for nearly two centuries.

We have now passed in review the political, ecclesiastical, and commercial administration of the Philippines in the olden time; and a general survey of some of the more striking results of the system as a whole may now be made. This is especially necessary on account of the traditional and widely prevalent opinion that the Spanish colonial system was always and everywhere a system of oppression and exploitation; whereas, as a matter of fact, the Spanish system, as a system of laws, always impeded the effectual exploitation of the resources of their colonies, and was far more humane in its treatment of dependent peoples than either the French or English systems.

If, on the one hand, the early conquistadores treated the natives with hideous cruelty, the Spanish government legislated more systematically and benevolently to protect them than any other colonizing power. In the time of the first conquests things moved too rapidly for the home government in those days of slow communication, and the horrors of the clash between ruthless gold-seekers and the simple children of nature, as depicted by the impassioned pen of Las Casas and spread broadcast over Europe, came to be the traditional and accepted characteristic of Spanish rule.[116] The Spanish colonial empire lasted four hundred years and it is simple historical justice that it should not be judged by its beginnings or by its collapse.

The remoteness of the Philippines, and the absence of rich deposits of gold and silver, made it comparatively easy for the government to secure the execution of its humane legislation, and for the church to dominate the colony and guide its development as a great mission for the benefit of the inhabitants.[117] To the same result contributed the unenlightened protectionism of the Seville merchants, for the studied impediments to the development of the Philippine-American trade effectually blocked the exploitation of the islands. In view of the history of our own Southern States, not less than of the history of the West Indies it should never be forgotten that although the Philippine islands are in the Tropics, they have never been the scene of the horrors of the African slave trade or of the life-wasting labors of the old plantation system.

Whether we compare the condition of the natives of the other islands in the Eastern Archipelago or of the peasants of Europe at the same time the general well-being of the Philippine mission villagers was to be envied. A few quotations from unimpeachable witnesses, travelers of wide knowledge of the Orient, may be given in illustration and proof of this view. The famous French explorer of the Pacific, La Pérouse, who was in Manila in 1787, wrote: "Three million people inhabit these different islands and that of Luzon contains nearly a third of them. These people seemed to me no way inferior to those of Europe; they cultivate the soil with intelligence, they are carpenters, cabinet-makers, smiths, jewelers, weavers, masons, etc. I have gone through their villages and I have found them kind, hospitable, affable," etc.[118]

Coming down a generation later the Englishman Crawfurd, the historian of the Indian Archipelago, who lived at the court of the Sultan of Java as British resident, draws a comparison between the condition of the Philippines and that of the other islands of the East that deserves careful reflection.

"It is remarkable, that the Indian administration of one of the worst governments of Europe, and that in which the general principles of legislation and good government are least understood,—one too, which has never been skillfully executed, should, upon the whole, have proved the least injurious to the happiness and prosperity of the native inhabitants of the country.

This, undoubtedly, has been the character of the Spanish connection with the Philippines, with all its vices, follies, and illiberalities; and the present condition of these islands affords an unquestionable proof of the fact. Almost every other country of the Archipelago is, at this day, in point of wealth, power, and civilization, in a worse state than when Europeans connected themselves with them three centuries back. The Philippines alone have improved in civilization, wealth, and populousness. When discovered most of the tribes were a race of half-naked savages, inferior to all the great tribes, who were pushing, at the same time, an active commerce, and enjoying a respectable share of the necessaries and comforts of a civilized state. Upon the whole, they are at present superior in almost everything to any of the other races. This is a valuable and instructive fact."[119]

This judgment of Crawfurd in 1820 was echoed by Mallat (who was for a time in charge of the principal hospital in Manila), in 1846, when he expressed his belief that the inhabitants of the Philippines enjoyed a freer, happier, and more placid life than was to be found in the colonies of any other nation.[120]

Sir John Bowring, who was long Governor of Hong Kong, was impressed with the absence of caste: "Generally speaking, I found a kind and generous urbanity prevailing,—friendly intercourse where that intercourse had been sought,—the lines of demarcation and separation less marked and impassable than in most oriental countries. I have seen at the same table Spaniard, Mestizo and Indian—priest, civilian, and soldier. No doubt a common religion forms a common bond; but to him who has observed the alienations and repulsions of caste in many parts of the eastern world—caste, the great social curse—the binding and free intercourse of man with man in the Philippines is a contrast worth admiring."[121] Not less striking in its general bearing than Crawfurd's verdict is that of the German naturalist Jagor who visited the islands in 1859-1860.

"To Spain belongs the glory of having raised to a relatively high grade of civilization, improving greatly their condition, a people which she found on a lower stage of culture distracted by petty wars and despotic rule. Protected from outside enemies, governed by mild laws, the inhabitants of those splendid islands, taken as a whole, have no doubt passed a more comfortable life during recent centuries than the people of any tropical country whether under their own or European rule. This is to be accounted for in part by the peculiar conditions which protected the natives from ruthless exploitation. Yet the monks contributed an essential part to this result. Coming from among the common people, used to poverty and self-denial, their duties led them into intimate relations with the natives and they were naturally fitted to adapt the foreign religion and morals to practical use. So, too, in later times, when they came to possess rich livings, and their pious zeal, in general, relaxed as their revenues increased, they still contributed most essentially to bring about conditions, both good and bad, which we have described, since, without families of their own and without refined culture, intimate association with the children of the soil was a necessity to them. Even their haughty opposition to the secular authorities was generally for the advantage of the natives."[122] Similar testimony from a widely different source is contained in the charming sketch "Malay Life in the Philippines" by William Gifford Palgrave, whose profound knowledge of oriental life and character and his experience in such divergent walks in life as soldier and Jesuit missionary in India, pilgrim to Mecca, and English consul in Manila, give his opinion more than ordinary value.

"To clerical government," he writes "paradoxical as the statement may sound in modern European ears, the Philippine islands owe, more than to anything else, their internal prosperity, the Malay population its sufficiency and happiness. This it is that again and again has stood a barrier of mercy and justice between the weaker and stronger race, the vanquished and the victor; this has been the steady protector of the native inhabitants, this their faithful benefactor, their sufficient leader and guide. With the 'Cura' for father, and the 'Capitan' for his adjutant, a Philippine hamlet feels and knows little of the vexations inseparable from direct and foreign official administration; and if under such a rule 'progress,' as we love to term it, be rare, disaffection and want are rarer still."

As compared with India, the absence of famines is significant; and this he attributes in part to the prevalence of small holdings. "Not so much what they have, but rather what they have not, makes the good fortune of the Philippines, the absence of European Enterprise, the absence of European Capital. A few European capitalist settlers, a few giant estates, a few central factories, a few colossal money-making combinations of organized labour and gainful produce, and all the equable balance of property and production, of ownership and labour that now leaves to the poorest cottager enough, and yet to the total colony abundance to spare, would be disorganized, displaced, upset; to be succeeded by day labour, pauperism, government relief, subscriptions, starvation. Europe, gainful, insatiate Europe would reap the harvest; but to the now happy, contented, satiate Philippine Archipelago, what would remain but the stubble, but leanness, want, unrest, misery?"[123]

The latest witness to the average well-being of the natives under the old system whom I shall quote is Mr. Sawyer. "If the natives fared badly at the hands of recent authors, the Spanish Administration fared worse, for it has been painted in the darkest tints, and unsparingly condemned. It was indeed corrupt and defective, and what government is not? More than anything else it was behind the age, yet it was not without its good points.

"Until an inept bureaucracy was substituted for the old paternal rule, and the revenue quadrupled by increased taxation, the Filipinos were as happy a community as could be found in any colony. The population greatly multiplied; they lived in competence, if not in affluence; cultivation was extended, and the exports steadily increased.—Let us be just; what British, French, or Dutch colony, populated by natives can compare with the Philippines as they were until 1895?"[124]

These striking judgments, derived from such a variety of sources, are a sufficient proof that our popular ideas of the Spanish colonial system are quite as much in need of revision as popular ideas usually are.

Yet one must not forget that the Spanish mission system, however useful and benevolent as an agency in bringing a barbarous people within the pale of Christian civilization, could not be regarded as permanent unless this life is looked upon simply as a preparation for heaven. As an educative system it had its bounds and limits; it could train to a certain point and no farther. To prolong it beyond that stage would be to prolong carefully nurtured childhood to the grave, never allowing it to be displaced by self-reliant manhood. The legal status of the Indians before the law was that of minors, and no provision was made for their arriving at their majority. The clergy looked upon these wards of the State as the school-children of the church, and compelled the observance of her ordinances even with the rod. La Pérouse says: "The only thought was to make Christians and never citizens. This people was divided into parishes, and subjected to the most minute and extravagant observances. Each fault, each sin is still punished by the rod. Failure to attend prayers and mass has its fixed penalty, and punishment is administered to men and women at the door of the church by order of the pastor."[125] Le Gentil describes such a scene in a little village a few miles from Manila, where one Sunday afternoon he saw a crowd, chiefly Indian women, following a woman who was to be whipped at the church door for not having been to mass.[126]

The prevalence of a supervision and discipline so parental for the mass of the people in the colony could but react upon the ruling class, and La Pérouse remarks upon the absence of individual liberty in the islands: "No liberty is enjoyed: inquisitors and monks watch the consciences; the oidors (judges of the Audiencia) all private affairs; the governor, the most innocent movements; an excursion to the interior, a conversation come before his jurisdiction; in fine, the most beautiful and charming country in the world is certainly the last that a free man would choose to live in."[127]

Intellectual apathy, one would naturally suppose, must be the consequence of such sedulous oversight, and intellectual progress impossible. Progress in scientific knowledge was, indeed, quite effectually blocked.

The French astronomer Le Gentil gives an interesting account of the conditions of scientific knowledge at the two Universities in Manila. These institutions seemed to be the last refuge of the scholastic ideas and methods that had been discarded in Europe. A Spanish engineer frankly confessed to him that "in the sciences Spain was a hundred years behind France, and that in Manila they were a hundred years behind Spain." Nothing of electricity was known but the name, and making experiments in it had been forbidden by the Inquisition. Le Gentil also strongly suspected that the professor of Mathematics at the Jesuit College still held to the Ptolemaic system.[128]

But when we keep in mind the small number of ecclesiastics in the islands we must clear them of the charge of intellectual idleness. Their activity, on the other hand, considering the climate was remarkable.[129] An examination of J.T. Medina's monumental work[130] on printing in Manila and of Retana's supplement[131] reveals nearly five hundred titles of works printed in the islands before 1800. This of course takes no account of the works sent or brought to Spain for publication, which would necessarily comprise a large proportion of those of general rather than local interest, including of course the most important histories. To these should be added no small number of grammars and dictionaries of the native languages, and missionary histories, that have never been printed.[132] The monastic presses in the islands naturally were chiefly used for the production of works of religious edification, such as catechisms, narratives of missions, martyrdoms, lives of saints, religious histories, and hand-books to the native languages. Simpler manuals of devotion, rosaries, catechisms, outlines of Christian doctrine, stories of martyrdoms, etc., were translated for the Indians. Of these there were about sixty in the Tagal, and from three to ten or twelve each in the Visayan, Vicol, Pampanga, Ilocan, Panayan, and Pangasinán languages.[133]

If, as is credibly asserted, the knowledge of reading and writing was more generally diffused in the Philippines than among the common people of Europe,[134] we have the singular result that the islands contained relatively more people who could read, and less reading matter of any but purely religious interest, than any other community in the world. Yet it would not be altogether safe to assume that in the eighteenth century the list of printed translations into the native languages comprised everything of European literature available for reading; for the Spanish government, in order to promote the learning of Spanish, had prohibited at times the printing of books in Tagal.[135] Furthermore, Zúñiga says explicitly that "after the coming of the Spaniards they *(i.e.* the people in Luzon) have had comedies, interludes, tragedies, poems, and every kind of literary work translated from the Spanish, without producing a native poet who has composed even an interlude."[136] Again, Zúñiga describes a eulogistic poem of welcome addressed by a Filipino villager to Commodore Alava. This *loa*, as this species of composition was called, was replete with references to the voyages of Ulysses, the travels of Aristotle, the unfortunate death of Pliny, and other incidents in ancient history. The allusions indicate some knowledge at any rate outside the field of Christian doctrine, even if it was so slight as not to make it seem beyond the limits of poetic license to have Aristotle drown himself in chagrin at not being able to measure the depths of the sea, or to have Pliny throw himself into Vesuvius in his zeal to investigate the causes of its eruption. The literary interests of the Indians found their chief expression however in the adaptation of Spanish plays for presentation on religious holidays. Zúñiga gives an entertaining description of these plays. They were usually made up from three or four Spanish tragedies, the materials of which were so ingeniously interwoven that the mosaic seemed a single piece. The characters were always Moors and Christians, and the action centered in the desire of Moors to marry Christian princesses or of Christians to marry Moorish princesses. The Christian appears at a Moorish tournament or vice versa. The hero and heroine fall in love but their parents oppose obstacles to the match. To overcome the difficulties in case of a Moor and Christian princess was comparatively easy. A war opportunely breaks out in which, after prodigies of valor, the Moor is converted and baptized, and the wedding follows. The case is not so easy when a Christian prince loves a Moorish lady. Since he can never forsake his religion his tribulations are many. He is imprisoned, and his princess aids in his attempt to escape, which sometimes costs him his life; or if the scene is laid in war time either the princess is converted and escapes to the Christian army, or the prince dies a tragic death. The hero is usually provided with a Christ, or other image or relic, given him by his dying mother, which extricates him from his many plights. He meets lions and bears, and highwaymen attack him; but from all he escapes by a miracle. If, however, some principal personage is not taken off by a tragic end, the Indians find the play insipid. During the intermission one or two clowns come out and raise a laugh by jests that are frigid enough "to freeze hot water in the tropics." After the play is over a clown appears again and criticizes the play and makes satirical comments on the village officials. These plays usually lasted three days.[137] Le Gentil attended one of them and says that he does not believe any one in the world was ever so bored as he was.[138] Yet the Indians were passionately fond of these performances.[139]

If one may judge from Retana's catalogue of his Philippine collection arranged in chronological order, the sketch we have given of the literature accessible to Filipinos who could not read Spanish in the eighteenth century would serve not unfairly for much of the nineteenth. The first example of secular prose fiction I have noted in his lists is Friar Bustamente's pastoral novel depicting the quiet charms of country life as compared with the anxieties and tribulations of life in Manila.[140] His collection did not contain so far as I noticed a single secular historical narrative in Tagal or anything in natural science.

Sufficient familiarity with Spanish to compensate for this lack of books of secular knowledge was enjoyed by very few Indians in the country districts and these had learned it mainly while servants of the curate. It was the common opinion of the Spanish authorities that the Friars purposely neglected instructing the Indians in Spanish, in order to perpetuate their hold upon them; but Zúñiga repels this charge as unjust and untrue.[141]

It is obvious that it was impracticable for the Indians to learn Spanish under the mission system. For the pastor of a pueblo of several hundred families to teach the children Spanish was an impossibility. A few words or simple phrases might be learned, but the lack of opportunity for constant or even frequent practice of the language in general conversation would make their attainments in it far below those of American grammar-school children in German in cities where that has been a compulsory study.[142] As long as the mission system isolated the pueblos from contact with the world at large, it of necessity followed that the knowledge of Spanish would be practically limited to such Indians as lived in Manila or the larger towns, or learned it in the households of the Friars. Slavery with its forced transplanting has been the only means by which large masses of alien or lower races have been lifted into the circle of European thought and endowed with a European language. If such a result is secured in the future in any large measure for the Filipino, it can be accomplished only by the translation of English or Spanish literature into the Tagal and other languages, on a scale not less generous than the work of the Friars in supplying the literature of religious edification. This will be a work of not less than two or three generations, and of a truly missionary devotion.

We have now surveyed in its general aspects the old régime in the Philippines, and supplied the necessary material upon which to base a judgment of this contribution of Spain to the advancement of civilization. In this survey certain things stand out in contrast to the conventional judgment of the Spanish colonial system. The conquest was humane, and was effected by missionaries more than by warriors. The sway of Spain was benevolent, although the administration was not free from the taint of financial corruption. Neither the islands nor their inhabitants were exploited. The colony in fact was a constant charge upon the treasury of New Spain. The success of the enterprise was not measured by the exports and imports, but by the number of souls put in the way of salvation. The people received the benefits of Christian civilization, as it was understood in Spain in the days of that religious revival which we call the Catholic Reaction. This Christianity imposed the faith and the observances of the mediæval church, but it did for the Philippine islanders who received it just what it did for the Franks or Angles a thousand years earlier. It tamed their lives, elevated the status of women, established the Christian family, and gave them the literature of the devotional life.

Nor did they pay heavily for these blessings. The system of government was inexpensive, and the religious establishment was mainly supported by the landed estates of the orders. Church fees may have been at times excessive, but the occasions for such fees were infrequent. The tenants of the church estates found the friars easy landlords. Zúñiga describes a great estate of the Augustinians near Manila of which the annual rental was not over $1,500, while the annual produce was estimated to be not less than $70,000, for it supported about four thousand people.[143] The position of women was fully as good among the Christian Indians of the Philippines as among the Christian people of Europe. But conspicuous among the achievements of the conquest and conversion of the islands in the field of humanitarian progress, when we consider the conditions in other European tropical colonies, have been the prohibition of slavery and the unremitting efforts to eradicate its disguised forms. These alone are a sufficient proof that the dominating motives in the Spanish and clerical policies were humane and not commercial. Not less striking proof of the comfortable prosperity of the natives on the whole under the old Spanish rule has been the steady growth of the population. At the time of the conquest the population in all probability did not exceed a half-million. In the first half of the eighteenth century according to the historian of the Franciscans, San Antonio, the Christian population was about 830,000. At the opening of the nineteenth century Zúñiga estimated the total at a million and a half as over 300,000 tributes were paid. The official estimate in 1819 was just short of 2,600,000; by 1845 Buzeta calculates the number at a little short of four millions. In the next half century it nearly doubled.[144]

In view of all these facts one must readily accord assent to Zúñiga's simple tribute to the work of Spain. "The Spanish rule has imposed very few burdens upon these Indians, and has delivered them from many misfortunes which they suffered from the constant warfare waged by one district with another, whereby many died, and others lived wretched lives as slaves. For this reason the population increased very slowly, as is now the case with the infidels of the mountain regions who do not acknowledge subjection to the King of Spain. Since the conquest there has been an increase in well-being and in population. Subjection to the King of Spain has been very advantageous in all that concerns the body. I will not speak of the advantage of knowledge of the true God, and of the opportunity to obtain eternal happiness for the soul, for I write not as a missionary but as a philosopher."[145]

The old régime in the Philippines has disappeared forever. In hardly more than a generation the people have passed from a life which was so remote from the outside contemporary world that they might as well have been living in the middle ages in some sheltered nook, equally protected from the physical violence and the intellectual strife of the outside world, and entirely oblivious of the progress of knowledge. They find themselves suddenly plunged into a current that hurls them along resistlessly. Baptized with fire and blood, a new and strange life is thrust upon them and they face the struggle for existence under conditions which spare no weakness and relentlessly push idleness or incapacity to the wall. What will be the outcome no man can tell. To the student of history and of social evolution it will be an experiment of profound interest.

Edward Gaylord Bourne
Yale University,
October, 1902.

PREFACE TO VOLUME I

The history of the Philippine archipelago is fitly introduced by presenting a group of documents which relate to Pope Alexander VI's Line of Demarcation between the respective dominions of Spain and Portugal in the recently-discovered New World. So many controversies regarding this line have at various times arisen, and so little on the subject has appeared in the English tongue, that we have thought it well to place before our readers the more important of the documents relating thereto, of which a brief synopsis is here given.

They begin with Alexander's Bulls—two dated on the third and one on the fourth day of May, 1493. The first of these (commonly known as *Inter cætera*) grants to. Spain all the lands in the West, recently discovered or yet to be discovered, which are hitherto unknown, and not under the dominion of any Christian prince. The second *(Eximiæ devotionis*, also dated May 3) grants to Spain the same rights in those discoveries which had formerly been conferred on Portugal in Africa. These grants are superseded by the Bull of May 4 *(Inter cætera)*, which establishes the Demarcation Line, and grants to Spain all lands west and south thereof which were not already in the possession of any Christian prince. Still another Bull (dated September 25 of the same year) authorizes Spain to extend her sovereignty also over lands which shall be discovered to the East, including India—thus practically annulling both the Demarcation Line and previous concessions to Portugal. The latter power's remonstrances against this infringement of her former rights lead to the Treaty of Tordesillas (June 7, 1494), in which, by mutual agreement between the sovereigns, a new line of demarcation is established to be drawn two hundred and seventy leagues farther west than that of Alexander VI; and another document (dated April 15, 1495) makes suitable arrangements for a scientific and equitable determination of this boundary. The final action of the Holy See in this matter is indicated by a Bull of Leo X *(Præcelsæ*, dated November 3, 1514) granted to Portugal; it confirms all previous papal gifts to that power of lands in the East, and grants to her both past and future discoveries and conquests, there and elsewhere. Disputes arising between Spain and Portugal over the ownership of the Moluccas or Spice Islands (see letters of Cárlos I to his ambassadors at Lisbon, February 4 and December 18, 1523; and the treaty of Vitoria, February 19, 1524), the Junta of Badajoz is convened (April 11-May 31, 1524) to settle this question; and that body fixes the Line of Demarcation three hundred and seventy leagues west of San Antonio, the most westerly of the Cape Verde Islands. (In this connection are presented the opinions of Hernando Colon, Sebastian Cabot, and other competent judges; and letters from Cárlos I to the Spanish deputies.) This settlement proving ineffectual, the Moluccas are relinquished to Portugal by the treaty of Zaragoza (April 22, 1529), Spain retaining possession of the Philippine Islands, although the terms of that treaty placed them outside of her jurisdiction.

Reverting to a somewhat earlier date, we note incidentally the Bull of Alexander VI *(Eximiæ*, November 16, 1501) which authorizes the Spanish monarchs to levy tithes on the natives and inhabitants of their newly-acquired possessions in the western world; and proceed to a summary of the life and voyages of Fernão de Magalhães (commonly known as Magellan). Synopses are given of many documents published by Navarrete, dated from 1518 to 1527: a contract by Magalhães and Falero to deliver to the House of Commerce of Seville one-eighth of all gains accruing to them from their future discoveries; a petition from the same men to Cárlos I regarding the expedition which they are about to undertake; remonstrances against the undertaking, by the Portuguese ambassador in Spain, Magalhães's request for more money; various appointments in the fleet; restriction of the number of seamen; instructions to Magalhães; a royal order that Ruy Falero shall not accompany the expedition; Magalhães's last will; the expense account of the fleet; an attempted mutiny on one of the ships; Francisco Albo'* journal of Magalhães's voyage; description of the cargo brought back to Spain by the "Victoria;" investigation of Magalhães's death; treaties with the natives of the Moluccas;

advice given to the emperor by Diego de Barbosa; Brito's account of Magalhães's voyage; and the confiscation of two of his ships by the Portuguese.

This résumé is followed by various supplementary documents. A royal mandate (March 22, 1518) authorizes Falero and Magalhães to undertake their expedition of discovery. A letter from Cárlos to King Manuel of Portugal (February 28, 1519) assures him that nothing in this enterprise is intended to infringe upon Portuguese rights. A document written (April 6, 1519) to Juan de Cartagena, appointed inspector-general of Magalhães's fleet, gives detailed instructions as to his duties in that office, especially in regard to the equipment of the fleet, its trading operations in the Orient, the royal share of profits to be derived therefrom, and the current accounts of the enterprise; he is also charged with the necessary arrangements for the colonization of lands to be discovered, and commanded to furnish to the King information as to the treatment of the natives by their Spanish conquerors, and the general conduct of the officers of the expedition, etc. The fleet is ordered (April 19, 1510) to proceed directly to the Spice Islands, and all persons belonging to it are exhorted to obey Magalhães. A letter (1522) to the King of Spain gives information about Magalhães's death, obtained from some Spanish ship-boys who had found their way to the Portuguese posts in India. The earliest published account of this noted expedition is the letter written (October 24, 1522) to Matthæus Lang, archbishop of Salzburg, by a natural son of his named Maximilian Transylvanus (then a student at Valladolid), relating the events of Magallanes's voyage to the Moluccas (1519-21), his death at the hands of hostile natives, and the further experiences of his followers in the Philippine archipelago and on their homeward voyage. The small remnant of this expedition—the ship "Victoria," and eighteen men—reach Spain on September 6, 1522, the first persons thus completing the circumnavigation of the globe.

At this point should appear in the present series the relation of Magalhães's voyage written by Antonio Pigafetta, who himself accompanied the great discoverer. Printed books gave Pigafetta's relation in abridged form, in both French and Italian, as early as 1525 and 1536 respectively; but apparently his own original work has never hitherto been adequately presented to the world. The

Editors of the present series, desiring to supply this deficiency, purpose to publish an exact transcription from Pigafetta's original manuscript, with accompanying English translation. They have not, however, been able to secure it in time for Volume II, where it should appear; it will accordingly be presented to their readers at a later period in this work.

The Editors

DOCUMENTS REGARDING THE
LINE OF DEMARCATION—1493-1529

Papal bulls: *Inter cætera* (May 3), *Eximiæ* (May 3), *Inter cætera* (May 4), *Extension de la concesion* (September 25)—1493. Treaty of Tordesillas—June 7, 1494. [Note on correspondence of Jaime Ferrer—1493-95.] Compact between the Catholic Sovereigns and the King of Portugal—April 15, 1495. Papal bull, *Præcelsæ*—November 3, 1514. Instructions from the King of Spain to his ambassadors—February 4, 1523. Letter from Cárlos I to Juan de Zúñiga—December 18, 1523. Treaty of Vitoria—February 19, 1524. Junta of Badajoz: extract from the records (April 14-May 13), opinions of cosmographers (April 13-15), letters to the Spanish delegates (March 21, April 10)—1524. Treaty of Zaragoza—April 22, 1529.

Sources: See Bibliographical Data at end of this volun

Translations: The Papal Bulls are translated by Rev. Thomas Cooke Middleton, D.D., O.S.A.; the Treaty of Zaragoza, by José M. Asensio; the remaining documents of this group are compiled, translated, and arranged by James A. Robertson.

Papal Bulls of 1493

Inter Cætera—May 3

Alexander, etc., to the illustrious sovereigns, our very dear son in Christ, Ferdinand, King, and our very dear daughter in Christ, Helisabeth [Isabella], Queen, of Castile and Leon, Aragon, Sicily, and Granada health and apostolic benediction. Among other works well pleasing to his divine Majesty, and cherished of our heart, this assuredly ranks highest that in our times especially the Catholic faith and the Christian religion be everywhere increased and spread, as well as that the health of souls be procured, and barbarous nations overthrown and brought to the faith itself. Wherefore inasmuch as by the favor of divine clemency, through no fitting merits of ours, we have been raised to this holy see of Peter, recognizing that as true Catholic kings and princes such as we have always known you to be, and as your illustrious deeds already known to almost the whole world declare, you not only eagerly desire but with every effort, zeal, and diligence, without regard to hardships, expenses, dangers, with the shedding even of your blood, are laboring to that end; recognizing besides that already you have long ago dedicated to this purpose your whole soul and all your endeavors—as witnessed in these times with so much glory to the divine name in your recovery of the kingdom of Granada from the yoke of the Moors—we therefore not unrighteously hold it as our duty to grant you even of our own accord and in your favor those things, whereby daily and with heartier effort you may be enabled for the honor of God himself and the spread of the Christian rule to accomplish your saintly and praiseworthy purpose so pleasing to immortal God. In sooth we have learned that, according to your purpose long ago, you were in quest of some far-away islands and mainlands not hitherto discovered by others, to the end that you might bring to the worship of our Redeemer and profession of the Catholic faith the inhabitants of them with the dwellers therein; that hitherto, having been earnestly engaged in the siege and recovery of the kingdom itself of Granada, you were unable to accomplish this saintly and praiseworthy purpose; but, at length, as was pleasing to the Lord, the said kingdom having been regained, not without the greatest hardships, dangers, and expenses, we have also learned that with the wish to fulfil your desire, you chose our beloved son Christopher Colon, whom you furnished with ships and men equipped for like designs, so as to make diligent quest for these far-away unknown countries through the sea, which hitherto no one has sailed; who in fine with divine aid nor without the utmost diligence sailing in the Ocean Sea, as said, through western waters towards the Indies, discovered certain very far-away islands and even mainlands, that hitherto had not been discovered by others. Therein dwell very many peoples living in peace, and, as reported, going unclothed, nor users of flesh meat. Moreover, as your aforesaid envoys are of opinion, these very peoples living in the said islands and countries believe in one God, Creator in heaven, besides being sufficiently ready in appearance to embrace the Catholic faith and be trained in good morals. Nor is hope lacking that, were they instructed, the name of the Savior, our Lord Jesus Christ, would easily be introduced into the said countries and islands. Besides on one of these aforesaid chief islands the above-mentioned Christopher has already had put together and built a fortress[146] fairly well equipped, wherein he has stationed as garrison certain Christians, companions of his, who are to make search for other far-away and unknown islands and countries. In the islands and countries already discovered are found gold, spices, and very many other precious things of divers kinds and species. Wherefore, as becoming to Catholic kings and princes, after earnest consideration of all matters especially of the rise and spread of the Catholic faith, as was the fashion of your ancestors, kings of renowned memory, you have purposed with the favor of divine clemency to bring under your sway the said countries and islands with their inhabitants and the dwellers therein, and bring them to the Catholic faith. Hence in heartiest commendation in the Lord of this your saintly and praiseworthy purpose, desirous too that it be duly accomplished in the carrying to those regions of the name of our Savior, we exhort you very earnestly in the Lord and insist strictly—both through your reception of holy baptism, whereby you are bound to our apostolic commands, and through the bowels of the mercy of our Lord Jesus Christ, that inasmuch as with upright spirit and through zeal for the true faith you design to equip and despatch this expedition, you purpose also, as is your duty, to lead the peoples dwelling in those islands to embrace the Christian profession; nor at any time let dangers or hardships deter you therefrom, with the stout hope and trust in your hearts that almighty God will further your undertakings. Moreover, in order that with greater readiness and heartiness you enter upon an undertaking of so lofty a character as has been entrusted to you by the graciousness of our apostolic favor, we, moved thereunto by our own accord, not at your instance nor the request of anyone else in your regard, but of our own sole largess and certain knowledge as well as in the fulness of our apostolic power, by the authority of almighty God conferred upon us in blessed Peter and of the vicarship of Jesus Christ which we hold on earth, do by tenor of these presents give, grant, and assign forever to you and your heirs and successors, kings of Castile and Leon, all and singular the aforesaid countries and islands thus unknown and hitherto discovered by your envoys and to be discovered hereafter, providing however they at no time have been in the actual temporal possession of any Christian owner, together with all their dominions, cities, camps, places, and towns as well as all rights, jurisdictions, and appurtenances of the same wherever they may be found. Moreover we invest you and your aforementioned heirs and successors with them, and make, appoint, and depute you owners of them with full and free power, authority, and jurisdiction of every kind, with this proviso however, that by this gift, grant, assignment, and investiture of ours no right conferred on any Christian prince is hereby to be understood as withdrawn or to be withdrawn. Moreover we command you in virtue of holy obedience, that, employing all due diligence in the premises, as you promise— nor do we doubt your compliance therewith to the best of your loyalty and royal greatness of spirit—you send to the aforesaid countries and islands worthy, God-fearing, learned, skilled, and experienced men in order to instruct the aforesaid inhabitants and dwellers therein in the Catholic faith, and train them in good morals. Besides, under penalty of excommunication *late sententie* to be incurred *ipso facto*,[147] should anyone thus contravene, we strictly forbid all persons of no matter what rank, estate, degree, order, or condition, to dare, without your special permit or that of your aforesaid heirs and successors, to go for the sake of trade or any other purpose whatever to the said islands and countries discovered and found by your envoys or persons sent thither. And inasmuch as some kings of Portugal, by similar apostolic grant made to them, discovered and took possession of islands in the waters of Africa, Guinea, and the Gold Mine,[148] as well as elsewhere, far which reason divers privileges, favors, liberties, immunities, exemptions, and indults were granted to them by this apostolic see, we through similar accord, authority, knowledge, and fulness of our apostolic power, by a gift of special favor, do empower you and your aforesaid heirs and successors, in the islands and countries discovered and to be discovered by you, to use, employ, and enjoy freely and legally, as is right, in all things and through all things, the same as if they had been especially granted to you and your aforesaid heirs and successors, all and singular these favors, privileges, exemptions, liberties, faculties, immunities, and indults, whereof the terms of all we wish understood as being sufficiently expressed and inserted, the same as if they had been inserted word for word in these presents. Moreover we similarly extend and enlarge them in all things and through all things in favor of you and your aforesaid heirs and successors, the apostolic constitutions and ordinances as well as all those things that have been granted in the letters above or other things whatsoever to the contrary notwithstanding. We trust in him from whom derive empires and governments and everything good, that with the guidance of the Lord over your deeds, should you pursue this saintly and praiseworthy undertaking, in a short while your hardships and endeavors will result in the utmost success to the happiness and glory of all Christendom. But inasmuch as it would be difficult to have these present letters sent to all places where desirable, we wish, and with similar accord and knowledge do decree that to copies of them, signed by the hand of a notary public commissioned therefor and sealed with the seal of any ecclesiastical officer or ecclesiastical court, the same respect is to be shown in court and outside as well as anywhere else, as would be given to these presents, should they be exhibited or shown. Let no one, therefore, infringe, or with rash boldness contravene this our exhortation, requisition, gift, grant, assignment, investiture, deed, constitution, deputation, mandate, inhibition, indult, exemption, enlargement, will, and decree. Should any one presume to do so, be it known to him that he will incur the wrath of Almighty God, and of the blessed apostles Peter and Paul. Given in Rome at St. Peter's, on the third day of May in the year one thousand four hundred and ninety-three, of the incarnation of our Lord, in the first year of our pontificate.

Gratis by order [of our most holy lord the Pope.]

B. Capotius
Coll. A. de Compania
D. Sorrano
N. Casanova

Alexander, etc., to the illustrious sovereigns, our very dear son in Christ Ferdinand, King, and our very dear daughter in Christ Elizabeth [Isabella], Queen of Castile, Leon, Aragon and Granada, health, etc. The sincereness and whole-souled loyalty of your exalted attachment to ourselves and the church of Rome deserve to have us grant in your favor those things whereby daily you may the more easily be enabled to the honor of Almighty God and the spread of Christian government as well as the exaltation of the Catholic faith to carry out your saintly and praiseworthy purpose and the work already undertaken of making search for far-away and unknown countries and islands. For this very day through our own accord and certain knowledge, as well as fulness of our apostolic power, we have given, granted, and assigned forever, as appears more fully in our letters drawn up therefor, to you and your heirs and successors, kings of Castile and Leon, all and singular the far-away and unknown mainlands and islands lying to the west in the Ocean Sea, that have been discovered or hereafter may be discovered by you or your envoys, whom you have equipped therefor not without great hardships, dangers, and expense; providing however these countries be not in the actual possession of Christian owners. But inasmuch as by this apostolic see have been granted divers privileges, favors, liberties, immunities, exemptions, faculties, letters, and indults to some kings of Portugal, who also by similar apostolic grant and donation in their favor, have discovered and taken possession of other countries and islands in the waters of Africa, Guinea, and the Gold Coast, with the desire to empower by our apostolic authority, as also is right and fitting, you and your aforesaid heirs and successors with graces, prerogatives, and favors of no less character; moved also thereto wholly by our own similar accord, not at your instance nor the petition of any one else in your favor, but through out own sole liberality as well as the same knowledge and fulness of our apostolic power, we do by tenor of these presents, as a gift of special favor, empower you and your aforesaid heirs and successors to the end that in the islands and countries, already discovered by you or in your name and to be discovered hereafter, you may freely and legally, as is proper, use, employ, and enjoy in all things and through all things exactly the same as if they had been granted especially to you and your aforesaid heirs and successors, all and singular the graces, privileges, exemptions, liberties, faculties, immunities, letters, and indults that have been granted to the kings of Portugal, the terms whereof we wish to be understood as sufficiently expressed and inserted, the same as if they had been inserted word for word in these presents. Moreover we extend similarly and enlarge these powers in all things and through all things to you and your aforesaid heirs and successors, to whom in the same manner and form we grant them forever, the apostolic constitutions and ordinances as well as all grants of similar kind made by letters to the kings of Portugal, as well as other things whatsoever to the contrary notwithstanding. But as it would be difficult to have these present letters sent to all places where desirable, we wish and with similar accord and knowledge do decree that to copies of them, signed by the hand of a public notary commissioned therefor, and sealed with the seal of any ecclesiastical officer or ecclesiastical court, the same respect is to be shown in court and outside as well as anywhere else as would be given to these presents should they be exhibited or shown. Let no one therefore, etc., infringe, etc., this our indult, extension, enlargement, grant, will, and decree. Should any one, etc. Given at Rome at St. Peter's, in the year, etc., one thousand four hundred and ninety-three, the third day of May, the first year of our pontificate.

Gratis by order of our most holy lord the Pope.

Jo. Nilis.
D Gallettus.

Inter Cætera—May 4

Alexander, etc., to the illustrious sovereigns, our very dear son in Christ, Ferdinand, King, and our very dear daughter in Christ, Helisabeth [Isabella], Queen of Castile and Leon, Aragon, Sicily, and Granada, health, etc. Among other works well pleasing to his divine Majesty and cherished of our heart, this assuredly ranks highest: that in our times especially the Catholic faith and the Christian law be exalted and everywhere increased and spread as well as that the health of souls be procured, and barbarous nations overthrown and brought to the faith itself. Wherefore inasmuch as by the favor of divine clemency, through no fitting merits of ours, we have been raised to so holy a see as Peter's, recognizing that as true Catholic kings and princes such as we have always known you to be, and as your illustrious deeds already known to almost the whole world declare, you not only eagerly desire but with every effort, zeal, and diligence, without regard to hardships, expenses, dangers, with the shedding even of your blood, are laboring to that end; that besides you have already long ago dedicated to this purpose your whole soul and all your endeavors, as witnessed in these times with so much glory to the divine name in your recovery of the kingdom of Granada from the yoke of the Moors, we therefore not unrighteously hold it as our duty to grant you even of our own accord and in your favor those things whereby daily and with heartier effort you may be enabled for the honor of God himself and the spread of the Christian rule to accomplish your saintly and praiseworthy purpose so pleasing to immortal God. In sooth we have learned that according to your purpose long ago you were in quest of some far-away islands and mainlands not hitherto discovered by others, to the end that you might bring to the worship of our Redeemer and the profession of the Catholic faith the inhabitants of them with the dwellers therein; that hitherto having been earnestly engaged in the siege and recovery of the kingdom itself of Granada you were unable to accomplish this saintly and praiseworthy purpose; but at length, as was pleasing to the Lord, the said kingdom having been regained, not without the greatest hardships, dangers, and expenses, that with the wish to fulfil your desire, you chose our beloved son, Christopher Colon, a man assuredly worthy and of the highest recommendations as well as furnished with ships and men equipped for like designs, to make diligent quest for these far-away, unknown mainlands and islands through the sea, where hitherto no one has sailed; who in fine, with divine aid, nor without the utmost diligence, sailing in the Ocean Sea discovered certain very far-away islands and even mainlands that hitherto had not been discovered by others, wherein dwell very many peoples living in peace, and, as reported, going unclothed, nor users of flesh meat; and, as your aforesaid envoys are of opinion, these very peoples living in the said islands and countries believe in one God, Creator in heaven, besides being sufficiently ready in appearance to embrace the Catholic faith and be trained in good morals. Nor is hope lacking that, were they instructed, the name of the Savior, our Lord Jesus Christ, would easily be introduced into the said countries and islands. Besides on one of these aforesaid chief islands the said Christopher has already had put together and built a well-equipped fortress, wherein he has stationed as garrison certain Christians, companions of his, who are to make search for other far-away and unknown islands and mainlands. In certain islands and countries already discovered are found gold, spices, and very many other precious things of divers kinds and species. Wherefore, as becoming to Catholic kings and princes, after earnest consideration of all matters, especially of the rise and spread of the Catholic faith, as was the fashion of your ancestors, kings of renowned memory, you have purposed with the favor of divine clemency to bring under your sway the said mainlands and islands with their inhabitants and the dwellers therein, and bring them to the Catholic faith. Hence in heartiest commendation in the Lord of this your saintly and praiseworthy purpose, desirous too that it be duly accomplished in the carrying to those regions of the name of our Savior, we exhort you very earnestly in the Lord and insist strictly both through your reception of holy baptism, whereby you are bound to our apostolic commands, and in the bowels of the mercy of our Lord Jesus Christ, that, inasmuch as with upright spirit and through zeal for the true faith you design to equip and despatch this expedition, you purpose also as is your duty to lead the peoples dwelling in those islands and countries to embrace the Christian religion; nor at any time let dangers nor hardships deter you therefrom, with the stout hope and trust in your hearts that Almighty God will further your undertakings. Moreover, moved thereunto by our own accord, not at your instance nor the request of any one else in your regard, but wholly of our own largess and certain knowledge as well as fulness of our apostolic power, by the authority of Almighty God conferred upon us in blessed Peter and of the vicarship of Jesus Christ, which we hold on earth, in order that with greater readiness and heartiness you enter upon an undertaking of so lofty a character as has been entrusted to you by the graciousness of our apostolic favor, by tenor of these presents should any of said islands have been found by your envoys and captains, we do give, grant, and assign to you and your heirs and successors, kings of Castile and Leon, forever, together with all their dominions, cities, camps, places, and towns, as well as all rights, jurisdictions, and appurtenances, all islands and mainlands found and to be found, discovered and to be discovered towards the west and south, by drawing and establishing a line from the Arctic pole, namely the north, to the Antarctic pole, namely the south, no matter whether the said mainlands and islands are found and to be found in the direction of India or towards any other quarter, the said line to the west and south to be distant one hundred leagues from any of the islands commonly known as the *Azores* and *Cabo Verde*. With this proviso however that none of the islands and mainlands found and to be found, discovered and to be discovered beyond that said line towards the west and south, be in the actual possession of any Christian king or prince up to the birthday of our Lord Jesus Christ just past in the present year one thousand four hundred and ninety-three. Moreover we make, appoint and depute you and your said heirs and successors owners of them with full and free power, authority, and jurisdiction of every kind; with this proviso however that through this gift, grant, and assignment of ours no right conferred on any Christian prince, who may be in actual possession of said islands and mainlands up to the said birthday of our Lord Jesus Christ, is hereby to be considered as withdrawn or to be withdrawn. Moreover we command you in virtue of holy obedience that, employing all due diligence in the premises, as you promise, nor do we doubt your compliance therein to the best of your loyalty and royal greatness of spirit, you send to the aforesaid main-lands and islands worthy, God-fearing, learned, skilled, and experienced men, in order to instruct the aforesaid inhabitants and dwellers therein in the Catholic faith and train them in good morals. Besides under penalty of excommunication *late sententie* to be incurred *ipso facto*, should any one thus contravene, we strictly forbid all persons of whatsoever rank, even imperial and royal, or of whatsoever estate, degree, order, or condition, to dare, without your special permit or that of your aforesaid heirs and successors, to go, as charged, for the purpose of trade or any other reason to the islands and mainlands found and to be found, discovered and to be discovered, towards the west and south, by drawing and establishing a line from the Arctic pole to the Antarctic pole, no matter whether the mainlands and islands found and to be found lie in the direction of India or towards any other quarter whatsoever, the said line to the west and south to be distant one hundred leagues from any of the islands commonly known as the *Azores* and *Cabo Verde*, the apostolic constitutions and ordinances and other decrees whatsoever to the contrary notwithstanding. We trust in him from whom derive empires and governments and everything good, that with his guidance, should you pursue this saintly and praiseworthy undertaking, in a short while your hardships and endeavors will result in the utmost success, to the happiness and glory of all Christendom. But inasmuch as it would be difficult to have these present letters sent to all places where desirable, we wish, and with similar accord and knowledge do decree, that to copies of them, signed by the hand of any public notary commissioned therefor, and sealed with the seal of any ecclesiastical officer or ecclesiastical court, the same respect is to be shown in court and outside as well as anywhere else as would be given to these presents, should they thus be exhibited or shown. Let no one therefore, etc., infringe, etc., this our recommendation, gift, grant, assignment, constitution, deputation, decree, mandate, prohibition, and will. Should any one, etc. Given at Rome at St. Peter's in the year, etc., one thousand four hundred and ninety-three, the fourth of May, and the first year of our pontificate.

Gratis by order of our most holy lord the Pope.

D. Gallectus.

For the registrar:

A. de Muciarellis.
Collator, L. Amerinus.

Extension of the Apostolic Grant and Donation of the Indies—September 25

Alexander, Bishop, servant of the servants of God, to the illustrious sovereigns, his very dear Son in Christ Fernando [Ferdinand], King, and his very dear Daughter in Christ Isabel, Queen of Castile, Leon, Aragon, Granada, health and Apostolic benediction. A short while ago through our own accord, certain knowledge, and fulness of our Apostolic power, we gave, conveyed, and assigned forever to you and your heirs and successors, kings of Castile and Leon, all islands and mainlands whatsoever, discovered and to be discovered towards the west and south, that were not under the actual temporal rule of any Christian owner. Moreover, investing therewith you and your aforesaid heirs and successors, we appointed and deputed you as owners of them with full and free power, authority, and jurisdiction of every kind, as more fully appears in our letters given to that effect, the terms whereof we wish to be understood the same as if they had been inserted word for word in these presents. But it may happen that your Envoys, Captains, or vassals, while voyaging towards the west or south might land and touch in eastern waters and there discover islands and mainlands that at one time belonged or even yet belong to India.

With the desire then to give you token of our graciousness, through similar accord, knowledge, and fulness of our power, by tenor of these presents and our apostolic authority, we do extend and enlarge our aforesaid gift, grant, assignment, and letters, with all and singular the clauses contained therein, so as to secure to you all islands and mainlands whatsoever that are found and to be found, discovered and to be discovered, are or were or seem to be in the route by sea or land to the west or south, but are now recognized as being in the waters of the west or south and east and India Moreover in all and through all, the same as if in the aforesaid letters full and express mention had been made thereof, we convey to you and your aforesaid heirs and successors full and free power through your own authority, exercised through yourselves or by the action of another or of others, to take corporal possession of the said islands and countries and to hold them forever, as well as to defend your right thereto against whomsoever may seek to prevent it. With this strict prohibition however to all persons, of no matter what rank, estate, degree, order or condition, that under penalty of excommunication *latae sententiae*, wherein such as contravene are to be considered as having fallen *ipso facto*, no one without your express leave or that of your aforesaid heirs and successors shall, for no matter what reason or pretense, presume in any manner to go or send to the aforesaid regions for the purpose of fishing, or of searching for any islands or mainlands. Notwithstanding any apostolic constitutions and ordinances or whatsoever gifts, grants, powers, and assignments of the aforesaid regions, seas, islands and countries, or any portion of them, may have been made by us or our predecessors in favor of whatsoever kings, princes, infantes, or whatsoever other persons, orders or knighthoods, who for any reason whatever may now be there, even for motives of charity or the faith, or the ransom of captives. Nor shall it matter how urgent these reasons may be, even though, based on repealing clauses, they may appear of the most positive, mandatory, and unusual character; nor even should there be contained therein sentences, censures, and penalties of any kind whatever, providing however these have not gone into effect through actual and real possession; nay even though it may have happened on occasion that the persons, to whom such gifts and grants were made, or their envoys, sailed thither through chance. Wherefore should any such gifts or grants have been made, considering the terms of our present decree to have been sufficiently expressed and inserted, we through similar accord, knowledge, and fulness of our power do wholly revoke the former. Moreover as regards countries and islands not in actual possession of others, we wish this to be considered as of no effect, notwithstanding what may appear in the aforesaid letters, or anything else to the contrary. Given at Rome at St. Peter's, on the twenty-fifth day of September in the year of the Incarnation of our Lord one thousand four hundred and ninety-three, the second year of our pontificate.

The Treaty of Tordesillas

[This treaty was signed by the respective representatives of the Spanish and Portuguese monarchs, June 7, 1494, at the city of Tordesillas. Full powers were conferred upon these representatives in special letters, that of the Catholic sovereigns being given June 5 at Tordesillas, and that of King Dom Joan of Portugal, March 8. The former sovereigns, as well as their son Don Juan, signed the treaty in person, at Arevalo, July 2; the King of Portugal, September 5, at Setubal—each ratifying it fully. The letter given by Ferdinand and Isabella to their representatives is as follows:]

Don Fernando and Doña Isabel, by the grace of God, King and Queen of Castilla, Leon, Aragon, Secjlia, Granada, Toledo, Valencia, Galisia, Mallorcas, Sevilla, Cerdeña, Cordova, Corçega, Murçia, Jahan, Algarbe, Algezira, Gibraltar, and the Canary Islands; count and countess of Barcelona; seigniors of Vizcaya and Moljna; duke and duchess of Atenas and Neopatria; count and countess of Rosellon and Cerdanja; marquis and marchioness of Oristan and Goceano: Inasmuch as the most serene King of Portugal, our very dear and beloved brother, sent hither his ambassadors and representatives [the names and titles follow] for the purpose of conferring and negotiating a treaty and compact with us and with our ambassadors and representatives acting in our name, in regard to the controversy existing between ourselves and the said most serene King of Portugal, our brother, concerning what lands, of all those discovered prior to this date, in the Ocean Sea, belong to ourselves and to him respectively; therefore we, having entire confidence that you Don Enrrique Enrriques, our chief steward, Don Guterre de Cardenas, deputy-in-chief of Leon[149] and our auditor-in-chief, and doctor Rodrigo Maldonado, all members of our council, are persons who will guard our interests, and that you will perform thoroughly and faithfully what we order and recommend, by this present letter delegate to you, specially and fully, all our authority in as definitive a form as possible,[150] and as is requisite in such cases, in order that you may, for us and in our name and in those of our heirs and successors, our kingdoms and seigniories,[151] and the subjects and natives of them, confer concerning, conclude, ratify, and contract and determine with the said ambassadors acting in the name of the most serene King of Portugal, our brother, whatever compact, contract, bound, demarcation, and covenant regarding the above, by whatever bounds of the winds, degrees of north latitude and of the sun, and by whatever parts, divisions, and places of the heavens, sea, and land,[152] may seem best to you. And we delegate our said power to you in such manner that you may leave to the said King of Portugal, and to his kingdoms and successors, all seas, islands, and mainlands that may be and exist within such bound and demarcation, which shall be and remain his.[153] And further, we delegate to you the said power so that in our name, and in those of our heirs and successors, and of our kingdoms and seigniories, and the subjects and natives of them, you may affirm, concur in, approve, and arrange with the said King of Portugal and the said ambassadors and representatives acting in his name, that all seas, islands, and mainlands that may be and exist within the bound and demarcation of the coasts, seas, islands, and mainlands which shall be and remain ours and our successors', may be ours and belong to our seigniory and conquest, and likewise to our kingdoms and the successors to the same, with such limitations and exceptions,[154] and with all other clauses and declarations that you deem best. [Furthermore we delegate the said powers] so that you may negotiate, authorize, contract, compact, approve, and accept in our name, and those of our said heirs and successors, and of all our kingdoms and seigniories, and the subjects and natives of the same, whatever covenants, contracts, and instruments of writing, with whatever bonds, decrees, forms, conditions, obligations, requirements, penalties, submissions, and renunciations you wish, and as may seem best to you, regarding all the aforesaid, and every part and parcel of the same, and every thing pertaining to it, or dependent upon it, or having even the slightest connection with it. And in regard to the foregoing you shall have authority to enact and authorize, and you shall enact and authorize, all and singular, of whatever nature and quality, weight and importance, they may or can be, although they may be such as by their terms should require in addition our signature and especial order, and of which especial and express mention should be made fully, and which we, in our own proper persons, could enact, authorize, and approve. Furthermore, we authorize you fully, to swear, and you shall swear, upon our consciences, that we, our heirs and successors, subjects, natives, and vassals, now and hereafter shall keep, observe, and fulfil, and that they shall keep, observe, and fulfil, really and effectually, all that you thus affirm, covenant, swear, authorize, and asseverate, without any deceit, fraud, duplicity, dissembling, or pretense. And in this manner, you shall, in our name, covenant, asseverate, and promise that we, in our own person, shall asseverate, swear, promise, authorize, and affirm all that you, in our name, asseverate, promise, and covenant in regard to the preceding, within whatever term and space of time you deem best, and that we shall observe and fulfil this, really and effectually, and under the conditions, penalties, and obligations contained in the treaty of peace[155] concluded and ratified between ourselves and the said most serene King, our brother, and under all other conditions whatsoever promised and determined upon by you, for all of which we promise, from this date, to pay the penalty if we violate them. For all the above, and each part and parcel of it, we grant to you the said authority with free and general powers of administration, and we promise and affirm by our kingly faith and word, we, our heirs and successors, to keep, observe, and fulfil everything, concerning all the aforesaid enacted, covenanted, sworn, and promised by you, in whatever form and manner; and we promise faithfully to maintain the same to the uttermost, now and forever, and neither ourselves nor our heirs and successors shall violate this compact, or any part of it, by any act of our own, or our agents, either directly or indirectly, under any pretense or cause, in judgment or out of it, under the express obligation of all our possessions, patrimonial and fiscal, and all other possessions whatsoever of our vassals, subjects, and natives, real and personal, acquired or to be acquired. In affirmation of the above we have caused this our letter of authorization to be given, and we sign the same with our names and order it sealed with our seal . . . [Signatures of the King, Queen, and Royal Secretary.]

[The letter of authorization granted by the King of Portugal follows. It is couched in much the same terms as the preceding. It opens as follows:]

Don Juan, by the grace of God, King of Portugal and the Algarbes, on either side of the sea in Africa, and Seignior of Guinea: To all who shall see this our letter of authority and powers of attorney, we proclaim: that inasmuch as certain islands were discovered and found by command of the most exalted, excellent, and powerful Princes, King Don Fernando and Queen Doña Ysabel [certain of their dignities follow] our very dear and beloved brother and sister, and other islands and mainlands may in future be discovered and found, regarding certain of which, known already or to be known, there might arise disputes and controversy between ourselves and our kingdoms and seigniories, and the subjects and natives of the same, because of our rights therein—which may our Lord forbid,— it is our desire, because of the great love and friendship between us, and in order to seek, procure, and maintain greater peace, and more enduring concord and tranquillity, that the sea, in which the said islands were and shall be found, be divided and allotted between us in some good, sure, and circumscribed manner; and inasmuch as at present we cannot attend to this in person, and confiding in you, Ruy de Sosa, Seignior of Usagres[156] and Berenguel, and Don Juan de Sosa, our intendant-in-chief, and Arias de Almadana, magistrate of civil cases in our court, and a member of our desenbargo (all members of our council), we grant you by the present letter our full and complete power and authority and our special command, and we appoint and constitute you all jointly, and two of you and one of you *yn solidun*,[157] in any manner whatsoever, if the others be prevented, as our ambassadors and representatives; and we do this in the most definitive form[158] possible and generally and specifically as is requisite in such cases,—in such manner that the general is not obscured by the specific nor the specific by the general. This we do so that, in our name, and those of our heirs and successors, and of all our kingdoms and seigniories, and the subjects and natives of the same, you may confer concerning, conclude, and ratify, and contract and determine with the said King and Queen of Castilla, our brother and sister, or with those empowered by the latter, whatever agreement, compact, limitation, demarcation, and contract regarding the Ocean Sea and the islands and mainlands contained therein, by whatever directions of winds and degrees of north latitude, and of the sun, and by whatever parts, divisions, and places of the heavens, land, and sea[159] you may deem best. [From this point the language is almost identical with that in the foregoing letter of authorization. The present letter is signed by the king and his secretary. The treaty proper follows:]

Thereupon it was declared by the above-mentioned representatives of the aforesaid King and Queen of Castilla, Leon, Aragon, Seçilia, Granada, etc.; and of the aforesaid King of Portugal and the Algarbes, etc.: That, whereas a certain controversy exists between the said lords, their constituents, as to what lands, of all those discovered in the Ocean Sea up to the present day, the date of this treaty, pertain to each one of the said parts respectively; therefore, for the sake of peace and concord, and for the preservation of the relationship and love of the said King of Portugal for the said King and Queen of Castilla, Aragon, etc., it being the pleasure of their Highnesses, they, their said representatives, acting in their name and by virtue of their powers herein described, covenanted and agreed that a boundary or straight line be determined and drawn north and south, from pole to pole, on the said Ocean Sea—from the Arctic to the Antarctic pole. This boundary, or line[160] shall be drawn straight, as aforesaid, at a distance of three hundred and seventy leagues west of the Cabo Verde islands, being calculated by degrees, or by any other manner, as may be considered the best and readiest, provided the distance shall be no greater than above said. And all lands, both islands and mainlands, found and discovered already, or to be found and discovered hereafter by the said King of Portugal and by his vessels on this side of the said line and bound determined as above, toward the east, in either north or south latitude, on the eastern side of the said bound, provided the said bound is not crossed, shall belong to, and remain in the possession of, and pertain forever to the said King of Portugal and his successors. And all other lands—both islands and mainlands, found or to be found hereafter, discovered or to be discovered hereafter, which have been discovered or shall be discovered by the said King and Queen of Castilla, Aragon, etc., and by their vessels, on the western side of the said bound, determined as above, after having passed the said bound toward the west, in either its north or south latitude, shall belong to, and remain in the possession of, and pertain forever to the said King and Queen of Castilla, Leon, etc., and to their successors.

Yten [Item]:[161] the said representatives promise and affirm by virtue of the powers aforesaid, that from this date no ships shall be despatched,—namely as follows: the said King and Queen of Castilla, Leon, Aragon, etc., for this part of the bound, and its eastern side, on this side the said bound, which pertains to the said King of Portugal and the Algarbes, etc.; nor the said King of Portugal to the other part of the said bound which pertains to the said King and Queen of Castilla, Aragon, etc.,—for the purpose of discovering and seeking any mainlands or islands, or for the purpose of trade, barter, or conquest of any kind. But should it come to pass that the said ships of the said King and Queen of Castilla, Leon, Aragon, etc., on sailing thus on this side of the said bound, should discover any mainlands or islands in the region pertaining, as above said, to the said King of Portugal, such mainlands or islands shall pertain to and belong forever to the said King of Portugal and his heirs, and their Highnesses shall order them to be surrendered to him immediately. And if the said ships of the said King of Portugal discover any islands and mainlands in the regions of the said King and Queen of Castilla, Leon, Aragon, etc., all such lands shall belong to and remain forever in the possession of the said King and Queen of Castilla, Leon, Aragon, etc., and their heirs, and the said King of Portugal shall cause such lands to be surrendered immediately.

Yten: In order that the said line or bound of the said division may be made straight and as nearly as possible the said distance of three hundred and seventy leagues west of the Cabo Verde islands, as hereinbefore stated, the said representatives of both the said parties agree and assent that within the ten months immediately following the date of this treaty, their said constituent lords shall despatch two or four caravels, namely, one or two by each one of them, a greater or less number, as they may mutually consider necessary. These vessels shall meet at the island of Grande Canaria [Grand Canary Island] during this time, and each one of the said parties shall send certain persons in them, to wit, pilots, astrologers, sailors, and any others they may deem desirable. But there must be as many on one side as on the other, and certain of the said pilots, astrologers, sailors, and others of those sent by the said King and Queen of Castilla, Aragon, etc., and who are experienced, shall embark in the ships of the said King of Portugal and the Algarbes; in like manner certain of the said persons sent by the said King of Portugal shall embark in the ship or ships of the said King and Queen of Castilla, Aragon, etc.: a like number in each case, so that they may jointly study and examine to better advantage the sea, courses, winds, and the degrees of the sun or of north latitude,[162] and lay out the leagues aforesaid, in order that, in determining the line and boundary, all sent and empowered by both the said parties in the said vessels, shall jointly concur. These said vessels shall continue their course together to the said Cabo Verde islands, from whence they shall lay a direct course to the west, to the distance of the said three hundred and seventy degrees, measured as the said persons shall agree, and measured without prejudice to the said parts. When this point is reached, such point will constitute the place and mark for measuring degrees of the sun or of north latitude either by daily runs measured in leagues, or in any other manner that shall mutually be deemed better. This said line shall be drawn north and south as aforesaid, from the said Arctic pole to the said Antarctic pole. And when this line has been determined as above said, those sent by each of the aforesaid parties, to whom each one of the said parties must delegate his own authority and power, to determine the said mark and bound, shall draw up a writing concerning it and affix thereto their signatures. And when determined by the mutual consent of all of them, this line shall be considered forever as a perpetual mark and bound, in such wise that the said parties, or either of them, or their future successors, shall be unable to deny it, or erase or remove it, at any time or in any manner whatsoever. And should, perchance, the said line and bound from pole to pole, as aforesaid, intersect any island or mainland, at the first point of such intersection of such island or mainland by the said line, some kind of mark or tower shall be erected, and a succession of similar marks shall be erected in a straight line from such mark or tower, in a line identical with the above-mentioned bound. These marks shall separate those portions of such land belonging to each one of the said parties; and the subjects of the said parties shall not dare, on either side, to enter the territory of the other, by crossing the said mark or bound in such island or mainland.

Yten: Inasmuch as the said ships of the said King and Queen of Castilla, Leon, Aragon, etc., sailing as before declared, from their kingdoms and seigniories to their said possessions on the other side of the said line, must cross the seas on this side of the line, pertaining to the said King of Portugal, it is therefore concerted and agreed that the said ships of the said King and Queen of Castilla, Leon, Aragon, etc., shall, at any time and without any hindrance, sail in either direction, freely, securely, and peacefully, over the said seas of the said King of Portugal, and within the said line. And whenever their Highnesses and their successors wish to do so, and deem it expedient, their said ships may take their courses and routes direct from their kingdoms to any region within their line and bound to which they desire to despatch expeditions of discovery, conquest, and trade. They shall take their courses direct to the desired region and for any purpose desired therein, and shall not leave their course, unless compelled to do so by contrary weather. They shall do this provided that, before crossing the said line, they shall not seize or take possession of anything discovered in his said region by the said King of Portugal; and should their said ships find anything before crossing the said line, as aforesaid, it shall belong to the said King of Portugal, and their Highnesses shall order it surrendered immediately. And since it is possible that the ships and subjects of the said King and Queen of Castilla, Leon, etc., or those acting in their name, may discover within the next twenty days of this present month of June following the date of this treaty, some islands and mainlands within the said line, drawn straight from pole to pole, that is to say, inside the said three hundred and seventy leagues west of the Cabo Verde islands, as aforesaid, it is hereby agreed and determined, in order to remove all doubt, that all such islands and mainlands found and discovered in any manner whatsoever up to the said twentieth day of this said month of June, although found by ships and subjects of the said King and Queen of Castylla, Aragon, etc., shall pertain to and remain forever in the possession of the said King of Portugal and the Algarbes, and of his successors and kingdoms, provided that they lie within the first two hundred and fifty leagues of the said three hundred and seventy leagues reckoned west of the Cabo Verde islands to the above-mentioned line,—in whatsoever part, even to the said poles, of the said two hundred and fifty leagues they may be found, determining a boundary or straight line from pole, to pole, where the said two hundred and fifty leagues end. Likewise all the islands and mainlands found and discovered up to the said twenty days of this present month of June, by the ships and subjects of the said King and Queen of Castilla, Aragon, etc., or in any other manner, within the other one hundred and twenty leagues that still remain of the said three hundred and seventy leagues where the said bound that is to be drawn from pole to pole, as aforesaid, must be determined, and in whatever part of the said one hundred and twenty leagues, even to the said poles that they are found up to the said day, shall pertain to and remain forever in the possession of the said King and Queen of Castilla, Aragon, etc., and of their successors and kingdoms; just as whatever is or shall be found on the other side of the said three hundred and seventy leagues pertaining to their Highnesses, as aforesaid, is and must be theirs, although the said one hundred and twenty leagues are within the said bound of the said three hundred and seventy leagues pertaining to the said King of Portugal, the Algarbes, etc., as aforesaid.[163]

And if, up to the said twentieth day of this said month of June, no lands are discovered by the said ships of their Highnesses within the said one hundred and twenty leagues, and are discovered after the expiration of that time, then they shall pertain to the said King of Portugal as is set forth in the above.

[The faithful observance by the respective sovereigns, of every point of this treaty is provided for in the fullest of terms by the commissioners, by virtue of the powers delegated to them; and this is sworn "before God, the Blessed Mary, and on the sign of the Cross." The instrument must receive also the sanction of the Pope, who will be asked to confirm the same by means of a bull in which the agreements of the treaty will be given.[164] The commissioners bind themselves under the foregoing oaths and penalties that, "within the one hundred days immediately following the date of this treaty, they will mutually exchange approbations and ratifications of the said treaty, written on parchment, and signed with the names of their said constituents, and sealed with their seals." Don Juan, heir to the Spanish crown, shall sign the instrument as well as Ferdinand and Isabella, and the whole shall be witnessed in proper manner.]

Note on Correspondence of Jaime Ferrer

[For lack of space, certain documents to and by Jaime Ferrer, regarding the line of demarcation, cannot be included in this series. These documents—a letter from the Cardinal Despanya, Archbishop of Toledo, Don Pedro de Mendoza, Barcelona, August 26, 1493; a letter from Ferrer to the Catholic sovereigns, Barcelona, January 27, 1495; Ferrer's opinion regarding the treaty of Tordesillas (undated, but probably in 1495); and a letter from the Catholic sovereigns, Madrid, February 28, 1495,—will be found in Navarrete, *Coll. de viages*, tomo ii, edition 1825, pp. 97-110; edition 1858, pp. 111-117, part of núm. lxviii; and a translation of all but the first in Dawson's *Lines of Demarcation* (printed in *Translations of the Royal Society of Canada*, 1899-1900, second series, vol. v, sec. ii, pp. 541-544,—also printed separately). Navarrete states that these documents, were printed in Barcelona in 1545, in a now rare book compiled by Ferrer under the title *Sentencias cathólicas del Divi poeta Dant*. In the first letter, signed "El Cardenal," Ferrer's presence is requested in Barcelona; he is to take with him his mappamundo and all his cosmographical instruments.]

Compact Between the Catholic Sovereigns and the King of Portugal, Regarding the Demarcation and Division of the Ocean Sea

Don Fernando and Doña Isabel, by the grace of God, King and Queen of Castilla, etc.: Inasmuch as, among other things in the treaty and compact regarding the division of the Ocean Sea, negotiated between ourselves and the most Serene King of Portugal and the Algarbes on either side of the sea in Africa, and Seignior of Guinea, our most dear and beloved brother, it was agreed and covenanted that, within the first ten months following the date of this treaty, our caravels and his, accompanied by astrologers, pilots, sailors, and others, agreed upon by ourselves and himself,—a like number on either side—shall be in the island of La Gran Canaria, in order to proceed to the determination and drawing of the divisional line of the said sea—which must be three hundred and seventy leagues west of the Cabo Verde islands, in a straight north and south line from the Arctic to the Antarctic pole, as covenanted between us by the said treaty of the division of the said sea, as is more fully set forth therein;—and inasmuch as we now consider that the line of the said division at the distance of the said three hundred and seventy leagues can be determined and calculated better, if the said astrologers, pilots, sailors, and others, come to a definite conclusion and agreement regarding the manner and order of procedure to be observed in the determination and marking of the said line, before the sailing of the said caravels, by so doing avoiding disputes and controversies that might arise regarding it among those going, if these had to be arranged after the departure; and inasmuch as it would be quite useless for the said caravels and persons to go before knowing that any island or mainland had been found in each one of the said parts of the said sea, and to which they must proceed immediately and orderly: Now therefore, in order that all this may be done to better advantage, and with the full and free consent of both sides, we agree and by this present letter consent that the said astrologers, pilots, sailors, and others determined upon with the said King, our brother—a like number on either side, and of sufficient number for this matter—must assemble and they shall assemble along any part of the frontier of these our Kingdoms and the Kingdom of Portugal. During the whole month of July first following the date of this letter these men shall consult upon, covenant concerning, and determine the manner of making the said divisional line of the said sea at the distance of the said three hundred and seventy leagues west of the said Cabo Verde islands, by means of a straight north and south line from the Arctic to the Antarctic Pole, as is set forth in the said treaty. And whatever they determine upon, unanimously, and whatever is concluded and marked out by them, shall be approved and confirmed through our letters-patent, by us and by the said King, our brother. And if after the said astrologers, pilots, and sailors, appointed as above said, shall have arrived at a conclusion, each one of the said parties going to that part of the said sea, according to the permission of the said treaty, and thereby observing the contents of said treaty, any island or mainland shall be found hereafter, which either of the parties consider to be so situated that the said line can be determined in accordance with the stipulations of the said treaty, and the one party shall cause notification to be given the other party that they shall cause the line abovesaid to be marked out, we and the said King, our brother, shall be obliged to have the said line determined and marked out, in accordance with the method determined upon by the astrologers, pilots, and sailors, and others abovesaid, and appointed as abovesaid, within the period of the first ten months reckoned from the date that either of the parties notified the other. And should it prove that the land thus found is not cut by the said line, a declaration of its distance from the said line shall be given, both on our own part and that of the said most serene King, our brother. They shall not, However, neglect to make the said declaration regarding any island or mainland which shall be found afterwards, during the period, nearer the said line. And in doing the aforesaid, they shall not neglect to observe the manner aforesaid, whenever any island or mainland is found in the neighborhood of the said line as aforesaid, and up to the said time of the said ten months after the notification of one party by the other, as aforesaid. It is our pleasure in this our letter to postpone and defer the departure of the said caravels and persons, notwithstanding the limit set and determined in the above-mentioned treaty in regard to it. And we therefore are pleased and consider it advantageous—for the better notification and declaration of the division of the said sea made by the said treaty between ourselves and the said King, our brother; and in order that both our subjects and natives and the subjects and natives of the said King our brother may be better informed henceforth as to the regions wherein they may navigate and discover,—to order (as in truth we shall order), under severe penalties, that the line of the said division be placed on all hydrographical maps made hereafter in our kingdoms and seigniories by those journeying in the said Ocean Sea. This line shall be drawn straight from the said Arctic to the said Antarctic pole, north and south, at the distance of the said three hundred and seventy leagues west of the Cabo Verde islands, as aforesaid, being measured as determined unanimously by the said astrologers, pilots, and sailors meeting as abovesaid. And we purpose and stipulate that neither this present letter nor anything contained herein, be prejudicial in any manner to the contents and compacts of the said treaty, but rather that they, all and singular, be observed throughout *in toto* without any failure, and in the manner and entirety set forth in the said treaty; inasmuch as we have caused the present letter to be made in this manner, simply in order that the said astrologers and persons shall assemble and, within the said time, shall determine the order of procedure and the method to be observed in making the said line of demarcation, and in order to postpone and defer the departure of the said caravels and persons, until the said island or mainland, whither they must go, is known to have been found in each one of the said parts, and in order to command that the line of the said division be placed on the said hydrographical maps,—all of which is set forth most fully in the above. We promise and asseverate on our kingly faith and word, to fulfil and observe all of the foregoing, without any artifice, deceit, or pretense in the manner and in the entirety set down in the above. And in confirmation of the above, we cause this our letter to be given, signed with our names, and sealed with our leaden seal hanging from threads of colored silk.

Bull, *Præcelsæ*, of Leo X

November 3, 1514

[This bull, called *Precelse denotionis*, confirms and extends certain bulls of Leo X's predecessors, Nicholas V and Sixtus IV, reciting the bulls so confirmed and extended—two of the former and one of the latter. In the first bull, *Dum diversas*, authority is granted to King Alfonso V of Portugal to make war upon the infidels, to conquer their lands, and to reduce them to slavery. It concedes also plenary indulgence for their sins to all taking part in the expeditions against the Moors, or aiding the expeditions with gifts.[166] Its date is June 18, 1452. The second bull is dated January 8, 1454, and is called *Romanus Pontifex*. In it Nicholas "after reviewing with praise the zeal of Prince Henry in making discoveries and his desire to find a route to southern and eastern shores even to the Indians, granted to King Alfonso all that had been or should be discovered south of Cape Bojador and Cape Non toward Guinea and 'ultra versus illam meridionalem plagam' as a perpetual possession."[167] The third bull, the *Eterni Regis* of June 21, 1481, confirms that of Nicholas V. It "granted to the Portuguese Order of Jesus Christ[168] spiritual jurisdiction in all lands acquired from Cape Bojador 'ad Indos.'" This bull also contained and sanctioned the treaty of 1480 between Spain and Portugal, by which the exclusive right of navigating and of making discoveries along the coast of Africa, with the possession of all the known islands of the Atlantic except the Canaries, was solemnly conceded to Portugal.[169] After thus reciting these bulls ("of our own accord . . . approve, renew, and confirm the aforesaid instruments"[170]) Pope Leo extends and amplifies them in the following words:]

And for added assurance, we do by virtue of the authority and tenor of the above instruments, concede anew, [to the King of Portugal] everything, all and singular, contained in the aforesaid instruments, as well as all other empires, kingdoms, principalities, duchies, provinces, lands, cities, towns, forts, dominions, islands, ports, seas, coasts, and all possessions whatsoever, real or personal, wherever they may be, and all uninhabited places whatsoever, recovered, found, discovered, and acquired from the above-mentioned infidels by the said King Emmanuel and his predecessors, or to be hereafter recovered, acquired, found and discovered, by the said King Emmanuel and his successors—both from Capes Bogiador and Naon[171] to the Indies and any district whatsoever, wherever situated, even although at present unknown to us. And likewise we do extend and amplify the instruments above-mentioned and everything, all and singular contained therein, as aforesaid, and in virtue of holy obedience, under penalty of our [wrath,] we do, by the authority and tenor of the foregoing, forbid all faithful Christians, whomsoever, even although possessing imperial, regal, or any other dignity whatsoever, from hindering, in any manner, King Emmanuel and his successors in the aforesaid, and from presuming to lend assistance, counsel, or favor to the infidels. [The Archbishop of Lisboa and the Bishops of Guarda and Funchal are ordered to see that the provisions of this bull are observed.[172]]

Instructions from the King of Spain to His Ambassadors in the Negotiations with Portugal

[In this document, written in Valladolid, February 4, 1523, and signed by the king and the chancellor and countersigned by the king's secretary Cobos, the king lays down the following points:]

First, that the course of action mapped out for you, our said notary-in-chief Barroso, in answer to your letter reporting your conversation with the duke of Berganza regarding this treaty, seemed then, and seems still right and proper; since by this course we declare in effect our purpose and wish to fulfil *in toto* toward the said most serene King, the treaty concerning the division and demarcation of the seas, negotiated between the Catholic sovereigns—my lords and grandparents—and King Don Juan of Portugal. I order you, likewise, to ascertain briefly what regions lie within the right of our conquest, and where are the limits of our demarcation, and those of the said most serene King of Portugal. And you shall ascertain in what manner restitution of whatever I may have appropriated of his possessions, with the profit accruing therefrom, may be made to the said most serene King, the latter making to our Royal crown the same restitution of whatever he may have appropriated, with all profits and revenues arising therefrom.

That we believe the reason for the refusal of the said most serene King to accept the expedients proposed, and for his recent reply to us, transmitted through you, the said notary-in-chief Barroso, was due to his not being informed thoroughly in regard to the said expedients, and of our past and present intention and wish to fulfil strictly in every point the said treaty; and to preserve and augment, by fair dealing on our part, our relations with, and love toward, the said most serene King. For these reasons we beseech him earnestly that he have the said expedients examined; that he treat and confer concerning them, singly and collectively; and that he inform us of whatever in them, singly or collectively, seems wrong or prejudicial to his rights—in order that we, through our great affection for him and our desire for its increase, may have his objections examined and discussed before our royal person by the members of our Council. This done we shall order what is unjust to be remedied, and the said most serene King, shall, in no wise, receive any hurt, in what by right pertains to him.

[The king orders further that his ambassadors confer discreetly and prudently with the Portuguese king and others, and advise him promptly as to the outcome, that he may take the proper steps. He continues:]

In case that you are unable to prevail upon the said most serene King to reëxamine the said expedients, and if he declares that he has seen them already, and that he has informed us, through you, the said notary-in-chief Barroso, of his dissatisfaction regarding them,—although without stating in detail his causes for dissatisfaction—and that he proposed now that we each send two caravels to determine the said demarcation, in the meantime neither himself nor myself despatching our fleets to Maluco, you shall reply in this manner: that whatever pertains to the sending of the said caravels to determine the said demarcation is in perfect accord with our desires, and we are quite well satisfied with the proposal, since such a procedure is in keeping with the said treaty, which will in this manner, be fulfilled so far as we are concerned. And you shall confer briefly with him and with those he shall appoint concerning the method of procedure—the tons burdens of the said caravels; the astrologers, cosmographers, notaries, pilots, and others who shall embark in each vessel; in what manner they shall be armed; and for what time victualed and provisioned. You shall stipulate that a certain number of our subjects shall embark in his caravels, and a like number of his subjects in ours, who shall all be designated by name, in order that the determination and measurements might proceed with more fairness and justice. Also all documents, both measurements and proofs, made for the verification of the above, shall be made in presence of the notaries sent in the said caravels by each of us. They shall be made before those notaries in such manner that one notary shall be present always for each one of us, and two others shall sign the said documents, which without such signatures shall be invalid. And you shall confer upon all other desirable topics, in order that the voyage be fair to us both, and the demarcation be made in accordance to the said treaty, and that those sailing in the said caravels have desire only to ascertain and declare the truth. Before concluding anything discussed and treated by you, you shall first advise us. But as regards saying that, during the time taken in fixing upon the said demarcation, neither of us shall send his fleets to the Maluco Islands, you shall reply to the said most serene King that, as he may see clearly, it is neither just nor reasonable to ask this of me, for the agreement and treaty neither prohibits nor forbids of it, and to do this would be to the detriment of my rightful and civil possession in the said Maluco Islands, and in the other islands and mainlands which will be discovered by my fleets during this time of fixing upon the said demarcation. He is aware that I am received and obeyed as king and lord of those Maluco Islands, and that those who, until the present, held possession of these regions, have rendered me obedience as king and rightful seignior, and have been, in my name, appointed as my governors and lieutenants over the said regions. He knows, too, that my subjects, with much of the merchandise carried by my fleet, are at the present time in these regions. For these reasons it is not reasonable to ask that I discontinue my possession of these districts during the time of determining the demarcation, especially since the said most serene King has never held possession, past or present, of any of the said Maluco Islands, or of any others discovered by me up to the present; nor has his fleet touched at or anchored therein.

You shall say to him that, inasmuch as I have not asked that he discontinue to hold his possessions in Malaca and other regions discovered by him, although I have been assured on many different occasions by many different persons of learning and judgment—a number of whom are natives of the Kingdom of Portugal—that these regions pertain to me and to my crown, being, as these men declare, within the limits of our demarcation, he will recognize quite fully the injustice of asking me to discontinue sending my fleets to Maluco and other regions where I am in civil and rightful possession, and am obeyed and regarded as legitimate seignior, as aforesaid.

Should the said most serene King propose to you that it would be a fair expedient to us both that, during the time of determining the demarcation, since we claim that Malaca and many other islands where he carries on trade lie within the limits of our demarcation and pertain to us, he will desist from despatching his vessels and fleets to those regions, provided that I do the same as regards whatever of the Maluco and other islands discovered by me in those regions, and claimed by him as lying within his demarcation; or should he propose any other expedient or innovation not in this present writing, you shall make answer that such expedient is new, and that we have no knowledge of it. On this account you shall request that he allow you to consult with us. After this discussion you shall advise me of the matter.

[The instructions conclude by urging the ambassadors to proceed prudently, and to impress the Portuguese monarch with the affection felt toward him by Carlos, and the latter's desire for its continuance. The ambassadors are to act in complete harmony with one another, and to carry on negotiations jointly at all times, one never presuming to act without the other's full knowledge. Exact reports must be submitted by them, in order that their king may give definite instructions.]

Letter of Carlos I of Spain to Juan de Zúñiga—1523

The King: Juan de Zúñiga, knight of the order of Santiago,[173] my servant. I have not hitherto written you of transactions in the negotiations respecting Maluco, to which the most serene and illustrious King of Portugal, my very dear and beloved cousin, sent his ambassadors, as I believed that, our right being so apparent, the treaty would be kept with us, or at least some good method of settlement would be adopted. This the ambassadors have not cared to do, although on our part we have done everything absolutely possible—much more than is usual between princes or relatives. I speak of this because my steadfast wish to preserve forever the kinship and love existing in the past and present between the most serene King and myself has been made manifest by my deeds. I am exceedingly sorry to find that this has been not only of no advantage, but rather, because of the meager results obtained, a disadvantage. And on this account the said ambassadors are returning without having come to any conclusion. By them I write to the said most serene King as you will observe in the copy of the letter enclosed herein.[174] Now because you should be informed of the transactions at this discussion,—both that you might, in our behalf, give a full account thereof to the said most serene King, and that you might discuss the same there [in Lisbon] wherever convenient,—I have determined to put you in possession of the facts in this letter, which are as follows. As soon as the said ambassadors had arrived, and after the letters from the most serene King had been presented to me, and their embassy stated by virtue of our faith in these letters, they requested me to appoint persons with whom they might discuss the questions upon which they were to mediate for their sovereign. I did this immediately, appointing for this purpose certain members of my Council whom I, considered the best informed for that particular negotiation, and men of straightforward principles. These men, in company with the aforesaid ambassadors, examined the treaty presented by the latter, which seemed to have been drawn up and authorized by the Catholic

King and Queen, my grandparents, and by King Don Manuel, his [King João III] father, of blessed memory. They listened to all the ambassadors had to say, and all together conferred regarding and discussed the questions many times. Afterwards, inasmuch as the said ambassadors besought me to give them a hearing, I did so, the above-named and others of my Council, whom I had summoned for that purpose, being present.

The result of their proposition was to present the said treaty to me and petition that I order the observance thereof, and in consequence thereof, have Maluco surrendered immediately to the said most serene King of Portugal. This they said we were bound to do, by virtue of the said treaty, which contained, they declared, a section whose tenor is as follows.[175]

In this manner they continued to assert that since Maluco had been found by the King of Portugal, we were bound to make petition for and accept it from him, if we claimed it as lying within the bounds of our demarcation, and not to take possession of it by our own authority; and that the King of Portugal being assured of our contention, which they neither denied nor mistrusted might prove correct, was quite prepared to surrender it to us immediately, according to the terms of the said treaty, of which, in the said name, he wished to make use, and they petitioned that we observe the same. And therefore, as being a matter in which all negotiations and conferences were in good faith, both because of the prominence of those engaged in them, and because of the relationship between them, they declared that they had no wish to profit by any other right or allegation, but only to petition that the contents of the said treaty be kept to the letter.

Certain members of our Council, being informed of the matter made answer that my wish and intention had ever been, and still was, to observe the said treaty, and not to violate it in any manner (as in truth is and has ever been so). When this treaty should be examined and understood in the true light of reason, it would be found to be in our favor; and our intention was clearly founded upon it; and especially were we acting in good faith, according to the declaration of the said ambassadors that it was only necessary to examine the tenor of the said treaty and abide by its contents. Furthermore, in the same section, upon which they, in the name of the said most serene King of Portugal, based their contentions, would be found also the declaration, that if the Castilian ships should find any mainland or island in the Ocean Sea, which the said most serene King of Portugal should claim or allege to have been found within the limits of his demarcation, we were bound to surrender it to him immediately; and he could not be ignorant, nor could he claim ignorance of this, since it was all together in one and the same section. Therefore it was quite evident, since Maluco had been and was found by Castilian and not Portuguese ships, as they declared, that we, according to the terms of the same treaty, held it lawfully, at least in the time taken in arriving at and concluding the true determination of demarcation; and the most serene King of Portugal, when he wished anything, must petition for, and ask it from us, and it being found to be in his demarcation, must accept it from us. All the above they said in my name; asserting that whenever it should appear to be as above stated, we should carry into effect and fulfil immediately everything according to the said treaty. They said that Maluco had been found and occupied first, as must be admitted, by our ships—a fact well known everywhere, as we believe you are aware—inasmuch as nothing else was ever heard or known. The present declaration of the ambassadors was a complete innovation, at which, and reasonably, we must express surprise, since the fact was so well known that no one could pretend ignorance of it.

And, in proof thereof (to continue the above), our present possession, which had been public and without any opposition by the said most serene King of Portugal, was sufficient. And this possession of ours had been continued with his knowledge, suffrance, and good grace, and had been likewise known and suffered by the most serene King Don Manuel, his father. It was now a cause for surprise, that, in an affair of such moment, after such a long interval, and after two generations had consented to it, the effort of obstruction and hindrance should be made, as if it were a matter that had just arisen. It was declared that whoever heard of it, believed it to be more for the purpose of vexing and annoying us at this time, seeing our necessities and our so just employment against the tyrants of Christendom,[176] than for the purpose of obtaining justice. For until the present we would have been able to have been advised of it, and to have informed ourselves, and therefore we, on our part, possessed the good faith in the observance and understanding of the said treaty, alleged by the said ambassadors.

Further, it could not be denied that Maluco had been found and taken possession of first by us, a fact supposed and proved by our peaceful and uninterrupted possession of it until now; and the contrary not being proved legally, our intention in the past and present is inferred and based upon this possession.

From the above it follows plainly that, inasmuch as we found and took possession of Maluco, and hold and possess it at present, as is quite evident that we do hold and possess it, if the said most serene King of Portugal, our brother, claims it, as being of his conquest and demarcation, he must petition us for it, and his representations proving correct, he must accept it from us. Herein is the said treaty obeyed to the letter, as the said ambassadors petition, and observed with the good faith alleged by them.

And in case anything has been obtained in Maluco, or any information has been acquired concerning Maluco, or any Portuguese has gone thither, or is there now, for the purpose of trade or barter, or for any other cause—none of which are known or believed to be so—it does not follow nor can it be asserted that Maluco was found by ships of the King of Portugal, as is required by the said treaty, and therefore the foregoing being, in fact, outside the terms of the treaty, we are outside of its jurisdiction and obligation.

Furthermore it was declared in our behalf, that, although Maluco had been discovered by ships of the King of Portugal— a thing by no means evident—it could not, on this account, be made to appear evident, or be said that Maluco had been found by him. Neither was the priority of time, on which he based his claims, proved, nor that it was discovered by his ships; for it was evident, that to find required possession, and that which was not taken or possessed could not be said to be found, although seen or discovered.

Leaving out of consideration the decision of the law, even the general opinion which was on my side and which comprehends and binds by virtue of common sense those who recognize no superior, and which all of us were and are bound to follow, pointed to the same thing, and it was proved clearly by the said treaty on which we both founded our pretensions, without any necessity arising of dragging *ab extra* any other right or allegation; because if he who found land, found it in the other's demarcation, he was bound to surrender it to him, according to the terms of the said treaty, it is evident, and follows plainly, that he who found the land must first hold and possess it, because not holding it he could not surrender it to the other, who petitioned him for it, on the grounds that it had been found within his demarcation. If any thing else should be declared, it was in violation of the terms of the said treaty, which must be understood and fulfilled effectually.

From the above it followed clearly that the finding of which the said treaty speaks, must be understood and is understood effectually. It is expedient to know, by taking and possessing it, that which is found; and consequently the most serene King of Portugal, nor his ships, can, in no manner, be spoken of as having found Maluco at any time, since he did not take possession of it at all, nor holds it now, nor has it in his possession in order that he may surrender it according to the stipulations of the said treaty.

And by this same reasoning it appeared that Maluco was found by us and by our ships, since possession of it was taken and made in our name, holding it and possessing it, as now we hold and possess it, and having power to surrender it, if supplication is made to us. It appearing to fall within the demarcation of the most serene King of Portugal, it follows from this, that supplication must be made to us by him, and if it is found to lie within his demarcation, he must receive it from us, and not we from him, in accordance with the said treaty, which being understood to the letter, as the ambassadors petition, thus proves and determines the question.

It was especially declared that we, in this reasoning, made no request of the King of Portugal. And inasmuch as we were the defendant we neither wished to, nor ought we to have any desire to assume the duties of the plaintiff, because if the King wished anything from us for which he should petition us, we were quite ready to fulfil in entire good faith all the obligations of the said treaty.

Furthermore it was declared that, supposing—which is not at all true—that the King of Portugal had found Maluco first, and that he should claim that we should restore it to him, asserting that he had been despoiled of it by our having taken possession of it on our own authority, when we should have petitioned and received it from him; or alleging that we did not disturb or trouble him in the possession of what he does not have, nor ever had in his possession, it was quite clear that the case was not comprehended in the said treaty. Neither was it provided for nor determined in the treaty, which was not to be extended, nor did extend to more than was expressly mentioned and set down therein, which it did determine. Rather this appeared to be a new case, omitted and unprovided for by the treaty, which must be determined and decided by common sense or common law.

Accordingly, since this matter was outside of the said treaty, we were not bound by the treaty, nor in any other manner to leave our right unexamined, nor was it either reasonable or proper to restore immediately in order to have to petition later, thus making ourselves, contrary to all ideas of equity and good faith, original criminal, prosecutor, or plaintiff; especially as it would be impossible or very difficult to recover what we should restore. For this very reason even the restitution of what was well known to be stolen was deferred by law, until the case of ownership was decided.

Furthermore the right of our ownership and possession was evident because of our just occupation. At least it could not be denied that we had based our intention on common law, according to which newly-found islands and mainlands, belonged to and remain his who occupied and took possession of them first, especially if taken possession of under the apostolic authority, to which—or according to the opinion of others, to the Emperor—it is only conceded to give this power. Since we, the said authorities, possessed these lands more completely than any other, and since the fact of our occupation and possession was quite evident, it followed clearly and conclusively that we ought to be protected in our rule and possession, and that whenever anyone should desire anything from us, he must sue us for it; and in such suit must be the occasion for examining the virtue and strength of the titles, the priority, and the authority of the occupation alleged by each party to the suit.

Meanwhile, and until it should be stated legally before one or the other, and that there ought to be a better right than ours, which we neither knew nor believed, we would base our intention upon common law. Therefore we held and possessed Maluco justly, since our title to acquire dominions therein was and is just and sufficient;

and from common law arose, both then and now, our good faith and just intention. Our good faith and the justice of our side was apparent by these and other reasons, by the said treaty in what falls within its scope, and by common law and common sense in what falls outside it, or by all jointly. There was no reason or just cause in what the ambassadors petitioned, as formerly in this matter of possession, Silveira, ambassador of our brother, the most serene King of Portugal, the first to come upon this business, had been given thoroughly to understand. Now inasmuch as my wish has ever been, past and present, to preserve the relationship existing between the said most serene King and myself, and in order that the affection and alliance we have ever had may continue to increase, as is in accordance with our desire and actions regarding this matter, as well as upon everything most intimately connected with it, I commanded the members of our Council to review this question in private, and with care; and I charged them in the strongest possible manner that upon God and their own consciences they should declare to me their opinion When it had been examined and discussed again thoroughly, all these members agreed, *nemine discrepante,* that, from everything observed up to the present, we held Maluco rightly. Now because, as you will understand, since all the members of my Council say the same thing, I ought to believe them, and it would neither be honest nor reasonable to disregard their opinion, especially in a matter upon which I acting alone could not nor can be well informed, I commanded that, according to the above, their opinion would be the answer to the said ambassadors, giving them to understand thoroughly the causes and reasons abovesaid, and others, which although clear and evident, the ambassadors would not accept. Rather they continued to persist that Maluco ought to be surrendered to them. They said they had information that Maluco had been found by the King of Portugal, and by his ships. But that information being unauthorized and in the same the witnesses being subjects of the King of Portugal, (you see how much advantage, honor, and increase it is to this nation to succeed in this undertaking), and it being a thing beyond the bounds of reason, and a matter of no credence or damage, we did not permit examination of it; for even though the evidence should prove damaging to the King of Portugal, he could not be compelled to abide by it, as it had not been presented in a regular court of law, nor sufficiently empowered by him. It was a departure from the principal matter of negotiation. And then too the said ambassadors, although other information better than their own was offered on my part, would not accept it, nor would they abide by it. Although, as you see, I ought not to depart from the said treaty, which was the only petition made me by the said ambassadors, they not wishing to stick to the truth, persisted obstinately in so doing, and then it was sufficient to have satisfied themselves as to its full observance.

But paying no heed to this, nor to the harm ensuing to us in persuading them, on account of my great affection to my cousin, the said most serene King of Portugal, and those causes already declared, proposals were made to the said ambassadors in my behalf, to wit, that it be considered immediately by the court of demarcation, and for this persons be appointed in accordance with the said treaty and the prorogation of it, and within a convenient period, which would not lengthen greatly the business in hand, nor be so short that it would seem that the matter could not be concluded in the time named, and the said declaration and demarcation should be determined. While this was being done, neither he nor I would despatch ships, nor engage in any new undertaking. This would be without hurt to either one of us, so that, if the demarcation was not determined in the time appointed, each one's right would remain and continue fully in force. This expedient, although, it was very prejudicial to our evident and peaceful possession to discontinue it by any compact, and withal a compact made with the side opposing us, the ambassadors would scarcely listen to, declaring that they were not empowered by the King of Portugal to discuss any halfway measures. And afterwards, although with great urging on our part they consented to write the latter concerning this question (and they say they did write him concerning it), they gave out that the reply received was in the way of a refusal.

And notwithstanding that it was seen and known that they did not wish to abide by the said treaty, nor to adopt a middle course or any reasonable conclusion, another expedient was proposed by certain members of our Council, to whom I committed the matter, namely, that while the court of demarcation was sitting, as aforesaid, each side should have entire liberty to despatch ships, if he so wished. For by this means the King of Portugal could take no offense, since this expedient was the same for both. Rather, if any harm resulted, it appeared to be against our right, for of our own free will we permitted them to make expeditions, from which would follow the disturbance of our peaceful and continued possession. Upon every point, although they were given the choice between the said expedients, they answered as at first maintaining an obstinate silence and asserting that they were not authorized. Thus by their own decision and choice they left everything to us.

Then because there remained nothing more to attempt, and in order to convince them thoroughly, and that the King of Portugal, our cousin, might know our intention thoroughly, it was proposed to them that since they were not abiding by the treaty upon which they based their pretensions, nor accepted the expedients proposed to them, that they themselves should propose other expedients, so that if they seemed proper (as were those proposed to them), they might be deliberated upon. To this they answered for the third time that they had no authority to discuss halfway measures, but that Maluco should be surrendered to them. Seeing that all these compliments and offers of expedients made to them on my part, which were submissions rather than compliments, rather proved a loss than a gain to the negotiations, they were abandoned, and the question remained as at first. Inform the most serene King of Portugal in regard to these entire proceedings, for it is the truth. And see that he understands fully my wish, which is as above stated to you; and that I have not failed on my part to do all required by the said treaty, nor to consider any proper and reasonable expedient. Advise me fully of all that is done in this matter. Pamplona, December 18, 1523. I the King.[177] [Countersigned by the secretary Cobos. Signature of the chancellor and of Carvajal]

Treaty Between the Emperor and the King of Portugal Concerning the Limits and Possession of Maluco

[This treaty was negotiated in the city of Vitoria, being signed February 19, 1524. The negotiators acting for Spain were the following: Mercurinus de Gatinara, Grand Chancellor of his Majesty; Hernando de Vega, Commander-in-chief in Castile of the order of Santiago; García de Padilla, Commander-in-chief of Calatrava; and

Doctor Lorenzo Galindez de Carvajal: "all members of the Council of the most exalted and powerful Princes, Don Cárlos, by the divine clemency Emperor ever august, and King of the Romans, and Doña Juana, his mother, and the same Don Cárlos, her son, by the grace of God King and Queen of Castilla, Leon, Aragon, the two Sicilas, Jerusalen, etc." Those acting for the Portuguese monarch were Pero Correa de Atubia, seignior of the city of Velas, and Doctor Juan de Faria, "both members of the Council of the most exalted and excellent Lord, Don Juan, by the grace of God, King of Portugal, of the Algarbes on this side of the sea and in Africa, seignior of Guinea, and of the conquest, navigation, and commerce of Ethiopia, Arabia, Persia, India, etc." The respective monarchs delegated full powers to these representatives to negotiate, in their names, this treaty, in which the ownership of Maluco was to be determined. The Spanish letter of authorization was signed in Vitoria, January 25, 1524. (Navarrete omits the Portuguese letter of authorization.) The treaty proper follows:]

Thereupon the said Representatives of the said King and Queen of Castilla, . . . etc., and of the said King of Portugal, . . . etc., said: That, inasmuch as some doubt exists, between the said Lords, their constituents as to the possession and ownership of Maluco, each one claiming that it falls within the bounds of his demarcation—which must be determined in accordance with the terms of the compact and treaty negotiated between the Catholic Sovereigns Don Hernando and Queen Doña Isabel, King and Queen of Castilla, . . . etc., and the most exalted and excellent King, Don Joan, King of Portugal, . . . etc., (may they rest in peace),—therefore they, jointly and severally, in the said names, and by virtue of the said powers, incorporated above, for the sake of peace and concord, and for the preservation of the relationship and affection between their constituents, authorize, consent to, and ratify the following:

First, there shall be appointed by each one of the parties to this treaty three astrologers, and three pilots and sailors, for the determination of the demarcation, which must be made according to the terms of the said treaty. These men must assemble, and they shall assemble, by the end of the month of March first following, or before that time if possible, at the boundary line of Castilla and Portugal, between the cities of Badajoz and Yelbes; in order that by the end of the month of May next following, of this present year, they may determine, in accordance with the terms of the said treaty, the said demarcation—taking a solemn oath as soon as they have assembled, and before attending to anything else, in the form prescribed by law and before two notaries (one for each side) with public declaration and testimony, swearing in the presence of God and the blessed Mary, and upon the words of the four holy Gospels, upon which they shall place their hands, that, laying aside all love and fear, hate, passion, or any interest, and with regard only to securing justice, they will examine the rights of the two parties involved.

Likewise three lawyers shall be appointed by each side, who, within the same period, and at the same place, and after having taken the said oath with all the solemn forms and in the manner abovesaid, shall inquire into the possession of Maluco, and receiving the proofs, documents, treaties, witnesses, and rights that shall have been presented before them, shall determine the possession, doing everything that seems necessary for making the said declaration, just as they would do in court. Of the three above-mentioned lawyers, he who is named first in the commission shall take charge of assembling all the other deputies of his side, in order that greater care may be exercised in the negotiations.

Further, during the said period and up to the end of the said month of May, next following, neither of the parties to this treaty shall despatch expeditions to Maluco, for purposes of trade or barter. But if, before the end of the said period the question of possession or ownership shall be determined, then the side, in whose favor the right of each of the said questions is declared, may despatch expeditions and may barter. And in case the question of ownership and demarcation is determined, then that of possession shall be understood to be decided and absorbed. If only the question of possession is determined by the said lawyers, without their being able to determine that of ownership, as aforesaid, then what still remains to be determined of the said ownership, and likewise of the possession of the said Maluco, shall, in accordance with the terms of the said treaty, remain in the same condition as before this present compact. All of the above must and shall be investigated without any prejudice to the rights of ownership and possession of either side, in accordance with the said treaty.

But if, before the conclusion of the said period, it shall appear to the lawyers first named in the commissions, as aforesaid, that the settlement can, in all probability, be concluded and determined with some further continuation of the time set, as above said; or if another good way or manner of procedure, by which this matter could be determined better under one head or another, to wit, that of possession or that of ownership, should offer itself to them, the two lawyers, as aforesaid, may, in either of these cases, prolong, for so long a time as seems convenient to them, the brief determination of the matter. During the period of the said continuation, these lawyers, and all the other deputies, each one in his own capacity, may investigate and ascertain, and they shall investigate and ascertain, just as if this extension of time were within the principal period named in their commission. But the said time shall be understood to be continued under the same conditions and obligations as hereinbefore stated.

And all the actions taken in this case shall be signed by the two notaries appointed in his name by each of the parties to this treaty, as aforesaid. Each notary shall write the actions taken by his side, and the other, after having confirmed and collated them, shall sign them.

Iten [Item]: each one of the sides must obtain the ratification and confirmation of these articles from their said constituents, within the twenty days first ensuing.

[The strict observance of the above is promised in the fullest of terms by the representatives of the two sovereigns, in the names of their respective constituents. The oath is taken in the usual way, "before God, and the blessed Mary, and on the sign of the Cross, upon which they placed their right hands, and upon the words of the four holy Gospels, wheresoever they are written most completely, and on the consciences of their said constituents, that they, jointly and severally, shall keep, observe, and fulfil all the above, and every part and parcel of it, really and effectually, casting out all deceit, fraud, and pretense; and they shall, at no time, nor in any manner, contradict it; and under the said oath they swore not to seek absolution from our most Holy Father, or from any other legate or prelate who may give it them, and even if it be given them, of his own accord, they shall make no use of it." Within twenty days of the date of the treaty, the respective representatives must exchange confirmations written on parchment and signed with the names and sealed with the hanging leaden seals of their constituents. The signatures affixed to the treaty are: Francisco de Valenzuela, secretary and knight of the order of Santiago; Pedro de Salazar, captain of their Majesties; Pedro de Ysasago, Contino[178] of their Majesties; Gregorio Casgas, Alvaro Mexia, and Sebastian Fernandez, servants of the said ambassador Pedro Correa de Arubia; Juan de Samano; and those of the negotiators.]

The Junta of Badajoz

Extract from the Records of the Possession and Ownership of the Moluccas

Record of Possession

April 11. On the bridge over the river Caya, situated on the boundary line between Castilla and Portugal the twenty-three deputies exhibited their authorizations. This first day passed in reading the treaty of Vitoria, negotiated February 19, 1524, and the letter of commission of the nine judges for Spain; the recall of Esteban Gomez, who *does not understand why he should take part in negotiations for our service*, and the appointment in his place of Fray Tomás Duran under date of Búrgos March 20, 1524; the appointment of the nine Portuguese judges; the appointment of one attorney for Spain, and two attorneys for Portugal; and a secretary for Spain, and the same for Portugal.

II They took the solemn oath to act in the sight of God and conscientiously.

III The judges ordered the attorneys of either side to state their side of the case, and to proceed with the matter.

IV The attorneys disputed as to who should act as plaintiff. Each one wished the other to act in this capacity. The Spanish attorney asserted that this affair was at the instance of Portugal, and that the ambassadors had been sent for this purpose by that country. The Portuguese attorney asserted that there was nothing upon the matter in the treaty, as was well known to Spain. In this wise passed the day.

April 14. On the said bridge. The Portuguese attorneys presented a notification, asserting that they made no petition; they said that the King had had possession of Maluco for more than ten years; therefore Spain ought to ask for and accept the witnesses which, according to the terms of the treaty of Vitoria, they were prepared to give as their proofs.

The Spanish attorney gave answer, insisting that the King of Portugal had moved first in this matter, and therefore should be the plaintiff. As to the rest he said that the suit was obscure, vague, and general, insufficient to form a case on possession, and to pass a sure sentence upon it, let them specify wherein they thought the treaty was not observed, and let them attempt the fitting remedy and interdict, and he will answer them.

April 20. In the chapter of the Cathedral church of San Juan at Badajoz. The attorney for Portugal said that it was not apparent from the records that his King had moved first in this matter, nor even if such a thing should be apparent, could it be called a provocation, because this matter was between those who could not be coerced into judgment, since they recognized no superior. As to the claim that their suit was vague, that was no reason why it was not a suit. They stated clearly that their King had been in possession ten years and more. Therefore Spain should act as plaintiff.

April 21. Under the same head. The attorney for Spain insisted upon what he said before, adding only that in regard to this matter being started by Portugal, they denied what they knew to be so, and such a thing could be proved quickly. As to Portugal's saying she had been in possession furnished no reason why Spain should be plaintiff.

April 22. *Ibid.* In a meeting of the judges, the three lawyers of Portugal gave expression to the following interlocutory opinion:

that each side should make cross-examinations according to law, in order that they might examine the witness produced by the attorneys. Thus the latter could offer any writs, proofs, and documents from which they hoped to gain aid in this case, so that, when everything was seen and examined, this case and the doubt as to whom the possession belonged could be determined.

The three Castilian lawyers declared that the petitions of the Portuguese attorneys had no place, and therefore within three days they would state and plead their right.

The Portuguese judges said that both informal opinions agreed in each side pleading its right, but the Castilian judges did not state in theirs whether they should be by court or by petition, and they therefore asked them to make such declaration. The Castilian attorney said that the opinion of his side was clear and there was no occasion for the suit.

The legal judges for Castilla made the same assertion.

May 4. In Yelves, in the town hall. The attorneys for Portugal replied that they would receive hurt from the opinion of the Castilian judges, because the latter claimed wrongly that they were the plaintiffs; that the two interlocutory decisions of either part were not the same. And they asserted that to be in accord with justice, and the treaty, which was in harmony with the opinion of their judges, they ought to form a court of cross-examination and furnish as proofs to the attorney for Castilla those things placed before them. And if they would not do this, then it was evident that the delay in the case was due to the Castilian judges and attorney.

May 6. *Ibid.* The attorney for Castilla denied that the parties to the suit could compel the arbitrators to submit to their opinions. He defended the opinion of his judges; demonstrated that the contrary was unjust and null and void, because they demand witnesses and proofs to be received without a suit, debate, or conclusion preceding, a thing quite contrary to all order in law. He impugned the secret motive that could provoke the Portuguese judges to their interlocutory opinion, the apparent meaning of which was to make a summary investigation concerning the possession in order thereby to clear the way for the decision of ownership, thus making defendant and plaintiff change places. This had no place in the proceedings because they could not prepare the decision in which they did not make investigations. Further it would be a perversion of the order given by the two sides, both for petitioner and possessor, and clearly what they would do would be null and void. For this and other reasons the opinion of the Portuguese judges had no value. They ought to conform to ours, and not doing so, it is evident that they are guilty of the time already lost and which will be lost.

May 7. *Ibid.* The Portuguese attorney shattered at length the reasons of Ribera with texts from Bartulo[179] and Baldo, and concluded by saying that the opinion of the Castilian judges was null and void and wrong, and ought to be rectified. Without doubt this was the instruction received from the court.

May 13. At Badajoz, in the council house of the said town. The attorneys for Portugal petitioned that the reply of the attorney for Castilla should not be read, because it should have been presented in the junta before the twelfth. There was a dispute on this point, but it was read. It contradicted the other side, and insisted on the same thing as before. At the end it threw the blame for the delay on the Portuguese deputies, inasmuch as they would not come to an agreement with the intention of their Majesties that the cases be determined in the time allotted. The same day, *ibid.* In the afternoon meeting Ribera said that the onslaught of the Portuguese deputies on the preceding afternoon had been expected, and it was understood that today was the first meeting at which he ought to speak. Therefore he asked that the petition which precedes be admitted and be placed on record. This was ordered.

May 18. *Ibid.* In the afternoon the vote of the Portuguese judges taken the morning of the same day was made public, namely, that they clung to their opinion, and threw the blame for the delay on the opposite side.

May 19. The vote of the Castilian judges was made public. It was to the same effect. They added that the judges of Portugal should consider whether they could find any expedient or legal form, whereby the remaining time should not be lost, without prejudice to their declaration. The Portuguese judges asserted the answer given at Yelves, whereupon Ribera presented a petition, setting forth the intention of their Majesties, and throwing the blame on the other side for not having even commenced the case by wishing for proof without suit or foundation.

May 23. In Yelves, in the town hall. The attorneys for Portugal said that, with regard to the fault of the others who would not make use of the remedies provided by law in such cases, they found no other expedient except the one they had set forth in their interlocutory opinion.

May 24. *Ibid.* The judges for Portugal declared they had a letter from their King, in which he told them that the Emperor was writing to his deputies to agree to resolve themselves into courts for cross-examination and to continue the time. In the afternoon the judges for Spain answered that they were ready for any good expedient and method whereby this negotiation could be brought to a speedy close, in accordance with their Majesties' wish. Those of Portugal replied that they did not answer whether they had such a letter from the Emperor, and if there was any delay, they were to blame.

May 25. *Ibid.* In the morning the judges for Castilla said that inasmuch as the matter upon which they had been notified was a weighty one, they would defer their answer until the next meeting on the twenty-seventh. Then the attorney Ribera presented a paper wherein he stated that the attorneys for Portugal ought to be compelled justly to act as plaintiffs, as in fact they had proved themselves to be in their petitions, conforming themselves therein with their sovereign who had provoked and commenced this negotiation. Therefore they were acting contrary to their words and deeds. The judges for Portugal ought to act in accordance with the interlocutory opinion of Castilia, so that the case might be valid. We did not have to solicit proofs and witnesses, since our rights were so well-known. But how could we solicit such things without a preceding sentence in accord with the suit depending upon the petitions, etc? Outside of this, since sentence must be passed jointly on possession and ownership, and the judges appointed for this purpose by the King of Portugal having placed a thousand impertinent obstacles in the way, it was evident that the deputies on the other side were avoiding the judgment and suit, and were eluding and losing the time of the compromise. Then he petitioned that they act in accord with his petition.

May 27. *Ibid.* The Emperor's deputies, in answer to the notification of the twenty-fourth, said that although it was proper that their interlocutory opinion be acted upon, nevertheless, because their Majesties wished the affair settled within the time agreed upon, they would agree that the attorneys of each side should plead their rights within three days.

In the afternoon meeting the deputies of Portugal responded saying that the answer was unsatisfactory. It was unnecessary to have the attorneys of each part plead, since such a thing had been ordered without avail on the eleventh of April. Therefore they insisted upon the interlocutory assembly.

May 28. *Ibid.* The attorneys for Portugal presented a writ to the effect that the time limit expired on the last of May, and the matter was in such shape that it would be finished briefly; for in regard to the ownership, their attorneys were unanimous on the three points, except in matters of slight moment, in which they could soon agree. In the matter of possession, the witnesses of both sides were present, and such an expedient could be adopted that this case could be determined immediately. "Therefore we petition," said they, "for a continuation of the time limit. In this will be done what ought to be done, and what the Emperor seems to wish, since he has told the ambassadors of our King that your graces could extend the time, and were empowered to do it by the said treaty."

The licentiate Acuña answered immediately that prorogation was an act of jurisdiction, and should be determined on the boundary line, where, according to the order, they must meet during the last three days; and that he was ready to discuss the matter on Monday, May 30 with the licentiate Acevedo, the member first named on their commission.

Acevedo consented, and they agreed to meet on the said day at seven in the morning.

May 30. When the deputies met on the boundary line Acevedo gave his vote, namely, that bearing in mind the treaty and that the matter could be settled briefly, the two cases be continued through June.

Acuña's vote was to the effect that it stipulated in the treaty that, if the case was in such shape it could be settled in a short time. In the matter of possession there was no case nor any sign that there would be one during the month. In that of ownership they differed from the very first point—some insisting that they should count from the island of La Sal, and others from that of

San Antonio. He thought the time spent here by the deputies would be lost, and his presence was necessary in the employment and discharge of his duty. He did not see any other expedient but to refer the matter to their principals. Therefore, it was his opinion that the matter should not be continued.

Immediately the attorneys for Portugal declared that their King had written to the Emperor, both upon the question of proceeding by means of courts of cross-examination and upon that of continuing the case, and as he expected a favorable reply within eight or ten days, they should at least prorogue it until that time. To this effect notification should be made by licentiates Acuña and Acevedo.

Acuña answered that he had given his final answer in his reply. On the thirty-first there would be no meeting in regard to the possession.[180]

Record of Ownership[181]

April 11. On the bridge of Caya River assembled the licentiates Cristóbal Vasquez de Acuña, a member of the council, Pedro Manuel, a member of the audiencia and chancery of Valladolid; Fernando de Barrientos, a member of the council of Ordenes; Don Hernando Colon, Simon de Alcazoba, Doctor Sancho de Salaya, master of theology; Fray Tomás Duran, Pero Ruiz de Villegas, Captain Juan Sebastian del Cano; likewise the licentiate Antonio de Acevedo Coutiño, Doctor Francisco Cardoso, Doctor Gaspar Vasquez, all of the desembargo of the King of Portugal; Diego Lopez de Sequera, of the King's council and his chief magistrate, Pedro Alonso de Aguiar, nobleman of the said King's household; Francisco de Mela, master of holy theology; licentiate Tomás de Torres, physician to the said King; Simon Fernandez, Bernaldo Perez, knight of the order of Christ—arbitrators appointed by Spain and Portugal. In the presence of the secretaries Bartolomé Ruiz de Castañeda and Gomez Yañes de Freitas, the treaty appointments, etc., were read. And the witnesses, Doctor Bernaldino de Ribera, attorney of the chancery of Granada, and attorney-general for Spain; and the licentiate Juan Rodriguez de Pisa, advocate to their Majesties; and the licentiate Alfonso Fernandez and Doctor Diego Barradas, attorneys-general for Portugal[182] took the solemn oath.

Upon this day, the Portuguese attorneys declared that Alcazaba could not take the oath or act as judge, inasmuch as he had fled from Portugal with intent to be disloyal to his King, who had, for good and sufficient causes, refused him certain rewards, and had ordered him tried for certain offenses committed in India. This was the reason for his flight, and therefore he was a suspicious person and ought not act as judge. The attorneys asserted strenuously that they would not assent to anything Alcazaba did, and that their King had written the Emperor to appoint another in his place.

Nevertheless the judges ordered that he be sworn and he took the oath with the others. Immediately Doctor Ribera, attorney for Spain, said that the reasons were trifling, and seemed to have been invented to delay the case. A copy was given to the attorneys for Portugal and the day of

April 12. *Ibid.* The latter said that they held their suspicions justly, and therefore the King had written to the Emperor, etc.

April 20. In the chapter of San Juan, the Cathedral church of Badajoz. A despatch from the King of Portugal was read, removing Bernardo Perez from participation in the case, "because of certain reasons that move us" [could he have been refused by the Emperor in reply to the refusal of Alcazaba? could the said Perez be a Spaniard?] and appointing in his place master Margallo. Another provision of their Majesties was read, removing Simon de Alcazaba, "because he must occupy himself with matters connected with our service," and appointing in his stead Master Alcarez; dated Búrgos, April 10, 1524.—Secretary Cobos. Margallo and Alcarez took the oath and the matter of the demarcation was begun, by the reading of the treaty of Tordesillas of June 5, 1494,[183] with the confirmation given to the same at Arevalo, July 2, of the same year; and the agreement of May 7, 1495, as to the prorogation of the ten months allowed to the caravels to determine the said demarcation.

April 23. *Ibid.* They began to treat formally of the matter, and in accordance with what had been discussed before, the attorneys propounded three questions.

1st. In what manner the demarcation should be determined.
2d. How the islands of Cabo Verde were to be situated and located in their proper place.

3d. From which of the said islands they should measure the three hundred and seventy leagues.

The judges for Spain voted that these questions should be examined in this order.

May 4. In Yelves, in the town hall. The attorneys for Portugal deferred their voting until this day, and voted that the order of examination should be in the inverse order. Immediately the deputies for Spain declared that in order to avoid discussions they made the declaration of the following writ. In substance this was reduced to saying that they ought to determine first the manner of locating the islands and to choose the meridian for the three hundred and seventy leagues. But this matter being easy and one of pure reason, it ought not obstruct the investigation of the other two, and therefore they would summon the attorneys within three days, to give their decision as to the first question. And they would treat immediately of the other two, since the time limit was short, and already they had lost time enough both because of the refusal to accept Alcazaba and the illness of certain Portuguese deputies.

The Portuguese deputies voiced the following expression in the afternoon: that the reason for not meeting sooner was because certain of the Castilian deputies were not empowered. Moreover they insisted that the first point to be discussed was the one declared by them, but they agreed to the declaration of the attorneys concerning it within three days.

May 6. *Ibid.* In the morning the attorneys discussed the matter. They sent for the sea-charts and globes of each side which each desired. Several examinations were made. The same discussion was continued in the afternoon, and voting was deferred until

May 7. *Ibid.* In the morning the Portuguese representatives said that sea-charts were not so good as the blank globe with meridians as it represents better the shape of the world. Then they discussed the best means of putting the lands, islands, and coasts upon it, as they were quite prepared to do this.

The judges for Spain said that they preferred a spherical body, but that the maps and other proper instruments should not be debarred, in order that they might locate the lands better upon the said body.

May 12. In Badajoz, in the chapter of the said church. The judges for Spain said that on May 4 they had ordered the attorneys to discuss the question of the island from which the three hundred and seventy leagues should be measured; that their intention was to hear them *viva voce*; that time was short, and they summoned them for the following day.

May 13. At Badajoz, in the town hall. Having given notification, the togated attorney of their Majesties and the licentiate Juan Rodriguez de Pisa, of the Council and advocate in this case, discussed the law. The attorneys for Portugal talked also. Then the judges for Spain voted as follows: as to the island from which we should begin to reckon the three hundred and seventy leagues, it is our opinion that it should be the most westerly, San Antonio. They proved this conclusively both by the natural meaning of words, and by the intention and purpose of the Portuguese King to have it as far west as possible. It was also evident from other documents [he alludes to the bull] that Portugal had one hundred leagues on the other side of the islands, and two hundred and seventy more were conceded to her. Then the three hundred and seventy leagues must begin from the most westerly, that of San Antonio. [This is doubtless the paper of Hernando Colon, for it says *spherical* and contains other sentences peculiar to it.] It was signed at the bottom by the astrologers and pilots alternately in the following order: D. Hernando Colon, Fray Tomás Duran, *Magister*, Doctor Salaya, Pero Ruiz de Villegas, Master Alcaraz, Juan Sebastian del Cano.

In the afternoon the judges for Portugal rendered the following vote: that the measurement of the said three hundred and seventy leagues should be made from the islands of La Sal or Buena Vista, which were on the same meridian. They adduced several trifling reasons which are not worth recording. They signed it at the bottom: Francisco de Melo, Diego Lopez de Sequera, Pedro Alfonso de Aguiar, Master Margallo, Licentiate Torres, Simon Fernandez.

May 14. *Ibid.* Having discussed the matter in regard to the judges for Portugal telling those for Castilla that they should give the form of their agreement, the latter presented the following writ: "The principal grounds upon which the judges for Portugal take their stand is, because in the treaty of 494 [*sic*] it is stated that the caravels shall sail from Canaria to the Cabo Verde Islands, of which the first and principal ones are La Sal and Buena Vista, as if that more than disposed of the voyage, and it was only necessary to finish the measurement." Then they confirmed the reasons given in their former paper and showed conclusively that the judges for Portugal ought to act in accord with them, or the blame for the delay would be theirs, etc.

May 18. *Ibid.* The judges for Portugal say that they cannot act in accordance with them, because the treaty states that the measurement shall begin at the Cabo Verde Islands, and this must not be understood indefinite, in such manner that it signifies all of them, but that it must be from a meridian where several islands are found. This is the case at the islands of La Sal and Buena Vista. They repeated this with the terms *á quo* and *ad quem*, and other subtle phrases, and concluded their long writ by saying that those of Castilla should act with them.

The judges for Castilla presented the following writ immediately: notwithstanding the contention in regard to the place from which they should calculate the three hundred and seventy leagues—to which they thought those from Portugal should conform themselves through fear of God—that they thought it best to pass beyond this question, and to locate the seas and lands on the blank globe. Much advantage would be derived from this. By so doing they would not be standing still and doing nothing. The location of the said lands and seas had no connection with the discussion, but perhaps it would prove to whom the Malucos belong no matter how the line be drawn. Therefore this ought to be done without awaiting the replies or debates which they have insinuated in their discussions, since they had not come here for debates nor to expect other agreement than the determining of justice. Then the judges for Castilla notified those of Portugal that they were acting up to what they said, and would continue to do so. And they would cast the blame upon them as acting contrary to right and law, and it could be seen that they were persisting in their attempt at delay, etc.

In the afternoon the judges for Portugal made answer asserting that their vote was in accordance with law, and they hoped those from Castilla would act in harmony with it. Moreover they agreed to pass on to the other matters of this negotiation.

May 23. In Yelves, in the town hall. The judges for Castilla said that, in accordance with the agreement, they had brought in the map showing the navigation from Castilla to the Malucos. In this was set down especially the cape of San Agustin in Brazil, in eight degrees of south latitude, and in twenty degrees of longitude west of the island of San Antonio; likewise was shown all the coast to the strait of the Malucos [Magallanes] whose entrance lies in fifty-two and one-half degrees of south latitude and four and one-half degrees of longitude farther west. The map contained also all the Maluco Islands, Gilolo, Burnel, Tincor, and many others which were named by Captain Juan Sebastian [del Cano], navigators who sailed in the "Victoria" and who were present at the assembly, and others who together with the foregoing discovered them, calling them the archipelago of the Malucos; and being situated in two degrees on each side of the equinoctial, and lying a distance of one hundred and seventy degrees from the meridian of the cape of San Agustin and one hundred and fifty from the divisional line. They handed this map to the judges for Portugal so that they might examine it, and petitioned them to show their navigation [eastward].

In the afternoon those acting for Portugal said that the foregoing map was of use only in determining the third point, for the Cabo Verde islands were not on it, with the exception of a portion of the island of San Antonio. "Many other lands were lacking and, above all the Line of Demarcation was drawn contrary to our opinion, nor is it sufficient to say that it was the navigation of Captain Juan Sebastian del Cano. Likewise we showed a similar map on which the Malucos were one hundred and thirty-four degrees distant [eastward] from La Sal and Buena Vista, quite different from theirs." But inasmuch as neither touched upon the case, they notified the Castilian deputies to present maps containing all the necessary lands, and "we would do the same."

Immediately the Castilian deputies petitioned that both maps be signed by the secretaries, and they showed theirs with all the Cabo Verde islands added to it, and some lands which the judges for Portugal passed by, so that on their part this did not remain to be done.

The Portuguese map contained Cape Verde with the Rio Grande to the Arbitro, but no more; and toward the north Cape Bojador, which lies thirteen and one-half degrees from Cape Verde; *Item*, an islet called La Ascencion, and then nothing to Cape

Buena Esperanza, which was a northwest direction with a north and south distance of fifty-two and one-half degrees, and a run of sixty degrees; *Item*, a nameless bay; *Item*, Cape Guardafui whither it was navigated from Buena Esperanza to the northeast, with a north and south distance of fifty and one-half degrees, and a run of fifty-six degrees; *Item*, Cape Comerin whither it was navigated from Guardafui in an east and west direction, one-half degree northwest, five degrees east, and a run of twenty degrees; *Item*, to Zamatra and up to the point called Ganispola, a run of fifteen and one-half degrees, from which point to the Malucos it was twenty-seven degrees.

Thereupon the judges for Portugal, with the exception of Francisco de Melo, who had departed, said they would answer the other points made by the deputies from Castilla in the morning.

May 24. *Ibid.* The judges for Castilla presented the following writ: "To say that the maps were only for the purpose of locating the Cabo Verde islands is strange, inasmuch as we are discussing the bringing by each side of our respective navigations, in order to determine the distance of the Malucos, as witness the members of the Council, who were and are present. It is also strange that among such persons they should withdraw the plans and maps of their navigation, and not allow us to examine them. In our navigation the only thing necessary is to see the distance in dispute, and we will locate on it anything else they wish. The line is drawn according to our opinion. Let them do the same on theirs meanwhile, in order that it may not prove an obstacle to the third point. As to what they say about their map being like ours, it is not so, for they have located only capes and points. We show the entire navigation up to the Malucos just as they saw it therein. As to the principal matter that there are one hundred and thirty-four degrees eastward from La Sal to Maluco, that is a matter we shall look into, and discuss, and say what we shall deduce as the truth. As to whether we have located the Cabo Verde islands properly, why was there no doubt about that when they agreed to it yesterday afternoon, comparing them in the book of Domingo Lopez de Sequerra, wherein the whole world is shown in meridian circles? Pero Alfonso de Aguiar assured the licentiate Acevedo, who showed doubt upon the matter, many times of this. But for greater abundance of proof we are going to bring back the maps so that they will be sure of it." [This writ seems to be an answer to the following one, but they are in the order written.]

Then the following writ of the judges for Portugal was read. In substance it said that the maps presented by Castilla located the Cabo Verde islands farther west than they should be; that it was unnecessary to present maps showing their navigations, since the only thing they ought to discuss was the location of the Cabo Verde islands.

Then the judges for Castilla offered for a second time their map with the Cabo Verde islands, from which the measurements were taken.

In the afternoon the Portuguese deputies said in substance that the navigations should not be examined, but only the locations of the Cabo Verde islands with their respective distances. This ought to be done in order to determine the meridian at the three hundred and seventy leagues.

The Castilian deputies declared immediately that they were ready to do this, without prejudice of going on to the decision of the negotiations.

Those from Portugal measured the maps, finding several differences between the one of Castilla and their two—a large one and a small one.

Those from Castilla petitioned that the differences be pointed out and that the Portuguese deputies should state what they considered the truth; and that they were quite ready to acquiesce.

May 25. *Ibid.* Those of Portugal declared that they found differences in this place of one degree, in that of five, which they should try to reconcile. Neither had those of Castilla shown the locations of the Canaries and Cape San Vicente, and it was necessary to have these lands indicated.

The Castilian deputies offered a map with the lands in question, saying that, if this was the opinion of the Portuguese deputies they would conform to it, only they would take back the map presented first, being ready to conform with this opinion in order to get rid of the disputes which were blocking the decision.

The Portuguese deputies said it was quite late, and they would give their answer on the next day.

May 27. *Ibid.* The judges for Portugal asserted in regard to the location of the Cabo Verde islands: "We locate the island of

Santiago in five and one-fourth degrees of longitude from Cape Verde; the islands of La Sal and Buena Vista in four; Sant Anton in eight; and San Nicolas in five and one-half."

The judges for Castilla gave immediately as their opinion that the island of Santiago was in five and two-thirds of longitude distant from the meridian of Cape Verde; those of La Sal and Buena Vista four and two-thirds; that of Sant Anton nine, being in eighteen degrees of latitude. [The original signatures of Colon, Duran, Salaya, Villegas, Alcaraz, and Cano follow.]

May 28. By common consent both sides presented globes showing the whole world, where each nation had placed the distances to suit themselves. The measurements were taken and the secretaries ordered to set them down.

The measurements followed in the afternoon. Numberless differences were found, such that the globe of the Portuguese deputies showed one hundred and thirty-seven degrees of longitude from the meridian of the islands of La Sal and Buenavista to the meridian passing through the Malucos; while that of the Castilians showed one hundred and eighty-three. Both were measured eastward with a difference of forty-six degrees.

At adjournment of this meeting they agreed to meet upon the thirtieth upon the bridge of Caya to discuss and examine everything needful for the negotiations.

May 30. Monday, on the said bridge. The judges for Portugal presented the following notification, read by Francisco de Melo: that because of the differences in the globes they believed it necessary to investigate and make certain of the longitudes in question. For this they proposed four methods, namely: The first, on land by taking distances from the moon to some fixed star, as might be agreed upon; the second, to take the distances of the sun and moon in their risings and settings, and this upon land having its horizon above the water; the third by taking a degree of the sky without any limit for sea and land; and the fourth, by lunar eclipses. "Let us examine the method that we must use," they say, "and let us consider how to end the negotiation. If the time remaining seems short, it should be prorogued as long as may be necessary and for such prorogation we notify," etc., and they did notify Acuña and Acevedo to prorogue it for all of June.

Acevedo gave his vote [the same as in the records of possession]. Acuña said that he heard it, and Don Fernando Colon read immediately the following writ, which in brief showed the subterfuges of the judges for Portugal, the differences between the said judges and the globes which they presented concerning the distance from the meridian of La Sal eastward to Maluco, for they say it is one hundred and thirty-seven degrees but in one globe there were one hundred and thirty-four degrees and in another one hundred and thirty-three, a difference which proved falsehood; that both word and drawing showed their [the Castilians'] truth, and reasons and experience proves the said distance to one hundred and eighty-three degrees, and by way of the west one hundred and seventy-seven. The principal matter could have been determined in the time set; and this proposition of methods, which would require a long time, proved that they wished to delay matters. Neither was one month sufficient for the examination by these methods foreign to the spirit of the treaty, and they were opposed to this thing. They notified the Portuguese deputies to vote definitely on the demarcation and ownership at four o'clock in the afternoon on the following and last day of the time set. If they did not do so they would be to blame . . . we protest that we shall vote, etc.

The licentiate Acuña immediately handed in a negative vote on the question of continuation, as is seen in the Records of Possession. The notification of Acevedo and the confirmation of Acuña are also the same as in the said Records.

May 31. *Ibid.* In reply to the deputies of Castilla; those of Portugal presented a writ to the following effect: that the case was far from being in a state to pass a definitive sentence upon it. Only three preliminary points had been touched upon, and discussion of the principal things passed by. Therefore they were to agree upon the distances by virtue of certain observations; to place, by common consent, the lands and seas on a blank globe; and to draw the line of demarcation. The difference in our globes proved nothing. Also they [the Castilians] had altered their only globe and map, based on the voyages of Juan Sebastian del Cano. Therefore believing that all the globes and maps were in error, we have proposed certain astrological methods. Meanwhile we cannot vote, etc.

Don Fernando Colon read immediately the following vote and opinion of the Castilian deputies:

Opinion of the Spanish Astronomers and Pilots[184]

The first thing required and presupposed in this matter of defining and determining the present case of the ownership of the Malucos is to ascertain where the divisional line passes; and secondly the location of the above-mentioned Malucos. As to the first—the location of the said line—we their Majesties' deputies declare: We have voted already for many reasons and causes that this line must pass west of the island of Sant Antonio, the measurement commencing from this place, as we have demonstrated by our words and drawings during the procedure of this case; and we declare the same now by our vote and decision. As to the second, we assert that the Malucos fall many degrees within their Majesties' demarcation. In verification of this assertion it is to be noted, that, since the sphere has a circumference of three hundred and sixty degrees, this number should, of necessity, correspond to the distance, demonstrated by the deputies of the King of Portugal, to be comprised between the meridian of the island of La Sal and the Malucos, plus our assertion of the distance westward to the same Malucos. And as this number of degrees not only is not attained in the said navigation, but the latter rather falls short of it by about fifty degrees, no other reason can be assigned for the shortage, except that it arises from the distance eastward being greater than they have shown it to be; and the error consists in their having shortened the said journey, which is suspected and proved conclusively according to the following.

First, because it is sufficiently clear evidence to note that, in the prosecution of this case, they attempted to make use of ends which were manifestly unjustifiable, and wished to delay and not arrive at a conclusion. This was quite apparent when they immediately *refused to admit Simon de Alcazaba,* because he had voyaged in those seas and lands with the Portuguese, and knew the truth concerning their distances, and the places where they shortened the distances; and because some days must pass before their Majesties' commission to elect another judge, could arrive from Búrgos. *Item:* because on Saturday, April 23, we [the Castilian deputies] voted upon the order of investigating the three points necessary in the prosecution of this case, namely, in what manner we should determine the demarcation,—whether on a plane or spherical surface,—what location we should assign to the Cabo Verde islands, and from which one of them we should commence to measure the three hundred and seventy leagues; they in a matter so apparent, and of so little inconvenience or room for speculation, would not vote until Wednesday, May 4, a space of eleven days, and in order to cause confusion they voted that the first thing to determine was from what island the three hundred and seventy leagues to the line were to be measured, it being beyond the bounds of reason to discuss such a thing before investigating or ascertaining the relative locations of these islands with regard to each other, examining them in some manner, in order afterwards to enable us to determine from which one such measurement should be made. This we showed most conclusively by the reasons brought forward in this case. But wishing the verification of the truth, we consented to proceed in the matter as they elected.

Item: when it came to a vote as to the island from which the three hundred and seventy leagues was to be measured, they voted for the islands of La Sal and Buena Vista. This was quite contrary to justice, inasmuch as the measurement should begin at the island of Sant Antonio, the most westerly of the Cabo Verde islands, as is apparent from reasons adduced by us. It is apparent also from these reasons that, at our last meeting in Yelves, they brought in a globe upon which the line of demarcation had been drawn by them twenty-one and one-half degrees west of the said island of Sant Antonio. This they tried to disavow so that the notaries could give no testimony regarding it, telling them they could give no other testimony than that they saw a reddish band just like many others on the globe. Nevertheless in downright truth, in a globe marked with the points of the compass as it was, on which the principal winds were shown in black, the mid winds in green, and the quadrants in lines of a reddish hue, there could not be a quadrant or colored band passing from pole to pole—especially since there was but one, all the others being black—which they were substituting for the north and south wind, blowing from one pole to the other, and which is placed on such globes instead of the wind or meridian line.

Therefore it is apparent from the above that they had drawn this line long before they voted for the line of demarcation, by the sphere which they showed to have been made long before; and which if it had other reddish lines girdling the sphere, these latter did not pass through the poles as this line did, but started from the center of the compasses placed on the equinoctial, and were in proportion to other circular lines. But this line was in proportion to no other line, saving one corresponding to the number of the three hundred and seventy leagues reckoned from the island of Sant Antonio, just as we voted it must be located. Therefore it is proved by this line and globe that the said line was in harmony with our vote in regard to the distance it must have from the said island of Sant Antonio and in regard to its passing from one pole to the other, according to the stipulation of the first treaty negotiated between the Catholic sovereigns and King Don Juan (may they rest in peace), and not in harmony with it, in regard to the other things maintained on this point in the said globe. Therefore it results that they voted contrary to justice, with intent to show that they had navigated a shorter distance, and to delay and cause disagreement in these negotiations because of this point. All the above is apparent and is proved by the records of this assembly, and it is inferred therefrom that they did not consider or regard as true the few degrees they had given out.

Item: having agreed that we should bring good maps on which we would show our voyages westward, and they theirs eastward, they produced a map, upon which were shown only a few points and principal capes, and those lately inserted thereon; so that their voyages could not be ascertained. Neither was it possible to verify in such a map what they compressed in it. As the said distance of degrees given by them was not true, as would be quite apparent if they brought a good map, and one made some time before, in which their said navigation should be contained, and as they had no just excuse to palliate such contention, they said that they brought the said maps only to locate the Cabo Verde islands, which by the very same map was proved to be contrary to the truth and was not a sufficient excuse, since the said islands were not located on this map, as is evident from the judicial records. Therefore because of all the above reasons, and because it might not be possible to verify later what had passed, they would not permit the judges and notaries of the case to examine the said map. More than this, having decided afterwards upon the location of the said islands, we were in agreement with a map on which they had located them. As the decision was not unanimous they locked up the said map and would not produce it again, although they were requested to do so by us. And therefore, they voted afterwards upon the location of the said islands contrary to their own determination of them in the said map, and contrary to what we voted in the said case. They did this contrary to all reason and right, as was proved afterwards by a globe that they showed, on which both the island of Sant Antonio and that of La Sal were exactly where we located them, as is evident from the judicial records of this case. Consequently they acted contrary to what they had declared and voted. In the same way it was proved by the said globe [the first one] that the voyage eastward from the said island of La Sal to the Malucos, was greater than they had declared at first; and the said globe did not conform with the map they had shown first, nor even with another globe they produced. It is adduced from all the above by, evidence and clear demonstration, that the said distance of degrees asserted by them is untrue. Therefore they sought and tried to delay these negotiations, alleging that maps and globes were insufficient instruments from which to ascertain the truth, and that the demarcation could not be determined by them. They begged insistently that other methods of eclipses and fixed stars be sought, not taking into account, as we have said, that these are causes for great delay; for the consideration of such eclipses, and the movement of the moon, and its visual conjunction with any fixed star, and all other like mathematical considerations can at present be of no advantage to us, *because of our being limited to such a brief period as two months*, in examining and determining this matter. From this [the short time] it is seen that it was not the intention of those sending us that such expedients should be sought or pursued. It can be well said from the above that he who has a poor proof, shows in detail the witnesses to that fact, and therefore, we shall demonstrate in the following more fully and specifically that the said distance is not what they assert, and that all reason, every document, and all experience contradict it.

First it is proved that they have on their part, lessened the number of degrees, for the voyage from Guinea *to* Calicut is shown to be greater than they assert or show, because from the time those lands were discovered until now, the said Portuguese have been shortening and lessening the said distance. [This assertion is proved by the various discoveries eastward made by the Portuguese navigators from the time of the Infante Don Enrique, (Prince

Henry the Navigator) namely, Cadamosto, the Venetian; Antonieto, the Genoese; Pedro Zinzio; Diego Cano; Bartolomé Diaz; and Vasco da Gama.[185] The distances navigated by these men are given as they themselves recorded them.] Therefore with apparent reason the *Itinerario Portugallensium*, translated from Portuguese into Latin by Archangelo Madrignano, and which was printed in 1508,[186] in chapter sixty, reckons a distance of three thousand eight hundred leagues, or fifteen thousand miles from Lisbona to Calicut, and declares in the last chapter that it is a three months' voyage from Calicut to Zamotra.

Item. the said distance is proved to be much greater, as we assert, because of certain persons who traveled through and navigated the lands and seas eastward from the sea Rojo [Red Sea] and recorded their voyages at a time when there was no suspicion of a discussion like the present. [Gerónimo de Santisteban, a Genoese, is given as an example. He sailed from Aden to Calicut in thirty days, and in eighty-three days from Calicut to Zaumotra (Sumatra), a distance of about fourteen hundred leagues. "With this number agree Marco Paulo (Marco Polo) and Juan de Mandevilla (John Mandeville) in the self-same voyages and travels made by them, as is stated very diffusely in their books." The three-year voyage of King Solomon's ships, as recorded in "the third book of the Kings"[187] to "Ofir and Zetin whence they brought the gold to build the Temple," and which places "all writers upon the sacred scriptures assert" to be "toward the most eastern part of India," agree with the same figures.] From all the above, therefore it is inferred that the navigation from the said Mar Rubro [Red Sea] to the eastern part of India is a much greater distance than the Portuguese say.

Item: it is well-known that the Portuguese themselves confessed that the said Maluco islands were so far to the eastward that they fell within their Majesties' territories. And this was so apparent that one of the deputies acting now in this cause for the said King, by name Master Margallo, in a philosophical book written by him, and but lately out of press, in showing the division between Castilla and Portugal, proves that the said Malucos fall and are within their Majesties' limits. And too, when they were discovered by the Castilian fleet, the King of Portugal desiring to have information regarding their location and boundary, considered himself perfectly assured when all those whom he ordered to assemble for this purpose concluded that they lay within the Castilian boundaries. And therefore the more than great caution exercised up to that time in not permitting sea charts to be taken from his realms was thereafter observed much more strictly, and many maps were burned, destroyed, and seized, and an order was sent forth that the routes in all maps should be shortened. And those maps they do give out for purposes of navigation, to those who must sail toward India, they give on account, so that they must be returned to the treasury in order that there might be no information in other places as to the longitude of this route. And all the abovesaid is confirmed more clearly, because, notwithstanding the great caution exercised in Portugal in not allowing maps to be taken outside of the kingdom, certain Portuguese and Castilians have taken and possessed some maps. We, the said deputies of their Majesties, wishing to become better informed concerning these maps, in order to pronounce better and more truly upon this case, for the greater assurance of our consciences, and for the purpose of securing the most indubitable knowledge in regard to this matter, summoned before us certain pilots and men, skilled both in navigation and in making maps, globes, and mappamundos. These men have always tried to inform themselves with great care, concerning the distances and routes of the said voyage, both of those who made the voyage, and of those who delineated and located the lands comprehended in the voyage. They stated under oath and before two notaries and the secretary of this case, that they knew that the said navigation and the location of these lands comprised more degrees than was declared and demonstrated by the said deputies of the King of Portugal, by their globes and maps. So much greater was the distance that it was evident they were now trying to shorten the said voyage again by more than twenty-five degrees of longitude of the distance until now declared by them.

Therefore, as is apparent from the said information of modern navigators and cosmographers, both Portuguese and those of other nations, and from the relation of the said pilots and sailors, it has been proved completely that the said distances and routes, declared by the said deputies of Portugal, are neither just nor true, and that the deputies have reported them much shorter than, in sober truth, they are. From this it can be presumed, that inasmuch as they shorten the said route each day, the said mistake of fifty degrees proceeds doubtless from their eastern part and not from our western part.

Item: it is to be observed that, notwithstanding the said distances, expressed, as is shown by the said pilots who determined them, as they should, on a spherical body, the said Malucos fall many degrees within the limits of our lord, the Emperor, and that they lie a much greater number of degrees east of the island of La Sal, than they had declared, inasmuch as, according to geometrical reasoning, the lands situated along the said eastern voyage, placed on a plane surface, and the number of leagues being reckoned by equinoctial degrees, are not in their proper location as regards the number and quantity of their degrees, for it is well known in cosmography that a lesser number of leagues along parallels other than the equinoctial, occupy a greater quantity of degrees. Now then as almost all the lands from the Cabo Verde islands to the Malucos, are, for the most part quite distinct from the equinoctial, it will take a much greater number of degrees when they are transferred and drawn on the spherical body. Calculating by geometrical proportion, with the arc and chord, whereby we pass from a plane to a spherical surface, so that each parallel is just so much less as its distance from the equinoctial is increased, the number of degrees in the said maps is much greater than the said pilots confess, and consequently these lands fall by a greater number of degrees inside their Majesties' limits. In order to verify the above we must examine the itineraries and navigation routes, and the angles and intersections made by the routes with the meridians and parallels encountered, which are styled angles *positionis* among cosmographers. This is the most certain method of determining lands on a spherical body, when calculating them from the plane surface, as the following will show.

[The distances of these itineraries are shown in evidence of the preceding. Maps of India made in Portugal "at the time when there was no suspicion that so great a number of leagues was to be subtracted as is proved now to have been the case," are cited and distances taken therefrom in proof of the assertions made by the Castilian deputies. As a result of these distances it is shown that the distance between the Moluccas and the island of Sant Antonio would be one hundred and eighty-four degrees to the eastward, to which number "must be added the degrees contained in the said three hundred and seventy leagues from the island of Sant Antonio to the line of demarcation." The following deductions are made:]

It is quite evident from the above that the distance of the navigation eastward assigned by the Portuguese in the proceedings is short by more than fifty degrees, being proved by the said old Portuguese relations and maps, which are not to be doubted. And it is evident that our calculation is true, both eastward and westward, and that from the said divisional line commencing from the island of Sant Antonio, the distance westward to the Malucos is not more than the said one hundred and fifty degrees.

[At this point the aid of the old authors, Ptolemæus and Plinius, is invoked to prove more conclusively that the distance was shortened by the Portuguese. The summary of the document is as follows:]

Therefore in concluding, we assert, both on account of the reasons abovesaid, and for many others which incite us to this decision, that we find the location of the Malucos not to lie in the longitude declared by the deputies of the King of Portugal, but where we claim and prove by our sea chart. Consequently we assert that they lie and are situated a distance of one hundred and fifty degrees west of the divisional line, as we have shown in these discussions. It results then that the distance eastward from the said line to the said Malucos is two hundred and ten degrees, and according to this the ownership and seigniory of the Malucos pertain to their Majesties. This is our vote and decision, and thus we declare to and notify the said deputies of the King of Portugal, that since our vote is just and in accordance with right, they conform to the same. Don Hernando Colon, Fray Tomás Duran, Doctor Zalaya, Pero Ruiz de Villegas, Master Alcarez, Juan Sebastian del Cano.

I have read the above vote and decision of their Majesties' said deputies in the presence of the deputies of the said King of Portugal. Thereupon the said deputies of their Majesties and their secretary all said for themselves that their opinion is in accordance with the above, and they ordered us, the said secretaries to set it down in the records. Then the said deputies of the said King of Portugal declared that they were opposed to the said vote and adhered to the writ presented by them yesterday, and to the one presented at this meeting today before the reading of the vote in question. They said they had other reasons to offer, which they would not give today for lack of time, but would present tomorrow, Wednesday, the first of June. They ordered us, the said secretaries to set it down thus in this record. And we, the said secretaries being present at this declaration, set it down in this record, and sign it with our names. Bartolomé Ruiz de Castañeda.

The Portuguese deputies answered that they adhered to their proposition. The formalities follow and the junta was adjourned, as was certified in the records by the secretaries Bartolomé Ruiz de Castañeda acting for Spain, and Gomez Yañes Freytas for Portugal.[188]

Opinion Rendered by Don Hernando Colon in the Junta of Badajoz Concerning the Ownership of the Malucos

Don Hernando Colon declares that, at the first meeting of the deputies who were to confer regarding the question of ownership, when discussing the method of procedure, it was his opinion that each one should set down in writing what he knew of this matter, thus furnishing reasons and information upon which to base his Majesty's right, and also material wherewith to answer the arguments, to which he thought they might be opposed *ex adverso*. Although this method was not approved by the said deputies, considering that it could not but result in some good to his Majesty's service, he presented his opinion in writing after the following Saturday, wherein he showed their Majesties' right not only to the Malucos, but also to all of Persia, Arabia, and India. [Thereupon it was decided that each one should present his opinion, "especially as each one will incite and spur on his fellows, and in case of any sickness or absence, what such and such a deputy knew of the matter would be known, and if we should decide upon nothing definite at this time, we shall leave a record of the truth for a future time." Colon says:]

First, inasmuch as the division of the sphere, which is an unknown quantity, is to be determined, we must determine and verify its size. This must be done by one of two methods, namely, by measuring the entire globe or body to be divided; or by ascertaining exactly the proportional relation between one portion of it and the corresponding portion of another body, whose size is known to us, as for instance the heavens, which learned men have divided into three hundred and sixty parts or degrees.

As to the first method of measuring the earth, besides being very difficult, it becomes also arbitrary unless measurements were always made by line. Much uncertainty is occasioned by this method, because, as we hear and say continually such and such leagues are very long, while others speak of them as small, each one judging according to his own opinion, and taking into consideration the time and rapidity it took him to walk them. On this account a much greater difference will result when the said leagues are measured by sea, for there are many more obstacles that alter or impede the correct calculation of them, such as, for instance, currents, tides, the ship's loss of speed, because of its meeting with strong head winds, or because of heavy seas coming athwart the bows, or from other directions. In addition to all these one may be deceived by the ship's burden and bulk; or by reason of the ship's bottom being cleaner or dirtier at one time than another; or whether it is towed or sailing alone; or whether it carries new or old sails and whether they are of good or ill pattern, and wet or dry; whether the day's run is estimated from the poop, prow, or amidships; and other special considerations that I pass by, such as the heaviness or lightness of the winds, the differences in compasses, etc. From the above then, I infer that it is difficult and unsatisfactory to determine the size of the earth by means of measuring it by traveling or sailing, and the same was maintained by Ptolemæus and other erudite men by actual test.

As to the second method, namely, by determining what portion of the earth corresponds to another known part of the heavens, it is more *probabile etiam per demonstrationem.* But the difficulty of this method lies in the fact that this proof or demonstration has been made by many learned and experienced men, and we discover a great diversity in their results, as I pointed out in my opinion when it was agreed that every one should commit *in scriptis* the number of leagues corresponding to each degree, of which the following is a copy.

> [Here follow the different calculations of the length of a degree and the circumference of the earth, beginning with Aristotle. Briefly these are as follows: Aristotle, 800 stadia to a degree, making the terrestial circumference, 12,500 leagues; Strabo, Ambrosius, Theodosius, Macrobius,[189] and Eratosthenes, each 700 stadia to the degree, and a circumference of 7,875 leagues; Marinus and Ptolemæus, 500 stadia to the degree, and a circumference of 5,625 leagues; Tebit, Almeon, Alfragano, Pedro de Aliaco[190] "in the tenth chapter of *De imagine mundi* and the author of the sphere in the division of the zones," Fray Juan de Pecan "in the fourth chapter of the treatise of the sphere," and the "first Admiral of the Indies,[191] as is evident from many papers made by him," each "fifty-six and two-thirds miles" or "fourteen leagues and two-thirds of a mile" to a degree, and a circumference of 5,100 leagues. "If no opposition is given to this latter *ex adverso mere voluntarie*," continues Colon, "then necessarily we must have recourse to verify it by experience, which is hindered by many obstacles." In further reasoning he says:]

It is clear from the above, that, supposing the measurement of the degrees to be conclusive, it is not reduced to such practical form that the place where such and such a number of leagues correspond to a degree can be told, nor is it easy to determine this; so that it will be necessary, both sides concurring, to select persons and instruments and the place for making the test. After these men had been ordered to proceed, instruction and advice must be given them, which being a huge matter and outside of the present discussion, I shall not dwell upon. If such practical experience is not acquired, then rightly and quite reasonably the measurement or size of degrees used by the authors of tables, or of almanacs and daily calculations of the stars, should be accepted; and such a view seems quite conclusive to whomever is not obstinate, since it is proved that the diversity of the relative positions of the superior bodies proceeds from the difference between the places of observation.

Supposing that the number of miles or leagues corresponding to each degree were to be verified by the care and skill of the men abovesaid, then another very long and difficult calculation would be necessary, namely, the appointment of experienced men to measure and determine the number of measures or degrees from one continent or province to another. And when they shall reach the half [one hundred and eighty degrees] counting from the line passing at the end of the three hundred and seventy leagues, at that place they shall establish a point or mark to show what pertains to each side. But as this manner of measuring degrees may be difficult from east to west, although easy from north to south, recourse must be had to certain fine and subtile methods, of which, although everybody is well informed concerning them, I shall not hesitate to state a few facts I have been able to acquire, in order to give these other deputies an opportunity to explain those facts of which I am ignorant.

[Various methods for estimating the length of a degree follow. Colon concludes thus:]

But inasmuch as the determination of the above methods seems to be and is difficult, each one of them must be employed, and each one put into execution, so long as one does not conflict with the other. Furthermore the day's run must conform to these methods, and pilots of great experience and judgment chosen. In this way it might be hoped to determine a division in which neither part would suffer and great loss or inconvenience. Inasmuch as, in another form, *rebus stantibus ut nunc*, I consider it impossible that one side can succeed in convincing the other by demonstrating that the Malucos fall within his territory, although one might show that it is more in accordance with equity and reason, and thus obtain his object, if the judges imagine that they could determine it according to rigorous and absolute judgment; therefore in order to accomplish my utmost as well as to do everything that I think can be of use in this question, upon the day determined by the assembly I shall present in writing all the evidences, documents, and drawings bearing upon this case that, to my mind, might prove useful.

Now to sum up in conclusion of the above, neither side can convince the other that he is trying to shift his ground; and therefore, I say, no sentence can at the present time be passed upon this case, except that it will be necessary to agree upon an expedition to compute the size of the degrees; and this done, ships and men must be chosen, for the purpose of measuring the longitude by one or the other of the various methods found to be best, and for definitely determining and marking the beginning and end of the said demarcation, and the lands falling in each part or hemisphere. [His signature and the notarial countersignature follow. The date of this document is April 13, 1524.]

Opinions of Fray Tomas Duran, Sebastian Caboto, and Juan Vespucci Rendered at the Junta of Badajoz Regarding the Ownership of Maluco

Inasmuch as you wish, it appearing to have some value, that each one should set down in writing his opinion regarding the demarcation that his Majesty commended to us, we, Fray Tomás Duran, Sebastian Caboto, captain and pilot, and Juan Vespuchi, pilot, concert together in setting down and explaining our opinion regarding this demarcation.

First we must calculate the leagues, giving as few at possible to the celestial degree, because giving fewer leagues [to the celestial degree] there will be fewer throughout the earth, which suffices quite well for their Majesties' service. However, as we pointed out formerly, it seems to us that we must employ the number used commonly by sailors both in Portugal and Castilla. These men assign to each heavenly degree seventeen and one-half leagues, to the first following point of the compass from the north [north by east] eighteen and one-half, to the northeast by north twenty, etc. The second fundamental is that we must conform ourselves to that most grave and practical astrologer Ptolemaeus, who, writing later than Pomponius, Marinus, Plinius, and Strabo, calculated sixty-two and one-half miles to each degree.

Thirdly we declare that there are two methods of procedure in this demarcation. The first is according to the conjectures and experiments made during many repeated voyages by skilled pilots. This method has been followed by all the writers on cosmography. The other most sure method is by proceeding in a northern altitude from north to south, and in an altitude from east to west, or by taking the east and west longitude. This is a difficult task, as this assembly is aware, and as each one has declared, and setting forth many methods for doing it that appear feasible to them, and finding fault with them all.

First let us examine this first method, and then the second. As to the first we must place the line of demarcation three hundred and seventy leagues from the island of San Antonio. This number of leagues is equal to twenty-two degrees and almost nine miles. Reckoning degrees from that parallel and from the island of San Antonio there is a distance of one hundred and eighty leagues to Cape Verde which equals ten degrees. Therefore it is thirty-two degrees from Cape Verde to the line of demarcation. We assert then, that by graduating these degrees in this manner, the Malucos fall within the boundaries of our lord the Emperor, however we may make the demarcation. For if we wish to determine it after the customary models and where voyages have been made up to this time, to wit, calculating five hundred and forty leagues from Cape Guardafuui to Cape Comori, five hundred and sixty leagues from Cape Comori to Malaca, and four hundred and twenty leagues from Malaca to the Malucos, in which way the voyage is always made, not only do the Malucos fall within his Majesty's demarcation but also Malaca and Zamatra. And if, perchance, we wish to determine the demarcation in accordance with the recently corrected Portuguese maps, which reckon a much less number of leagues between the above-named places, to wit, from Cape Guardafuui to Cape Comori, Cape Comori to Malaca, and from Malaca to the Malucos, we still assert that the Malucos fall within the demarcation of our lord the Emperor. For according to these maps corrected recently in this way, the demarcation or line of demarcation falls near Gilolo, an island near the Malucos. This is so on the plane surface of their map. When this plane surface is reduced to a spherical one, because of the rotundity of the sea where these voyages are made—the latter being in addition along parallels other than that of the equinoctial and where the degrees are less than those of the equinoctial, (the same league being assigned to the different degrees)—so that when this reduction is made, five degrees are gained, or nearly this number, which we have measured and proved to be so, then it comes to pass, from their own map, that the line of demarcation falls outside the Malucos, and the Malucos are in the territory of the Emperor our sovereign.

Item: let us suppose, for instance, that when the Catholic Sovereigns and King Don Juan of Portugal ordered the demarcation of the seas to be made, by commanding a line to be drawn from the Arctic to the Antarctic pole at a distance of three hundred and seventy leagues from the Cabo Verde islands, they had ordered also the demarcation made on the eastern side, which his Majesty orders us to do now—though at that time neither Persia, Arabia, nor the Cabo Buena Esperanza [Good Hope] was discovered—it is quite certain that this north and south line must pass on the eastern side through the mouth of the river Ganges. This is a fact, because Ptolemaeus with great care described and located the cape of Catigara in accordance with the long experience of those voyaging through the spice region, as is discussed in the fourteenth chapter of the first book of his cosmography. He makes a distance of one hundred and eighty degrees from the Canarias to Catigara or the Metropol of the Chinese. Therefore subtracting the thirty-two degrees—the distance of the divisional line west [of the Cape Verde Islands], the line on the other side passes through the mouth of the river Ganges, which lies in one hundred and fifty degrees of longitude. Therefore Malaca, Zamatra, and Maluco fall within the demarcation of his Majesty.

Item: it can not be denied that the island of Gilolo, lying near the Maluco Islands, is the cape of Catigara, inasmuch as the companions of Magallanes journeyed westward upon leaving the strait discovered in fifty-four degrees of south latitude, sailing such a distance west and northeast that they arrived in twelve degrees of north latitude where were found certain islands, and one entrance to them. Then running southward four hundred leagues, they passed the Maluco islands and the coast of the island of Gilolo, without finding any cape on it. Then they took their course toward the Cabo Buena Esperanza [Good Hope] for Spain. Therefore then the cape of Catigara can only be the said island of Gilolo and the Malucos.

Item: Ptolemaeus locates this cape of Catigara at the point of the gulf Magnus, next to the gulf of the Ganges and the Cresonensus bay, which conforms wholly to the account now discovered, so that the description and figure of Ptolemaeus and the description and model found recently by those who came from the spice regions are alike and not only alike in appearance, but in name. That region is now called China; Ptolemæus styled it *regio Sinarum;* the barbarians also compressing the *s* say Sina instead of China; and the Portuguese themselves place China in this region. Therefore it being asserted that the island of Gilolo and the Maluco islands are Cape Catigara, as is a fact, the line of demarcation falls thirty-two degrees more to the westward and passes through the mouth of the Ganges. Therefore Zamatra, Malaca, and the Malucos fall within our demarcation.

Item: in everything discovered by the Portuguese of which Ptolemaeus has any notice, the former conform in their navigation to the latter. They locate China north of the Malucos in the gulf Magnus, just as Ptolemaeus locates it. For these and other reasons, which will be adduced by wiser than we, it seems to us that the Malucos, Malaca, and Zamatra fall thirty-two degrees within his Majesty's demarcation, as we stated above. This is the opinion of all three of us, and as such we give it, signed with our names this fifteenth of April, one thousand five hundred and twenty-four, in the city of Badajoz. Fray Tomás Duran, *Magister.* Sebastian Caboto. Juan Vespucci. [The notarial countersignature follows.]

Memorandum Relative to the Right of
His Majesty to the Dominion and Ownership of Maluco,
Presented by Don Hernando Colon

Don Hernando Colon asserts that the first section of the treaty ratified between the Catholic sovereigns (may they rest in peace) and King Don Juan of Portugal, sets forth a certain division of seas and lands of which, the people having no definite knowledge or understanding, the public report has originated and been sown broadcast that they had divided the world between themselves. From this supposition it resulted that the people inferred another general conclusion, namely, that having divided the world, it followed immediately that they divided it into equal parts. So wide spread is this that the above report gives rise to a so deep-rooted impression in these men whom his Majesty sent at present to inquire into the question of ownership, that they have persuaded themselves that it is really the truth. And although they have seen and read the said treaty many times, this does not suffice to make them recognize in their method of procedure that such a supposition is untrue, especially since the contrary was not declared by his Majesty's Council in their assembly. Neither did they appreciate the fact that the assembly did not say they should understand it in this or that manner, but fulfil the stipulations of the first treaty in accordance with the new treaty and commissions delegated to you.

Therefore, inasmuch as many inconveniences result from this, which occasion not only great damage to his Majesty's service, but also a great delay in the settlement of the present business, on account of this vicious understanding being the cause of their trying to direct it by unsuitable and senseless methods, and to wrangle and dispute not only with the Portuguese, but even among themselves in regard to obtaining certain other things, it seems to me that the present negotiations would move more briskly and advantageously if they should do the very contrary of what they are striving to do, namely, to locate the line of demarcation as far westward as possible; I the said Don Hernando beg your graces, the lawyers Acuna, Manuel, and Barrientos, as being members of his Majesty's Council, and the licentiates Pisa, and Doctor Ribera, as being his advocate and official attorney, both in order to fulfil his Majesty's command, namely that we ask your advice, and in order that the above command might be obeyed by your graces, that, since this point consists principally in law and not in astrology or cosmography, you set forth and declare in writing, for our good understanding, what we ought to do in this case, and what understanding we should have of it; so that we may all give a good account of what was commanded us, which we should do now, for we know the intent of the Portuguese, and what they wish or show that they wish; and are about to come to certain conclusions with them. And especially since a fortnight has passed since I proposed this doubt to your graces by word and writing, it is to be supposed that you will have come to a decision regarding it; and in closing I beg that a definite decision be rendered in the case.

Don Hernando Colon.

[The official recognition of the notary dated Wednesday, April 27, 1524 follows.]

Letters from the Emperor to the Deputies Appointed to Treat of the Ownership of the Malucos in the Junta of Badajoz

[The first letter is an open proclamation and order to the "Council, court, *regidores*,[192] knights, squires, officials, and good people of the city of Badajoz." The King announces that he is sending "to this said city the licentiates de Acuña, of my Council; the licentiate Pedro Manuel, auditor of our audiencia of Valladolid; the licentiate Barrientos, of my Council of Las Ordenes,"[193] Don Hernando Colon, Simon de Alcazaba, other astrologers, pilots, and other lawyers and persons, who are to investigate, in our name, the demarcation, with other deputies and representatives of the most serene and excellent King of Portugal." He orders that the utmost hospitality be extended to those representatives. They must be given free and (not in inns) good lodging. No overcharges must be made in food and other necessities, and they must not be bothered with noises or questionings. All courtesy must likewise be extended to "the ambassadors of the said most serene King . . . as it is proper in a matter of such import to these kingdoms, that I should receive from you courteous behavior." Vitoria, March 8, 1524.]

[In accordance with the terms of the treaty negotiated in Vitoria, February 19, 1524, *(q.v.* above) which make it incumbent upon the king to appoint "a notary before whom, together with another notary appointed by the said most serene King of Portugal the said case and all its proceedings must be conducted," Bartolomé Ruiz de Castañeda is appointed "as notary for our side, so that, together with him who shall be appointed by the said most serene King of Portugal, you may inquire into it, and all the proceedings shall be conducted in your presence, and you shall do whatever else, in accordance with the above compact, that is necessary," Búrgos, March 20, 1854.]

[Two letters follow, both bearing the date, March 21, 1524, and sent from Búrgos. The first is addressed to the licentiates Acuña, Pedro Manuel, and Barrientos "our deputies." The second is to Hernando Colon, Simon de Alacazaba, Doctor Salaya, Pero Ruiz de Villegas, Fray Tomás Duran, and Captain Juan Sebastian [del Cano], "our astrologers and pilots." Each letter contains the following injunction, couched in the same words:]

Inasmuch as, as you will understand, this matter that you are to examine and determine is of so great caliber and import to us and the good of these kingdoms, that it should be considered with great care and vigilance, and that in the determination of it, there should be great moderation and discretion; and inasmuch as there should be no want of harmony among yourselves, I charge and order you that before conferring with the deputies of the said most serene King of Portugal, that you shall have discussed and conferred on the matter among yourselves, so that you may take a common resolution as to what you shall answer or plead in our favor, and so that you may all speak with one mouth.

[The second letter contains the additional injunction:]

And in order that you may be better informed, you shall always listen to the opinions and arguments of our astrologers and pilots, and others, who by our command, accompany you for the purpose of informing you as to our rights, in order that everything might be done in a suitable manner. And it will be advisable for you to hold discussions with the licentiates Acuña and Pedro Manuel, and the licentiate Hernando de Barrientos, our deputies, as often as possible, so that all that should be done for our service and the good of the said negotiation be done better and unanimously.

[A letter from Búrgos, April 10, 1524, and addressed to the licentiates Acuña, Pedro Manuel, and Hernando de Barrientos, states that the King of Portugal has requested the removal of "one of our deputies, the astrologer Simon de Alcazaba, as he was formerly a vassal and is a native of that kingdom (Portugal)," as he is suspicious of him; and that another be appointed in his stead. Accordingly Cárlos appoints one master Alcarez, although declaring that Alcazaba entered his service with the knowledge and consent of the Portuguese monarch. This change goes into effect provided that no former Spanish subjects be appointed on the commission by the King of Portugal. It is reported that two Spaniards—the bachelor Maldonado, who fled from Spain for various offenses, and

Bernardo Perez, a citizen of Noya, kingdom of Galicia—had been appointed by the latter. Should these be retained, or should other former vassals of Spain be appointed, then "the said Simon de Alcazaba shall enjoy what was committed to him, until as abovesaid, both the above-mentioned men be removed and displaced, or whichever of them is appointed, or any one else, who may be our vassal, subject, or native of our kingdoms."

[On the same date the King writes to the same licentiates as follows:]

I have your letter of the sixth instant, and your memoranda of your doubts since your meeting and conference with the deputies of the most serene and excellent King of Portugal, our very dear and beloved cousin, and you have done well in advising me of it.

As to what you say about having difficulty in the place where you must meet for your investigations in the determination of this matter, for the reason that no place on the boundary line is suitable for it; and because, as you have seen by the compact negotiated in Vitoria, the stipulation was relaxed so that the meeting might take place wherever agreed upon between yourselves and the deputies of the most serene King of Portugal, therefore you may agree, as you say, to remain there in Badajoz one week, or what time you determine, and an equal period in Yelves, in order that you may be well lodged and have a good meeting place. You do well in wishing that the first meeting be held there in Badajoz, since it is not to be believed that the deputies of the most serene King, my cousin, will wish any thing else or oppose any objection, nor should you consent to anything else.

As to the departure of Simon de Alcazaba, he will have arrived already, for this post brought news hither that the day of its arrival here, he would have arrived there in Badajoz. Therefore the negotiations will not be delayed on his account.

As to what you say about the astrologers, pilots, and other persons whom we sent thither to furnish reasons and information concerning our right, namely, that, because they were not named on the commission, our astrologers and pilots who were appointed as deputies, will not receive them in their assembly as not bearing our special writ of appointment, I am much surprised, for it was here repeated again and again that they must summon to their council all those going thither at our command for the above said purpose, and they must confer with them and discuss with them concerning the demarcation; for otherwise their being there was useless. I am sending orders to these deputies to the effect that from this moment they do this. And I therefore order you to give them my letter, and to see to it that whenever the said pilots and astrologers shall meet to discuss and confer in regard to the matter committed to them that they summon to their council all those who are there at my behest, to wit, Master Alcarez, the bachelor Tarragona, our chief pilot, the other pilots of the India House of Trade,[194] and Diego Rivero; and that they confer with and discuss with them everything necessary for their information and the elucidation of our right; they shall always be careful to preserve a mutual harmony, as I now recommend to you.

In regard to your lodging, I am giving orders to the *corregidor*[195] that he look after the same and provide the rooms. You shall be careful that whenever the deputies of my cousin, the most serene King, shall come there, that they be well lodged and treated as is fitting.

This post brings the moneys asked for by the treasurer for the payment of the witnesses there at Badajoz, and if more are necessary, they will be sent.

I will have the bulls and other documents favoring our rights that you ask for, looked up, and will send them to you. Likewise I will have secured the hydrographical maps of which you say you have been advised, and which are in the possession of Francisco de Lerma, an inhabitant of this city, and the one that the pilot Estéban Gomez gave to Colonel Espinosa. These latter I shall send by another messenger, for this one does not take them, in order not to be detained.

I have ordered sent you with the present letter the copy of the letter you mention that I wrote to my ambassador in Portugal, and in which I give the reasons for our right, and reply to the reasons brought forward on the side of the most serene King.[196]

This mail bears a packet of letters written by the ambassadors of the most serene and excellent King, my cousin, residing at my court, to the licentiate Antonio de Acevedo, his chief magistrate, or to whatever other such official resides in the city of Yelves as his deputy. As it is a thing which concerns this negotiation in my service, as soon as this post arrives, you are to give or send this packet to him with all care, and you shall make him certify that it has been delivered to him, and shall send me the certification.

[The letter closes with the king prescribing the order in which the deputies shall be seated at their general councils.]

[Another letter of the same date as the preceding commands the astrologers and pilots named as deputies to summon to their councils those who, though not named on the commission are there to give their opinion and advice. They are commanded "whenever you assemble among yourselves to consider and discuss regarding this matter, you shall summon the persons above named, and shall discuss and confer with them, and shall listen to their words and opinions, and after having heard all of them, according to this order, you shall determine what you shall reply or plead when you meet with the deputies of the most serene and excellent King of Portugal, my cousin, and you shall always advise me fully of every thing that happens."]

The King. Licentiates Acuña, of my Council, Pedro Manuel, auditor of Valladolid, and Licentiate Barrientos, of my council of Las Ordenes, our commissaries in the city of Badajoz, investigating the affair of the Spice Islands: I saw your letter, and the records and papers you sent me of what occurred there in regard to the possession of the Maluco islands, at which proceedings you were present; also in what shape affairs are at present, and the manner in which you have managed them. My Council of the Indies has discussed it, and consulted with me regarding it. What you have done seems good, and as was to be expected from your learning and prudence. And inasmuch as I have ordered a full reply to be made in regard to the matters upon which you have consulted me, as you will see by the memorandum accompanying this letter, signed by my grand chancellor, I therefore command and charge you to examine it, and in accordance with it direct affairs, so that, so far as we are concerned, it will be evident that nothing remains to be done for the fulfilment of what we agreed upon. You must accomplish this secretly and in the good manner I expect from you. You shall give a very secret account of everything to the licentiate de Pisa.

I am writing to our deputies—the astrologers and pilots—to place entire confidence in you. You shall discuss with them in the best and most reserved manner possible what pertains to them in accordance with the section of the said memorandum that treats of the demarcation, and in regard to the advices given by Don Hernando on the true understanding of the treaty. Búrgos, May 7, 1524. I the King. By command of his Majesty: Francisco de los Cobos.

The King. Our deputies in the city of Badajoz, who are considering the demarcation: I saw what you wrote me, and am pleased with you. I hold in mind all you say, which is as I expected from you. And inasmuch as I am writing fully to the licentiates Acuña, Pedro Manuel, and Barrientos, our commissaries, who will discuss with you in my behalf what you should know of it; therefore I command and charge you that, placing entire faith and credence in them, you shall execute this as I wish, and that you shall in all this business have the watchfulness I expect from you, so that the said demarcation be established justly and truly. Búrgos, May 7, 1524. I the King. By command of his Majesty: Francisco de los Cobos.

The Treaty of Zaragoza

[This treaty was negotiated at Zaragoza (Saragossa) between the representatives of the Spanish and Portuguese monarchs, and signed by them April 22, 1529. It was ratified the following day by Cárlos I at Lerida, and by João III, at Lisboa (Lisbon), June 20, 1530. The usual letters of authorization precede the treaty proper, the Spanish letter being given at Zaragoza, April 15, 1529, and the Portuguese at Lisboa, October 18, 1528. The Spanish deputies were: Mercurio de Gatinara, count of Gatinara, and grand chancellor; Fray García de Loaysa,[197] bishop of Osma and confessor of the emperor; and Fray García de Padilla, commander-in-chief of the order of Calatrava,[198] all three members of the emperor's council. The Portuguese deputy was the licentiate Antonio de Azevedo *coutiño*, member of the Portuguese council and the King's ambassador. The treaty follows:]

After said authorizations were presented by the said representatives it was declared that: inasmuch as there existed a doubt between the said Emperor and King of Castilla, etc., and the said King of Portugal, etc., concerning the ownership, possession, and rights, or possession or quasi possession, navigation, and trade of Maluquo and other islands and seas, which each one of the said lords, the emperor and king of Castilla and the King of Portugal declares as his, both by virtue of the treaties made by the most exalted, powerful, and Catholic sovereigns, Don Fernando and Doña Isabel, rulers of Castilla, grandparents of the said emperor and the King, Don Joam the Second of Portugal (may they rest in glory) about the demarcation of the Ocean Sea and by virtue of other rights and privileges which each one of the said emperor and monarchs asserts to belong and pertain to said islands, seas, and lands belonging to him of which he is in possession; and inasmuch as the said emperor and monarchs considering the very close relationship and great affection existing between them, and which, not only should very rightly be preserved, but as far as possible be increased; and in order to free themselves from the doubts, complaints, and disputes that might arise between them, and the many troubles that might ensue among their vassals and subjects and the natives of their kingdoms; the said emperor and monarchs and the said attorneys acting in their names, have covenanted and agreed as to the said doubts and disputes in the following form and manner:

First, the said grand chancellor, the bishop of Osma and the commander-in-chief of Calatrava, attorneys of the said emperor and sovereign of Castilla declared that they, in his name, and by virtue of their said power of attorney would sell and in fact did sell from this day and for all time, to the said King of Portugal, for him and all the successors to the crown of his kingdoms, all right, action, dominion, ownership, and possession or quasi possession, and all rights of navigation, traffic, and trade in any manner whatsoever; that the said emperor and king of Castilla declares that he holds and could hold howsoever and in whatsoever manner in the said Maluquo, the islands, places, lands, and seas, as will be declared hereafter; this, with the declarations, limitations, conditions, and clauses contained and stated hereunder for the sum of three hundred and fifty thousand ducats of gold, paid in the current money, of gold or silver, each ducat being valued in Castilla at three hundred and seventy-five maravedis. The said King of Portugal will give and pay this amount to the said emperor and king of Castilla, and to the persons whom his majesty may appoint, in the following manner: one hundred and fifty thousand ducats to be paid at Lixbona, within the first fifteen or twenty days after this contract, confirmed by the said emperor and king of Castilla, shall have arrived at the city of Lixboa, or wherever the said King of Portugal may be; thirty thousand ducats to be paid in Castilla—twenty thousand at Valhadolid and ten thousand at Sevilla, by the twentieth day of the month of May of this present year; seventy thousand ducats to be paid in Castilla at the May fair of Medina del Campo of this same year, at the terms of the payments of said fair;[199] and the hundred thousand ducats remaining at the October fair at the said town of Medina del Campo of this same year, at the terms of the payment of the same—all to be paid over and above the rate of exchange. If necessary, notes will be given for the said time; and, if said emperor and King of Castilla wishes to take in exchange the said hundred thousand ducats at the said May fair of this said year in order to avail himself of their use, he shall pay the said King of Portugal exchange at the rate of five or six per cent, the rate which his treasurer, Hernand Alvarez, is accustomed to exact from fair to fair. The aforesaid sale is made by the said emperor and king of Castilla to the said King of Portugal on condition that, at whatever time the said emperor and king of Castilla or his successors, should wish to return, and should return, all of the said three hundred and fifty thousand ducats without any shortage to the said King of Portugal or his successors, the said sale becomes null and void and each one of the said sovereigns shall enjoy the right and authority which he now holds and claims to hold, both as regards the right of possession or quasi possession, and as regards the proprietorship, howsoever and in whatever manner they belong to him, as if this contract were not made, and in the manner in which they first held possession and claimed to hold it, and this contract shall cause no prejudice or innovation.

Item. It is covenanted and agreed by the said attorneys, in the names of their said constituents, that, in order to ascertain what islands, places, lands, seas, and their rights and jurisdiction, are sold, henceforth and forever, by the said emperor and king of Castilla, by this contract under the aforesaid condition, to the said King of Portugal, a line must be determined from pole to pole, that is to say, from north to south, by a semicircle extending northeast by east nineteen degrees from Maluquo, to which number of degrees correspond almost seventeen degrees on the equinoctial, amounting to two hundred and ninety-seven and one-half leagues east of the islands of Maluquo, allowing seventeen and one-half leagues to an equinoctial degree. In this northeast by east meridian and direction are situated the islands of Las Velas and of Santo Thome, through which the said line and semicircle passes. Since these islands are situated and are distant from Maluquo the said distance, more or less, the deputies determine and agree that the said line be drawn at the said two hundred and ninety-seven and one-half leagues to the east, the equivalent of the nineteen degrees northeast by east from the said islands of Maluquo, as aforesaid. The said deputies declare that, in order to ascertain where the said line should be drawn, two charts of the same tenor be made, conformable to the chart in the India House of Trade at Sevilha, and by which the fleets, vassals and subjects of the said emperor and king of Castilla navigate. Within thirty days from the date of this contract two persons shall be appointed by each side to examine the aforesaid chart and make the two copies aforesaid conformable to it. In them the said line shall be drawn in the manner aforesaid; and they shall be signed by the said sovereigns, and sealed with their seals, so that each one will keep his own chart; and the said line shall remain fixed henceforth at the point and place so designated. This chart shall also designate the spot in which the said vassals of the said emperor and king of Castilla shall situate and locate Maluquo, which during the time of this contract shall be regarded as situated in such place, although in truth it is situated more or less distance eastward from the place that is designated in the said charts. The seventeen degrees eastward shall be drawn from the point where Maluquo is situated in said charts. For the good of this contract the said King of Portugal must have said chart, and in case the aforesaid be not found in the House of Trade of Sevilha, the said persons appointed by the said sovereigns shall make said charts within one month, signed and sealed as aforesaid. Furthermore navigation charts shall be made by them, in which the said line shall be drawn in the manner aforesaid, so that henceforth the said vassals, natives, and subjects of the said emperor and king of Castilla shall navigate by them; and so that the navigators of either pa shall be certain of the location of the said line and of the aforesaid distance of the two hundred and ninety-seven and one-half leagues between the said line and Maluquo.

It is covenanted and agreed by the said deputies that, whenever the said King of Portugal should wish to prove his right to the proprietorship of Maluco, and the lands and seas specified in this contract, and although at that time the said emperor and king of Castilla shall not have returned the price abovesaid, nor the said contract be canceled, it shall be done in the following manner, namely, each one of the said sovereigns shall appoint three astrologers and three pilots or three mariners who are experts in navigation, who shall assemble at a place on the frontier between the kingdoms, where it shall be agreed that they assemble, within four months of the time when the emperor and king of Castilla, or his successors, shall be notified by the said King of Portugal to appoint a day. There they will consult, covenant, and agree upon the manner of ascertaining the right of said proprietorship conformable to said treaty and contract made between the said Catholic sovereigns, Don Fernando and Doña Isabel, and the said King Dom Joam the Second of Portugal. In case the said emperor and king of Castilla be judged to have the right of said proprietorship, such sentence will not be executed nor used until the said emperor and king of Castilla or his successors shall first have actually returned all the said three hundred and fifty thousand ducats, which by virtue of this contract shall have been given. If the right of proprietorship be conceded to the said King of Portugal, the said emperor and king of Castilla or his successors shall be obliged actually to return the said three hundred and fifty thousand ducats to said King of Portugal or his successors within the first four years ensuing after the date of such sentence.

Item. It was covenanted and agreed by said deputies, in the names of their said constituents, that, since this contract of sale shall be valid and hold good henceforth from date, if any spices or drugs of any sort whatever be brought to any ports or parts of the kingdoms and seigniories of either of the said constituents, in charge of the vassals, subjects or natives of the kingdoms of the said emperor and king of Castilla or by any other persons whomsoever who may not be vassals, subjects, or natives of said kingdoms, then the said emperor and king of Castilla in his kingdoms and seigniories, and the said King of Portugal in his, shall be obliged to order and cause, and they shall order and cause, the said spices or drugs to be deposited securely, without him to whose kingdom they have been brought being so notified to do so by the other side; but they shall be deposited in the name of both, in the power of the person or persons whom each one of the said sovereigns shall have ordered to take charge of said deposit in his lands and seigniories. The said sovereigns shall be obliged to order and cause such deposit to be made in the manner abovesaid, whether the said spices or drugs are found in the possession of those who brought them, or in the power of any other person or persons, in whatsoever regions or districts they shall have been found. The said emperor and kings shall be obliged to give notification to this effect henceforth throughout all their kingdoms and seigniories, so that these instructions may be complied with and no one may plead ignorance of them. The said spices or drugs having been taken to any ports or lands that do not belong to either one of said sovereigns, provided they are not those of enemies, either one of them, by virtue of this contract, may require, in the name of both, and without showing any further provision or power of the other to the justice of the kingdoms and seigniories where said drugs or spices happen to be or to have been found, and they may order them to be deposited, and they shall be deposited. In whatsoever ports said drugs or spices are thus found, they will be under embargo and deposited by both until it is known from whese demarcation they were taken. In order to ascertain if the places and lands from which the said spices or drugs are taken and brought, fall within the demarcation and limits which by this contract remain to the said King of Castilla, and if they contain the said spices or drugs, the said emperor and kings shall despatch two or four ships, an equal number being sent by both. In these an equal number of persons from both sides, sworn to fulfil their obligation, will sail to those places and lands whence the said spices or drugs were said to have been taken and brought in order to ascertain and determine within whose demarcation are situated the said lands and places whence the said spices or drugs are said to have been brought. Should it be found that said places and lands are within the demarcation of the said emperor and king of Castilla, that the said spices and drugs exist there in such quantity that they could reasonably be carried away; then the said deposit shall be given up and freely delivered to the said emperor and king of Castilla, without his being obliged to pay any costs, expenses, interests, or any other thing. If, on the other hand, it be discovered that said drugs or spices were taken from the districts and lands belonging to the said King of Portugal, the said deposit shall be ceded and delivered in like manner to the said King of Portugal without his being obliged to pay any costs, expenses, interests, nor anything whatsoever. The persons who thus imported said drugs or spices shall be penalized and punished by the said emperor and king of Castilla or by his justices, as violators of peace and faith, according to law. Each one of the aforesaid, the emperor and king of Castilla and the King of Portugal, shall be obliged to send as many ships and persons as may be required by the other. As soon as the said spices or drugs shall be deposited and placed under embargo in the manner aforesaid, neither the said emperor and king of Castilla, nor his agents, nor any one with his favor or consent, shall go or send to the said land or lands whence were taken the said drugs or spices in this manner. All that is set forth in this section about the deposit of the spices or drugs, shall not be understood to refer to the spices or drugs which may come to any places whatsoever for the said King of Portugal.

Item: It is covenanted and agreed, that, in all the islands, lands, and seas within the said line, the vessels and people of the said emperor and king of Castilla or of his subjects, vassals or natives of his kingdom, or any others (although these latter be not his subjects, vassals, or natives of his kingdoms) shall not, with or without his command, consent, favor, and aid, enter, navigate, barter, traffic, or take on board anything whatsoever that may be in said islands, lands, or seas. Whosoever shall henceforth violate any of the aforesaid provisions, or who shall be found within said line, shall be seized by any captain, captains, or people of the said King of Portugal and shall be tried, chastised and punished by the said captains, as privateers and violators of the peace. Should they not be found inside of said line by the said captains or people of the said King of Portugal and should come to any port, land, or seigniory whatsoever of the said emperor and king of Castilla, the said emperor and king of Castilla, by his justices in that place, shall be obliged and bound to take and hold them. In the meantime the warrants and examinations proving their guilt in each of the abovesaid things, shall be sent by the said King of Portugal, or by his justices, and they shall be punished and chastised exactly as evildoers and violators of the peace and faith.

Item. It is covenanted and agreed by said deputies that the said emperor and king of Castilla shall not, personally or through an agent, send the natives of his kingdoms, his vassals, subjects, or aliens (and although these latter be not natives of his kingdoms, or his vassals or subjects), to the said islands, lands, and seas within said line, nor shall he consent nor give them aid or favor or permit them to go there, contrary to the form and determination of this contract. Rather he shall be obliged to forbid, suppress, and prevent it as much as possible. Should the said emperor and king of Castilla, personally or through an agent, send natives of his kingdoms, or his vassals, subjects or aliens (although these latter be not natives of his kingdoms, or his vassals or subjects), to the said islands, lands, or seas within the said line or consent to such a thing, giving them aid, or favor, or permitting them to go contrary to the form and determination of this contract; and should he not forbid, suppress, or prevent it, as much as possible, the said agreement of *retro vedendo* becomes null and void; and the said King of Portugal shall no longer be obliged to receive the said sum, nor to sell back the rights and dominion which the said emperor and king of Castilla might have therein in any manner whatsoever, but which he has sold, renounced and delivered to the said King of Portugal by virtue of this contract, by this very act, the said sale shall remain complete and valid forever, as if at first it were made without condition and agreement to sell back. However, since it may happen that, when the aforesaid subjects, natives, or vassals of the said emperor and king of Castilla navigating as aforesaid in the southern seas, should meet with winds so tempestuous or contrary that they would be constrained by necessity to continue their course and navigation within the said line, they shall in such case incur no penalty whatever. On the contrary, when, in such circumstances, they shall come to and anchor at any land included within the said line, pertaining by virtue of this contract to the said King of Portugal, they shall be treated by his subjects, vassals, and inhabitants of said land as the vassals of his brother, as in the same manner the emperor and king of Castilla would command the Portuguese subjects to be treated who should in like manner arrive at ports in his lands of Nueva España or in any other of his ports. It is understood, however, that, when such necessity ceases, they shall immediately set sail and return to their part of the southern seas. Should the aforesaid subjects cross said line through ignorance, it is herein covenanted and agreed that they shall incur on that account no penalty whatsoever, and as long as it is not fully evident that they know themselves to be within the said line, they shall not turn about and go outside of it, as is covenanted and agreed in case of entering on account of tempestuous and contrary winds or necessity. But, when such a fact is quite evident, if it shall be proved that they have entered the line maliciously, they shall be punished and dealt with as those who shall enter the line as aforesaid and as is set forth in this contract. Should the aforesaid discover any islands or lands, while navigating within the said line, such islands or lands shall belong freely and actually to the said King of Portugal and his successors, as if they were discovered, found, and taken possession of by his own captains and vassals, at such time. It is covenanted and agreed by said deputies that the ships and vessels of the said emperor and king of Castilla and those of his subjects, vassals, and the natives of his kingdoms, may navigate and pass through the seas of the said King of Portugal, whence his fleets sail for India, only as much as may be necessary to take a due course toward the strait of Magalhanes. And if they violate the abovesaid, and sail farther over the said seas of the said King of Portugal than is mentioned above, both the said emperor and king of Castilla, if it is proved that they did it by his order, countenance, aid, or consent, and those sailing in this manner and violating the abovesaid, shall incur the above penalties, in the completeness set forth above in this contract.

Item. It was covenanted and agreed that if any of the subjects of the said emperor and king of Castilla or any others shall henceforth be seized and found within the said limits above declared, they shall be imprisoned by any captain, captains, or subjects whatsoever of the said King of Portugal and shall be tried, chastised, and punished as privateers, violators, and disturbers of the peace by the said captains. Should they not be discovered within the said line, and should afterwards come to any port whatever of the said emperor and king of Castilla, his majesty and his justices shall be obliged to seize and imprison them, until the warrants and testimonies sent by the said King of Portugal, or his justices, shall have been presented. If proved guilty of the aforesaid offenses they shall be punished and chastised to the limit as evil-doers and violators of the faith and peace, and of everything else set forth in this contract in regard to the crossing of said line by any subjects of the said emperor and king of Castilla, or any others by his command, consent, favor, or aid. It is understood that these penalties shall apply from the day when the subjects and people of the said Emperor now in and navigating those seas and regions shall be notified. Before such notification they shall not incur said penalties. It is to be understood, however, that the aforesaid refers to the people of the fleets of the said Emperor, which have until now gone to those parts and that no others be sent without incurring said penalties from the day of the signing of this contract, and henceforth during the time that the said sale be not canceled in the aforesaid manner.

Item. It was covenanted and agreed by the said deputies that the said King of Portugal shall not build nor order built for himself, or any other, any new fortress whatever in Maluco, nor within twenty leagues of it, nor any nearer Maluco than the line which is to be drawn according to this contract. It is covenanted unanimously by the said deputies of both sides that this provision shall take effect, namely, from the time that the said King of Portugal can send there a notification to make no new fortress whatever; that is to say, in the first fleet which shall sail for India from the said kingdom of Portugal, after this contract shall have been confirmed and approved by the said constituents, and sealed with their seals. There shall be no new work whatsoever undertaken on the fortress which is already built at Maluquo, from the said time henceforth; it shall only be repaired and kept in the same condition in which it may be at the aforesaid time, if the said King of Portugal so desires; to the above he shall swear and promise full compliance.

Item. It was covenanted and agreed that the fleets, which heretofore have been despatched to those regions by the said emperor and king of Castilla, be well treated in every way, by the said King of Portugal and his people; and that no embargo or obstacle to their navigation or traffic be imposed upon them. If there should be any damage, which is not looked for however, which they shall have received or shall receive from his captains or people, or shall anything have been seized from them, the said King of Portugal shall be obliged to give satisfaction, restore, make good and pay immediately all such damages suffered by the said emperor and king of Castilla, and his subjects and fleets; he shall order the offenders to be punished and chastised and he shall allow the fleets and people of the said emperor and king of Castilla to come and go as they please, freely without any obstacle whatever.

Item. It is covenanted that the said emperor and king of Castilla command letters and instructions to be given immediately to his captains and subjects who are in the said islands that they do no more trading henceforth and return at once, provided that they be allowed to bring freely whatever goods they shall have already bartered, traded, and taken on board.

Item. It is covenanted, agreed, and provided that in the instructions and letters relating to this covenant and contract, which are to be given and despatched by the said emperor and king of Castilla, it shall declare that this statement, instruction, and contract as above made is as binding as though it were made and passed in the general courts, with the express consent of the attorneys thereof; and to make it valid by his royal and absolute power, which, as king and natural lord, recognizing no temporal superior, he may exercise and shall exercise, abrogate, abolish, repeal, and annul the supplication made by the attorneys of the cities and towns of these kingdoms at the court held in the city of Toledo, in the past year, five hundred and twenty-five, concerning the trade of the said islands and lands, the reply given to it, and any law that was made on this subject in the said courts or in any others that may conflict with this.

Item. It is hereby covenanted that the said King of Portugal promises to command manifest, sincere, and summary justice to be executed, because certain subjects of the said emperor and king of Castilla and other aliens of his kingdoms who entered his service complain that their possessions have been seized by his House of Trade in India and in his kingdoms, without any respect to the annoyance caused them thereby, because they have entered the service and did serve the said Emperor.

Item. It was covenanted and agreed by the said deputies in the names of their said constituents that the treaties negotiated between the said Catholic sovereigns, Don Fernando and Doña Ysabel and the King Dom Joam the Second of Portugal in regard to the demarcation of the Ocean Sea shall remain valid and binding *in toto* and in every particular, as is therein contained and declared, excepting those things which are otherwise covenanted and agreed upon in this contract In case the said emperor and king of Castilla returns the sum which according to this contract is to be given in the manner aforesaid, thus canceling the sale, the said treaties negotiated between the said Catholic sovereigns Don Fernando and Doña Ysabel and the said King Dom Joam the Second of Portugal, shall remain in full force and power, as if this contract were not made; and the said constituents shall be obliged to comply with it in every respect, as is therein stated.

Item. It is covenanted and agreed by the said attorneys that although the rights and dominion which the said emperor and king of Castilla claims to possess in the said lands, districts, seas, and islands and which he sells to the said King of Portugal in the manner abovesaid are worth more than half of the just price given, and the said emperor and king of Castilla has certain definite knowledge through exact information of persons who are experts on the subject, and who have investigated and ascertained definitely, that said rights are of much greater value and worth, more than half of the just price that the said King of Portugal gives to the said emperor and king of Castilla he is pleased to make him a gift of it, as he does in fact, which from the said day henceforth shall be valid between the living, of the said excess in value above the half of the just price, however great that excess may be. This excess in value above the half of the just price, the said emperor and king of Castilla relinquishes for himself and his successors, and disunites the same from the royal crown of his kingdoms forever, and delivers it entire to the said King of Portugal, to him and to his successors and crown of his kingdoms, really and effectually, in the aforesaid manner, and during the time of this contract.

[The treaty provides further that he who may violate its provisions in any way, shall lose all his rights therein, and shall in addition pay a fine of two hundred thousand ducats to the other. The Pope is to be asked to confirm it by a bull, imposing the penalty of excommunication for its violation. The deputies promise most fully and under oath that their respective constituents shall observe all the provisions.]

PAPAL BULL, *EXIMIÆ*

November 16, 1501

Source: See Bibliographical Data at end of this volume.

Translation: By Rev. Thomas Cooke Middleton, O.S.A.

Bull, *Eximiæ*—November 16, 1501

Alexander, bishop, servant of the servants of God: to the Catholic sovereigns of Spain—Ferdinand the king, dearest son in Christ, and to Elizabeth [Isabella] the queen, dearest daughter in Christ, health and Apostolic blessing. The sincerity of your great devotion and the unswerving faith with which you honor us and the Roman Church merit, and not unworthily, that your wishes, especially those relating to the spread of the Catholic faith, and the overthrow of infidel and barbarous nations, should be freely and promptly granted. Indeed, on your behalf, a petition recently laid before us set forth that, impelled by pious devotion for the spread of the Catholic faith, you greatly desire—inasmuch as quite recently, and not without great expense and effort on your part, you began and from day to day continue to do more toward the capture and recovery of the islands and regions of the Indies, to the end that in those lands wherever any accursed belief obtains, the Most High should be worshiped and revered; and inasmuch as for the recovery of the islands and regions aforesaid, it will be incumbent upon you to incur heavy expenses and undergo great perils, it is expedient that for the conservation and maintenance of the said islands, after their capture and recovery by you, and for the defraying of the expenses necessary for the conservation and maintenance of the same,—you should be empowered to exact and levy tithes[200] on the inhabitants of the aforesaid islands and dwellers therein for the time being. On this account we have been humbly petitioned on your behalf to deign through our apostolic graciousness to make in the premises suitable provision for you and your state. Therefore yearning most eagerly for the spread and increase of that same faith particularly in our own days, we commend in the Lord your loving and praiseworthy purpose, and being favorably disposed thereto we hereby through our apostolic power in virtue of these presents do as a special favor grant to you and your successors for the time being that in the aforesaid islands after their capture and recovery (as observed) you may receive a tithe from the inhabitants thereof and the dwellers therein for the time being, and levy the same freely and lawfully, providing after dioceses shall there be established (whereon we charge your consciences as well as your successors'), you first from your own and their estate shall really and effectively devise a sufficient revenue for the establishment of churches in those islands through you and your aforesaid successors, whereby the incumbents of the same and their administrators may support themselves suitably, carry on the necessary work of those churches for the time being, as well as celebrate rightly the divine worship of Almighty God, and fulfil all diocesan requirements. The Lateran Council, other apostolic constitutions and ordinances or other decrees, to the contrary notwithstanding. Let no one then infringe this our grant, nor dare with rashness to contravene its provisions. But should any one presume to set it at naught, let him recognize that he has thereby incurred the displeasure of Almighty God, and of the Blessed Apostles Peter and Paul. Given at Rome at St. Peter's, in the year of the incarnation of our Lord one thousand five hundred and one, the sixteenth day of November, the tenth year of our Pontificate.

[The signatures and authorizations follow.]

LIFE AND VOYAGE OF
FERNÃO DE MAGALHÃES—1518-27

[Résumé of contemporaneous documents—1518-27.] Letter of
authorization to Falero and Magallánes—March 22, 1518. *Carta
de el-rei de Castella para El-rei D. Manuel—February 28, 1519.
Instructions to Juan de Cartagena—April 6, 1519. *Carta de rei de
Castella a Fernando de Magalhães e a Ruy Falero—April 19, 1519.
*Extracto de una carta de las Indias—1522. De Molvccis Insulis:
Maximilianus Transylvanus—1523.

Sources: See Bibliographical Data at end of this volume.

Translations: The first and the fifth of these documents are translated
by James A. Robertson; the second and fourth by José M. Asensio;
the third by Francis W. Snow; the sixth by Frederic W. Morrison;
for the last, we use the translation made by the late Henry Stevens
(published in his *Johann Schöner.*)

Resume of Contemporaneous Documents—1518-27

[Prefatory Note: The scope of the present series does
not demand the publication *in extenso* of many documents
on this subject. Those who wish to study it in detail will
find abundant material in volume iv of the *Coleccion de viages*
published by Navarrete (Madrid, 1829); we present only a
brief resumé of these documents, inserted here to preserve
the continuity of our narrative, and to indicate to students
the extent and scope of such material.[201]

---

*   Documents marked by an asterisk are here presented in both the original text and
English translation.

Navarrete precedes these documents by a brief and somewhat imperfect summary of early discoveries; a biographical sketch of Magalhães, with proofs, citations, etc., by way of authentication thereof—these citations being drawn from the authors Fray Antonio de San Roman, Herrera, Gomara, Muñoz, Quintana, Barros, Maximilianus Transylvanus, Argensola, and others; a letter by Ruy Falero; extract from Magalhães's will;[202] a memorandum addressed by him to the emperor;[203] and a compilation from early authors and from the documents that follow, giving full citations of authorities. The documents here mentioned are given by Navarrete in the appendix to volume iv, at pp. 110-406; some of them have been already presented in connection with the Line of Demarcation.]

Valladolid, February 23, 1518. Rui Faller (Ruy Falero) and Fernando Magallánes,[204] both Portuguese, bind themselves to deliver to the factor of the India House of Trade at Seville the eighth part of everything they may find in their discoveries in the spice regions. This is promised in the following words: "Know all ye who shall see this public testament that we, Rui Faller, citizen of Cunilla, in the kingdom of Portugal, and Fernando de Magallánes, citizen of the city of Puerto [Oporto], in the same kingdom, consent, make manifest, and declare that, inasmuch as it has been agreed between us, as parties of the first part, and you, Juan de Aranda, Factor for the King, our Lord, and citizen of the city of Burgos, in the House of Trade of the Indies of the city of Sevilla, as party of the second part, that of all gain and income pertaining to us from the discovery of lands and islands (which if God wills we are to discover and find in the lands, limits, and demarcations of our Master the King, Don Cárlos) you shall have the eighth part. And we shall give this to you from all the income and gain accruing to us therefrom, whether in money, allotment, or rent, or by virtue of our office, or in anything else whatever, of whatever quantity and quality, without any shortage, and without deducting or excepting anything whatever of our possessions." They promise this in extended terms and under oath. The factor approves the document and promises to abide by all its provisions. (No. i, pp. 111-113.)

March, 1518. The same two men in an unsigned document petition the king on various matters connected with the proposed expedition. To each section is appended the monarch's objections, approbations, or other remarks.

1. That no permit be given for ten years to any other person to make an expedition of discovery in those regions "where we are about to go, . . . if we desire to undertake such discovery, with as sufficient equipment and as many ships as the other;" and that they be informed of such tentative expeditions, so that they may go themselves or commission agents.

2. That they receive the twentieth part of all profits after expenses are paid, with the title of admiral, and the governorship for themselves and heirs of all lands discovered.

3. That they be allowed to employ in the newly-discovered lands as they see fit, one thousand ducats worth of merchandise (first cost) each year, giving to the king the twentieth part, without other rights or taxes.

4. That they be allowed to choose for themselves two islands, if the number discovered exceeds six, giving to the crown ten per cent of all profits therefrom.

5. That one-fifth of all net profits derived from the expedition be allotted them on its return, and that each year they may carry one hundred quintals' weight of merchandise in any ship sailing from those regions.

6. That the twentieth part of all profits accruing from the royal ships or any others be given them for ten years.

7. That if his Highness undertake at his cost the armament of the fleet, they promise to prove to him the vast wealth of the lands and islands that will be discovered within his dominions.

8. That if one of them die on the expedition the other, or his heirs and successors, be ordered to fulfil everything as if both were living.

9. That the king order the strict observance of the above.

If the king prefers them to assume the expenses of the expedition they propose the following:

1. That all the lands and islands discovered by them or their agents belong to them "with all traffic, seigniory, and government," giving to the crown one-fifth of all net profits.

2.   That no other ships, either of the king or any other person, be allowed to trade in such lands, under penalty of confiscation by the petitioners.

3.   That no other commissions for expeditions of discovery be given for ten years.

4 and 5. Provision in case of death, and provision for fulfilment. (No. ii, pp. 113-116; *vide infra,* "Instructions to Carthagena," p. 280.)

Zaragoza, July 20, 1518. The King writes to the officials of the House of Trade, approving the contemplated expedition, and regarding the expenditures of moneys and the fitting out of the fleet.[205] (No. v, pp. 122, 123.)

October 24, 1518. Magallánes writes the king enumerating and amplifying certain information and requests concerning the fleet, contained in a letter written by him to his majesty on the fifteenth of the same month. This letter had been despatched by a post sent by the House of Trade. Besides giving a full account of the preparations of the fleet,[206] it begs that the balance of the 16,000 ducats, "without which we cannot finish" be provided; and that the 5,400 ducats lacking be taken from the 11,000 ducats in the house. He asks also an increase of the 3,000 ducats for merchandise, "since the profits accruing therefrom might be twenty-fold, estimating conservatively; and therefore I desired all the gain to be your Highness's." Also, he asks that the officials pay for the armament, weapons, and powder of the fleet, which have been paid out of the 16,000 ducats, but which the king was to provide. He complains of the antagonism of the officials at Seville, relating a serious conflict that had taken place two days before. He had caused his banners, bearing his arms to be flung from one of the vessels. The Spaniards, incited thereto, claimed that they were those of the King of Portugal, and attempted to arouse sentiment against him and cause his arrest. This evil treatment, in which he did not receive the aid and countenance of the officials, he says, was not done to him "as Fernando de Magallánes, but as your highness's Captain."[207] (No. vii, pp. 124-127.)

March 30, 1519. By a royal decree Luis de Mendoza is appointed treasurer of the fleet, and 60,000 maravedis are assigned as his annual salary during the voyage. Juan de Cartagena is appointed inspector-general, "and he shall exercise the duties of that trust in accordance with the instructions *[q. v. post]* given him under the King's signature." He is to receive "70,000 maravedis from the time of the departure of the fleet from Spain until its return." The latter is also appointed "Captain of the third ship of the fleet of Fernando Magallánes and Rui Falero," "with an annual salary of 40,000 maravedis." (Nos. viii-x,[208] pp. 127, 128.)

April 6, 1519. Gaspar de Quesada is appointed "Captain of the fourth or fifth ship of the fleet in the expedition of discovery of the spice regions, and Antonio Coca accountant, who shall have account of everything contained in the ships, giving note of everything to the Treasurer." The latter is to receive 50,000 maravedis a year. (Nos. xi, xii, pp. 128, 129.)[209]

Barcelona, May 5, 1519. A letter from the king to the "officials of the House of Trade of the Indies" states that there are to be two hundred and thirty-five men[210] in the fleet, and orders, "because calculation would have to be made for them in the provisioning and in other things, if there were a greater number," "that they do not allow, or give place in the said fleet, for any reason whatsoever, for more than the two hundred and thirty-five men." They may even specify a less number if it seems expedient. "All the seamen who sail in the said fleet shall be received under the supervision of our Captain Fernando de Magallánes, as he is the most experienced in such things." Full declarations in writing must be made of the route to be followed and a copy shall be given to each pilot. The officials are ordered to buy from Magallánes the excess of powder, arms, etc., that has been provided for the fleet, "since it can be used in other things," paying him what it cost. (No. xiii, pp. 129, 130.)

Barcelona, May 8, 1519. The instructions given to Magallánes and Falero discuss more or less fully such points as the method and manner of navigation (information as to routes given to the other captains and pilots, method of signaling at night, and manner of procedure in case the vessels become separated); treatment of natives found, treatment of other vessels found trading in these spice regions, "within our demarcation," such treatment differing if the vessels are those of Christians or of Moros (Mahometans); ransoms and exchange of prisoners; trade with the natives; division of prize-money; reprovisioning the ships; giving of rations; keeping of accounts; regulations concerning firearms; penalties for disobedience to the captain-general; the taking of oaths; morals; discoveries; weights and measures in trading; deaths of officers of the fleet, and the cargo. Above all, the domains and demarcation of the Portuguese monarch must be respected. The exact location of all lands must be noted, and if these are inhabited they are to "try to ascertain if there is anything in that land that will be to our interest." The natives must be well treated, in order that food and water may be obtained. When the land of spices is reached "you will make a treaty of peace or trade with the king or lord of that land." As high a valuation as possible is to be placed on the articles traded from the ships. The inspector-general and accountant shall note everything in their books. Other vessels found in the spice regions shall, if Christians, be warned not to trade further without permission, under penalty of seizure and confiscation of property; if Moros, "not of the lands of our demarcation, you shall seize them in fair war," and the gold, etc., found in their ships must be noted carefully in the books. Moros who may, by their rank, avail for ransom are to be well treated, but they may be sold as slaves. If Moros are found "who are of our demarcation," they must be well treated; and a treaty must be made, if possible, with their king or seignior. If they do not desire peace, then the Castilians may exercise a certain amount of cruelty against them to serve as a warning. Of the prize money or merchandise of captured ships, certain percentages are to be given to all, these portions varying. The King's share (one-fifth of the amount remaining, after deducting certain sums that go to the captain-generals, and the one-twentieth for the redemption of captives) is to be set apart for him. One-fifth of what remains shall be given the captain-generals. The remainder is to be divided into three parts, "of which two parts are for us and the ships, and one for the crews." Of the latter, ten parts are to be used for religious purposes. Good treatment is to be accorded the natives in order that pleasant trade-relations may be established. The physicians and surgeons are to take no money from the natives for medical services, not even from their enemies who are wounded in war. And the captain-generals must see that the men have no intercourse with the native women. Entire freedom must be accorded to every one to write what he pleases to Spain; and no letter must be seized, under penalties to be imposed by the captain-generals. They must guard against fire. In case of the death of any of the crew, it is advisable to get slaves to fill their places. Rations are to be given every two days, "and if it becomes necessary to shorten rations, they shall be shortened." Dissatisfaction as to the length of the voyage must not be expressed. The firearms are not to be discharged on any newly-discovered land, "because the Indians fear this more than anything else." No weapons shall be sold, under penalty of loss of all property to the one so doing. Blasphemers, and card- and dice-players are not to be allowed to ship with the crew. The captain-generals have power to devise and execute punishments against disobedient men of their crews. Oath shall be taken before the captain-generals by all their crews to observe obedience and the King's service. If it is necessary to seize water and provisions because of the hostility of the natives, it shall be done, but with as little scandal and show of force as possible. Samples of all products must be brought from the lands discovered. "Ready-made clothes and other articles to give to the kings and other princes of these lands shall be carried." "And if the kings or seigniors of the land give any jewels or presents, they shall be ours, and the inspector-general or accountant shall place them in charge of the treasurer." No presents shall be given without permission of the officers of the fleet. Everything traded must be noted carefully and minutely in the books of the inspector-general and accountant. If the return cargo is spice, it must be obtained as clean as possible. The ships' cargoes must be traded first before any private affairs are attended to. Full notices must be made in the books regarding each member of the crew—his father and mother, whether he is single or married, etc., in order that his heirs may be known. Each person before embarking must have attended confession and communion. In case any officer dies, another is to be elected in his stead; but one-half of all the pay, etc., that would fall to the said officer shall be given to his heirs, and the other half shall go to the one taking his place. Any Portuguese or other Christians found in the lands discovered must be treated well, in order to gain information from them. "If by any chance you should meet ships from Portugal within our limits, bid them quietly to leave the land, because in their own requirements given by our very dear and well-loved uncle and brother, it is forbidden to them to enter or discover in the lands and limits belonging to us, and the same is forbidden to you by us." The cargoes must be given up by such ships, if not peaceably, then by means of force, provided "you can seize it without much loss to yourself." A list is appended of the amount of freight that each one may take in the vessels. A copy of these instructions is to be given to Juan de Cartagena, the inspector-general. This document was copied from his books by the secretary Joan de Samano in 1524. (No. xiv, pp. 130-152.)

Seville, 1519. The officials of the house of trade show to Magalhães an order from the King (dated at Barcelona, July 26, 1519), "by which his Highness orders that the commander Rui Falero remain behind and not go as captain jointly with him in the fleet which his Highness orders to be prepared for the spice regions; and also that the said official judges name and appoint the stewards sailing in the said fleet, and as secretaries of the ships of the said fleet shall go those appointed by the said commander [Magalhães] if they are natives [of his kingdom]." Juan de Cartagena is appointed in Ruy Falero's place as *conjunta persona*, and Francisco, brother of Ruy, is appointed captain of one of the ships. Magalhães says in his communication to the officials of the House of Trade that he consents to Falero remaining behind, provided the latter surrender to them and to him the "elevations of east and west longitude, with all the rules accompanying them, that they may remain in the said house and be kept in the said fleet." He justifies, the first appointment of two Portuguese stewards, both of whom he declares to be good and faithful men. "If they should prove unfaithful then they shall be removed." As for his Highness ordering that "no Portuguese seamen sail in the fleet," these men had been accepted by the masters of the said ships, and Magalhães "received them as he did many other foreigners,—namely, Venetians, Greeks, Bretons, French, German, and Genovese,—because, at the time he took them, natives of these kingdoms were lacking." He signifies his willingness to accept others in place of the Portuguese, provided they make no extra expense. In regard to the order not to ship Portuguese, if such a cause could be shown in the contract that he and Falero made with the King at Barcelona he would keep it; but otherwise he "would keep only the contract and instructions given to him in Barcelona." He would not observe anything contrary to this contract, even if ordered by the King and Council. That the King wishes no change in the instructions is evident, because Juan de Cartagena has been ordered not to make any innovation.

Magalhães notifies the officials not to interfere with his taking the Portuguese who had shipped in the fleet; the blame will be theirs if, now, when everything is in readiness, they obstruct in any way the expedition. The officials of the house of trade reply, asking Magalhães to keep the commands that have come from the king. Ruy Falero will give up all that is needed. They believe that the two Portuguese stewards appointed by Magalhães are honest men; but it is against the king's orders to carry men of that nation. Letters from the king are cited to the effect that Magalhães and Falero take only four or five Portuguese apiece. They urge him to live up to these orders. (No. xvi, pp. 156-162.)

September, 1519. On setting out upon his voyage Magalhães leaves for the king a memorandum of the latitudes and location of the Spice Islands, and the shores and principal capes in the Castilian demarcation, "because some time the Portuguese King may try to declare that the islands of Maluco are within his demarcation." He bids the king keep this memorandum carefully, for there may be a time when it is necessary. (No. xix, pp. 188, 189.)

On the nineteenth of April, 1520, while at port San Julian, Magalhães ordered an investigation of a petition presented by Alvaro de la Mezquita, captain of the ship "San Antonio." The petition states that on the first of April Gaspar de Quesada and Juan de Cartagena appeared at Mezquita's ship, took him prisoner, and made themselves masters of the vessel. Quesada refused to liberate the prisoner at the request of the master, and checked the intended resistance of the remaining officers and crew of the "San Antonio" by severely wounding the master, Juan de Elorriaga and ordering the others disarmed. The mate was taken prisoner, and carried to the "Concepcion." Antonio de Coca, accountant of the fleet, was a party to the conspiracy. Juan de Sebastian del Cano, master of the "Concepcion," was placed in command of the captured vessel, which was put in a state of defense, all guns being mounted in place. Mezquita asks for a thorough investigation of this case, so that the fleet may be cleared of traitors. The charges of wastefulness and cruelty preferred against him, he wishes examined; and, if he is worthy of punishment, let it be administered. This petition was presented on the fifteenth, and acknowledged on the seventeenth. The testimonies were given before a notary on and after April 19, and certified on the twenty-sixth. In the investigations the depositions were taken of the chaplain of the fleet, and of the notary, the pilot, a sailor, the boatswain, the steward, and the master of the "San Antonio." In the main they are all alike, exonerating Mezquita from all charges and condemning Quesada and his accomplices. On the return to Seville of the "Victoria" (in which Mezquita was carried a prisoner), these depositions were presented, through the efforts of Diego Barbosa, to the alcalde-in-ordinary (May 22, 1523). (No. xx, pp. 189-201.)

Seville, May 12, 1521. The accountant Juan Lopez de Recalde writes to the bishop of Búrgos on this date of the arrival of the "San Antonio" at the port of Seville, Las Muelas. The captain of the vessel now was "Gerónimo Guerra, a relative and servant of Cristobal de Haro, and its pilot Esteban, a Portuguese." "They brought as prisoner Alvaro de la Mezquita, eldest son of Magallánes's brother, who was appointed captain of this said ship in place of Juan de Cartagena." Mezquita was transferred to a prison on shore, at which Barbosa, "Magallánes's father-in-law, showed much resentment, saying that he ought to be set free and those who brought him imprisoned." The letter relates the discord between Magalhães and certain of the other officers of the fleet; the imprisonment of Mezquita by Cartagena; the attempted mutiny; the tragic deaths of Mendoza, the treasurer, and Quesada; and other vigorous measures of Magalhães in quelling the outbreak. He relates the separation in the strait of the "San Antonio" from the other vessels, and the determination of the men of this vessel to return to Spain, notwithstanding the opposition of Mezquita. The latter coming to blows with the pilot Esteban Gomez was arrested and "they came direct to this port, eating three ounces of bread each day, because their provisions had failed. In the judgment and opinion of those who have come, the said Magallánes will not return to Castilla." (No. xxi, pp. 201-208.)

A journal or log of Magalhães's voyage was written by Francisco Albo, covering the voyage from cape San Agustin in Brazil until the "Victoria" [the first ship to circumnavigate the globe] returned to Spain. The log begins November 29, 1519, and ends September 4, 1522. The entries are for the most part very brief. It shows that the fleet sighted or touched at various points, among them "a mountain shaped like a hat, which we called Monte Vidi, now corruptly called Santo Vidio [today Montevideo],[211] and between it and Cape Santa

Maria . . . a river called the Patos River;" also, farther on, "a very great river . . . Solis [today Rio de la Plata]." The record for October 21-December 1, 1520, says: "On the twenty-first of the said month we took the sun in fifty-two degrees at a distance from land of five leagues. And there we saw an opening like a bay; at its entrance toward the left was a long sandy point. The cape we discovered before this point is called Cape Las Vírgines. The point of sand lies in fifty-two degrees of latitude and fifty-two and one-half degrees of longitude. From this sand-point to the other side is about five leagues. Inside this bay we found a strait of about one league in width. From this entrance to the sand-point it is straight east and west. On the left side of the bay is a large angle in which are many sunken rocks. But as you enter you keep toward the north, and as you enter the strait you go toward the southwest by a mid channel. And as you enter you observe some shoals in front at a distance of three leagues from the mouth, and afterward you will find two sandy islets, and then the open channel, and you can doubtless sail at will therein. Passing this strait we found another small bay, and then another strait like unto the first. From one entrance to the other the direction is east and west, and the strait runs from the northeast to the southwest. After we had passed through the two mouths or straits we found a very large bay, and some islands. In one of the latter we anchored and took the altitude, which we found to be fifty-two and one-third degrees. From this point we sailed southeast and found a point to the left, at a distance from the first entrance of about thirty leagues . . . There are many turns in this strait, and the mountains are very high and covered with snow. Afterward we sailed northeast by east, passing many islands on the way. At the farther end of the strait the coast turns northward. At the left we saw a cape and an island, and we named them Cape Fermoso and Cape Deseado. It lies in the same altitude as Cape Las Virgines, which is the first point at the entrance. From the said Cape Fermoso we sailed northeast, north, and north-northwest, for two days and three nights, and on the next day we saw land . . . and this land we saw the first day of December." On the twenty-fourth of January, 1521, they find an islet, which they name San Pablo. On the sixth of March two small islands are sighted, and they see many small sails. A further note of this same day says "The islands of the Ladrones are three hundred leagues from Gilolo."

March 16, they sight more islands, giving names to two, Suluan and Yunagan—the first island of the archipelago of San Lázaro [the Philippines]. They land successively at the islands of Gada, Seilani, and Mazava, and pass by or anchor at Matan, Subu, Baibai. "We left Subu sailing southeast . . . between the Cape of Subu and an island named Bohol; and on the western side of the Cape of Subu is another island, by name, Panilongo, inhabited by blacks. This island and Subu have gold and quantities of ginger . . . We anchored at the island of Bohol." Thus the log continues without date for some time, the islands of Quipit, Quagayán, Poluan, and Borney being noted. At the latter place in a brush with the natives, they seize a junk, on which "was a son of the king of Luzon, which is a very large island." The ship passes on through the Moluccas, which are named: "Terrenate, Tidori, Mare, Motil, Maquiam, Bachian, Gilolo—these are all that have cloves." On the fourth of May, 1522, the Cape of Good Hope is founded. (No. xxii, pp. 209-247.)

The cargo of cloves brought by the "Victoria" amounted to three hundred and eighty-one sacks, with a net weight of five hundred and twenty-four quintals, twenty-one and one-half libras. This was delivered to Cristóbal de Haro, through an agent, in accordance with a royal decree of October 10, 1522. The cargo also contained other spices, and a feather ornament, besides the private stores. (No. xxiii, pp. 247, 248.)

October 18, 1522. Certain questions are to be put to those coming in the "Victoria." These included: the cause of the discord between Magalhães and Cartagena and others; the reason for the capture and killing of Mendoza, and if any reward were promised to Espinosa for killing him; the reason for Magalhães's abandonment of Cartagena and the ecclesiastic, and if he acted right toward Quesada, Mendoza, and others; whether the punishments were meted out for the purpose of putting the Portuguese accompanying him, and who were kin to him, in command of the ships; the reason for Magalhães's long delays in various ports, thus wasting provisions and losing valuable time; questions affecting trade; as to the manner in which Magalhães met his death from the Indians, and why some say he died in another manner; those who were left behind at the island where Magalhães had been killed, and whether they could be rescued. Answers are given to these questions by Juan Sebastian Del

Cano, captain, Francisco Albo, pilot, and Fernando de Bustamente, barber, all of the "Victoria." (No. xxv, pp. 285-294.)

The expedition begun by Magalhães made treaties of peace with various petty kings or governors among the islands. One was made with the seignior of Poluan, a vassal of the king of Borneo. The interpreter in this treaty was "a Moro who was seized in the island of the king of Lozon and knew some Castilian." Presents were made to seal the peace. Treaties were made also in Tidori, Cebu, and Gilolo. (No. xxvii, pp. 295-298.)

1523. Diego de Barbosa presents a memorandum to the king regarding some events of Magalhães's voyage, and the methods for trading in the spice regions. He cites the memorandum left by the latter on his departure from Seville in 1519. He adds "And now, . . . I believe that the time has come when this must be investigated, and I determined to present this memorandum to your Majesty in order that you may not be deceived in the routes, and in the trade of those regions which you have in your power, since it was discovered at so great expense and toil to Magallánes, and his death . . ." He justifies the conduct of the latter, and urges the king to see justice done. Speaking of the trade he says, "Your Majesty should believe that the sport of this business that you have in your power is of what extent you may desire, only your Majesty must know the game well, because in these first beginnings lies its good. Whence I say, that before all else your Majesty ought, in this case, to give such examples to those sailing in the fleet which you expect to have prepared, so that those who go shall not be betrayed . . . as happened in the past, and that the captain-general . . . be one who knows thoroughly what he must do, and that those accompanying him go so instructed that after telling him their opinion, they shall not dare to instruct him in his duties; for where confusion exists there is the whole mistake." He urges a powerful fleet in order to be able to show sufficient force to the natives, and to punish those who killed Magalhães. He cites the example of the Portuguese who send large fleets to the east, and gain respect through fear, "for if the King of Portugal has prestige in the Indies, it is because he has always tried to demonstrate his power there, sending as large a fleet as possible each year. Therefore not only did he rule those lands with love and good works, but to a greater degree by means of fear." In the matter of trading, the king should keep control; for if traders are allowed to trade on their own account they will ruin everything, and will sell lower, being content with thirty or forty per cent when they might gain one hundred per cent or more. He advises the king that trading should be under the control of his Majesty's factor. (No. xxviii, pp. 298-301.)

Chainho, 1523. Antonio Brito writes to the king of Portugal in regard to events in India and the voyage of Magalhães. "I arrived at Tidore May 13, 522 [sic]. The Castilians had been there and loaded two of the five vessels that sailed from Castilla; and I learned that the one had left there four months before, and the other one month and a half." On October 20, news is brought of a ship. Brito orders it brought to port, and finds, as he had supposed, that it is a Castilian vessel. Of their crew of fifty-four men, thirty had died. Their maps and instruments are seized; and the ship and cargo confiscated, the wood of the former being used in the fortress. "They said that the bishop of Burgos and Cristóbal de Haro had fitted out this fleet." A short account of the voyage is given. From Rio de Janeiro the Castilians "sailed to the river called Solís, where Fernando Magallánes thought a passage would be found; and they stayed there forty days . . . They coasted along shore to a river called San Juan, where they wintered for four months. Here the captains began to ask where he was taking them, especially one Juan de Cartagena . . . Then they tried to rise against Magallánes and kill him." The flight of the "San Antonio" is narrated, "and it is not known whether it returned to Castilla or whether it was lost." The discovery of the strait is noted, with a brief description of its location. The succeeding events—the death of Magalhães, the election of two captains (Duarte Barbosa, "a Portuguese, and brother-in-law of Magallánes; . . . and Juan Serrana, a Castilian"), and the death of Barbosa and thirty-five or thirty-six men at the hands of natives, are briefly narrated. "They sailed to an island called Mindanao . . . and had an interview with the king, who showed them where Borneo lay," whither they next journeyed. Here they were taken by the natives for Portuguese, and were well treated. They asked for pilots to conduct them to the Moluccas, but the king gave them only as far as Mindanao "on the opposite side from which they had come, where they would get other pilots. Mindanao is a very large and fertile island." Brito relates further the disposition made of the Castilians and their cargo. (No. xxx, pp. 305-311.)

Valladolid, August 2, 1527. Investigations are instituted by the Council of the Indies in regard to the seizure and confiscation by the Portuguese of the "Trinidad," one of Magalhães's vessels. This court of inquiry is in charge of the bishop of Ciudad, Rodrigo, who examines under oath the captain of the vessel, Gonzalo Gomez de Espinosa and the two pilots Ginés de Mafra and Leon Pancado. The investigation brings out, in the form mainly of question and answer, the communication of the Castilians with the Portuguese, and the confiscation of their ship and cargo. (No. xi, pp. 378-388.)

Letter of Authorization to Falero and Magallanes

Inasmuch[212] as we have commanded a certain contract and agreement to be made with you, Ruy Falero, bachelor, and Fernando de Magalhayns, knight, natives of the Kingdom of Portogal, in order that you make an expedition of discovery in the Ocean Sea; and inasmuch as for the said voyage we have ordered five ships to be armed, manned, provisioned, and supplied with whatever else is necessary for said voyage, having confidence that you are such persons as will guard our service, and that you will execute fully and loyally what we command and entrust to you: it is our will and pleasure to appoint you—as by this present we do—as our captains of the said fleet. We also authorize you so that, during the time of your voyage and until (with the blessing of Our Lord) you shall return to these kingdoms, you may and shall hold office as our captains, both on sea and land, in your own names and those of your lieutenants, in every case and in everything relating and pertaining to said office. You shall see that there is proper execution of our justice in the lands and islands that you shall discover, according to and in the manner followed by those who have been our sea captains hitherto. By this our letter, we command the masters, mates, pilots, seamen, roustabouts, boys, any other persons and officials of the said fleet, and whatsoever persons may see this present, and shall reside in the said lands and islands that you shall discover, and whomsoever the contents of this letter may concern or affect in any manner whatever, that they regard, accept, and consider you as our captains of the said fleet. As such, they shall obey you and fulfil your commands, under the penalty or penalties which, in our name, you shall impose or order imposed, and which, by this present, we impose and consider as imposed. We authorize you to execute sentence on their persons and goods, and that they observe and cause to be observed all the honors, favors, grace, privileges, liberties, preeminences, prerogatives and immunities, which as our captains, you should hold and enjoy, and which must be kept for you. It is our pleasure and we command that, if during the voyage of said fleet, there should be any disputes or differences, either on land or sea, you shall be empowered to sentence, judge, and execute justice in brief form, summarily and without process of law. We authorize you to decide and judge the said disputes, and to execute all the remaining contents of this our letter and whatever is incumbent upon and pertains to said office of captain, with whatever may be incident, dependent, or connected in any way with the same; and neither yourselves nor others shall act contrary to this.

Given at Valladolid, the xxij day of March, of the year one thousand five hundred and eighteen. I, the King. I, Francisco de los Covos, Secretary of the Queen[213] and of the King, her son, our Sovereigns, write it by their command.

> [*Endorsed:* "Authorization as sea-captains, given to Fernando Magallayns and the bachelor Ruj Fallero for the time while they shall be in the fleet which your Highness ordered to be equipped, until their return to España. Johanes le Sauvaige. Fonseca, archbishop and bishop. Registered. Juan de Samana. (Seal) Guilhermo, chancellor."]

Carta de El Rei de Castella para El Reid Manuel

+

Smo y muy ex_te_ Rey y principe mj muy caro y muy amado hr_o_ y tio Recebi vra letra de xij de hebrero con q he avido muy gran plazer en saber de vra salud, y de la *Sma* Reyna vra muger mj muy cara y muy amada hermana especialment del contentamjento q me escreujs q tenys de su compañja q Lo mjsmo me escreujo Su Ser_d_ asi la he esperado sienpre y: demas de conplir lo q deveys a

165

vra Real persona a mj me hazeys en ello muy singular conplazencia porq yo amo tanto a la dicha *Sma* Reyna mj hermana, q es muy mas lo q la qero q el debdo q con ella tengo. afectuosamente vos Ruego sienpre me hagays saber de vra salud y de la suya q asi sienpre os hare saber de la mja y lo q de present ay de mas desto q dezires q por cartas q de alla me han escrito he sabido q vos teneys alguna sospecha q del armada q mandamos hazer para yr a las Jndias de q van por capitanes hernando magallanes y Ruy falero podria venjr algun perjuizo a lo q a vosos perteneçe di aqllas partes de las Jndias bien crehemos q avn q algunas personas qaran jnformas dealgo desto q vos terneys por cierta ñra voluntad y obra para las cosas q os tocare q es la q el debdo y amor y la Razon lo reqere mas porq dello no os qde pensamjento acorde de vos escreujr po q sepays q nra voluntad ha sido y es de muy cumplidamente guardar todo lo q sobre la demarcaciõ fue asentado y capitulado con los cathocos Rey y Reyna mjs señores y abuelos q ayan *glra* y q la dicha armada no yra ni tocara en parte q en cosa perjudiq a vro *drho* q no solamente q remos esto mas avn qrriamos dexaros de lo q a nos perteneçe y tenemos y el primer capitulo y mandamjeto nro, q lleban los dichos capitans es q guarden la demarcaciõ y q no toque en njnguna manera y so graves penas en las partes y terras y mares q por la demarcaciõ a vos os estan señaladas yos pertenece y asi lo guardarã y complirã y desto no tengays ninguna dubda. *Smo* y muy ex_te_ Rey & *pn*cipe nro muy caro y muy amado hr_o_ y tio nro Señor vos aya en su especial guarda y Recomjenda de barcelona a xxviij dias de hebrero de dxjx as. Yo Elrey. Couos, sect?

(*Sobrescripto*:) *Smo* y muy ex_te_ Rey * * * cipe de portugal * * * muy caro y muy * * o hermano y tio.

Letter from the King of Castile to the King Don Manuel

+

Most Serene and very excellent King and Prince and very dear and beloved brother and uncle: I received your letter of the twelfth of February and I was extremely pleased to learn concerning the state of your health and that of the most serene queen, your wife, my very dear and much loved sister; and especially was I gratified to hear of the pleasure you take in her company, of which her serene highness likewise wrote me. So I have always wished it, and, besides fulfilling what you owe your royal character, you do me therein very great pleasure, for I love the most serene queen, my sister, so much, that my love for her far exceeds that which is due her from me. I pray you affectionately always to inform me concerning your health and hers, and I will always let you hear as to mine. And now with regard to what is further to be said, I have been informed by letters which I have received from persons near you that you entertain some fear that the fleet which we are dispatching to the Indies, under command of Hernando Magallanes and Ruy Falero, might be prejudicial to what pertains to you in those parts of the Indies. We believe that, in spite of the fact that certain persons desire to imbue you with such an idea, you are assured of our good will and deed in all matters affecting you, which are such as love, duty, and reason demand. Nevertheless, in order that your mind may be freed of anxiety, I thought it best to write to you to inform you that our wish has always been, and is, duly to respect everything concerning the line of demarcation which was settled and agreed upon with the Catholic king and queen my sovereigns and grandparents (may they rest in glory); and that the said fleet will not in any way enter a district so that your rights would be at all injured; and not only do we desire this but would even wish to give over to you that which belongs to and is held by us. And our first charge and order to the said commanders is to respect the line of demarcation and not to touch in any way, under heavy penalties, any regions of either lands or seas which were assigned to and belong to you by the line of demarcation; and that they will keep and fulfil this injunction I beg you to entertain no doubt. Most Serene and very excellent King and Prince, our very dear and well beloved brother and uncle, may our Lord have you in his special keeping and recommendation. Barcelona xxviij February dxjx. I, the King; Covos, secretary.

[*Superscription:* "Most Serene and very excellent King, [pr]ince of portugal [our][214] very dear and well [belov]ed brother and uncle."]

Instructions to Cartagena

I, the King. That which you, Juan de Cartagena our captain, are to do in the fulfilment of your duties as our inspector-general of the fleet, which we are sending under command of Ruy Falero and Fernando de Magallãins, our captains, knights of the order of San Tiago, on the voyage of discovery which, with the blessing of Our Lord, they are about to undertake as our captain-generals of said fleet, is as follows:

First: in order that you may go well-informed, the instructions and agreement made with our said captains for the voyage of discovery are as follows:

I, the King. Inasmuch as you, Fernando de Magallãins, knight, native of the kingdom of Portogal and bachelor Ruy Falero, also native of said kingdom, wish to do us signal service, binding yourselves to discover within the boundaries which pertain to and belong to us in the Ocean Sea, within the limits of our demarcation, those islands and mainlands, riches, spices, and other things with which we shall be well pleased and these our kingdoms well profited, we order herewith the following agreement to be made with you:

First: in order that you may and shall with good fortune go on a voyage of discovery in that part of the Ocean Sea within our limits and demarcation; and as it would not be just that since you are going yourselves to perform the aforesaid, other persons should venture to do the same; and considering that you are to have the hardship of this enterprise: it is my will and pleasure (as I now promise) that, for the term of the first ten years ensuing we shall not permit any other person to go on a voyage of discovery by the same route and course that you may take; and that if anyone else should wish to undertake it and ask permission, it shall not be granted until you have been informed thereof, so that, if at the same time you should so desire, you may undertake it also, being as well prepared, equipped, and furnished with as many vessels as equally well-conditioned, equipped, and manned as those of the other persons wishing to make the said discovery. But it is to be understood that if we should wish to order or permit other persons to undertake such an enterprise by the western route, in the district of those islands, with Tierra Firme and all other places already discovered, towards the desired direction, for the purpose of seeking the strait of those seas, we may so order or permit to these others. If they should wish to start on their discoveries from Tierra Firme or from the island of Sant Miguel, and go through the southern sea, they may do so. Likewise if the governor or people who, by our mandate, are now, or may be in the future, in the said Tierra Firme, or any others of our subjects and vassals should wish to set out on a voyage of discovery in the southern sea, wherein such discovery is permitted; and if they wish to send out ships for further discoveries; then our said governor, vassals, and any other persons who, according to our pleasure, should go upon such discovery in that direction, may do so, notwithstanding the aforesaid of any section and clause whatever in this agreement. But we also desire that if you should wish to do so, you may discover by any of these said routes, provided the place be not already discovered or found.

The aforesaid discovery must be made in such manner that you do not discover or do anything to his prejudice, within the demarcation and limits of the most serene king of Portogal, my very dear and well beloved uncle and brother, but only within the limits of our demarcation.

And acknowledging your wish to serve us which has moved you to undertake the said discovery; the service which we shall receive therefrom; and the benefit of our royal crown—as a remuneration for the labor and danger which you will have to undergo, it is our will and pleasure, and our desire in all the islands and mainlands that you may discover, to grant you—as we do in this present—that of all the profit and gain from all the lands and islands you may so discover, both rents and rights, and whatever else accrues to us in any way, you shall have and take the twentieth part (after first deducting all expenses which may be involved); also you shall have title as our *adelantados*[215] and governors of said lands and islands, you, your children, and lawful heirs forever. This shall be on condition that the supremacy of the same shall pertain to us and to the kings after us, and if your children and heirs are natives of our kingdoms and married therein; and if the said government and title of *adelantado* shall descend to your son or heir after your death. We shall have your letters and privileges to this effect sent to you in proper form.

We also grant you grace and give you license and power, so that each year hereafter you may take and send, and you shall send, either in our vessels or in any others that you may prefer, to said islands and lands that you shall discover, as above, the value of one thousand ducats first cost. This is to be employed at your risk, and in the place and manner you may deem best. And you can sell this there and use it as you shall decide and desire. You shall bring the returns thereof to these kingdoms, paying us as our rights the twentieth part thereof, without being obliged to pay any other taxes whatsoever, those usually imposed or those which may be newly levied. It is to be understood, however, that this is to be after the return from the first voyage, not during the same.

Moreover, it is our will and pleasure that if the islands, which you shall discover in this manner, exceed six in number, having first chosen six [for us], you may assign to yourselves two of those that remain. Of these you shall have and take the fifteenth part of all the profit and gain of rent and rights pertaining to us, left clear, over and above the expenses involved.

Yten: We wish and it is our will and pleasure that, considering the expenses and labors involved by you on said voyage, to grant you grace—as we do by this present—that at the return of this first fleet and for this once you shall have and take the fifth part of whatever pertains to us in the things that you bring from those regions, which remains clear, over and above the expenses involved in the said fleet. In order that you may accomplish the aforesaid better, and that the necessary caution may be observed, I shall order five ships to be armed for you, two of one hundred and thirty tons, two of ninety and one of sixty tons, all to be sufficiently manned, provisioned, and armed. It should be known that said ships shall be provisioned for two years and shall have two hundred and thirty-four persons to manage them, counting masters, mariners, deck hands and all others necessary, according to the memorandum of the same. This we shall order to be put into effect immediately by our officials of the India House of Trade who reside in the city of Sevilla.

Because it is our will and pleasure that the aforesaid should be kept and complied with in every respect, we desire that, if, in the prosecution of the aforesaid, either of you should die, the contents of this present instrument shall be observed and fulfilled by the remaining one, and as faithfully as it must be kept, should both live. Furthermore, in order that there may be justice and a good account of the aforesaid, and the suitable caution as regards our estates, we are to appoint, and we shall appoint a treasurer, accountant, and clerks for said ships, who shall keep and record the account and calculation of every thing, and before [whom shall pass][216] and be delivered everything acquired by the said fleet.

This I promise you and I pledge on my royal faith and word that I will order it kept and observed in every particular, according to the contents herewith. I order this present instrument given, signed with my name. Given at Valladolid, March twenty-two, one thousand five hundred and eighteen. I, the King. By command of the King: Francisco de los Covos.

Then when you shall come to the city of Sevilla, you shall show our officials of the India House of Trade, residing there, the despatch which you bring concerning your said office, informing them fully and specifically of the method which you think you ought to employ in guarding the interests of our estates; also of the said voyage, and the contents of this instruction.

Yten: You will cause our accountant of said fleet to take note of everything spent and which will be spent in said fleet; everything in the cargo taken in the ships from the said city of Sevilla; and the wages and provisions, the merchandise carried, both that belonging to us, and that belonging to others who may supply anything for the furnishing and maintenance of the said fleet. You must see to it that a book is kept in which you will make entry of all that is loaded in the holds. These things must be marked with your mark, each different class of merchandise being by itself; and you must designate particularly what belongs to each person, because, as will be seen later, the profits must be allotted at so much to the pound, in order that there may be no fraud.

Yten: You will ask the said officials of Sevilla to give you, before the departure of said fleet, an inventory of all the merchandise and other articles placed on board, both on our account and for any other persons. Our accountant must put all this in the charge of our treasurer of said fleet, entry being made in the books of both, in order that, when, with the blessing of Our Lord, said fleet shall return, they may give an account and calculation of everything which can be easily verified and explained. And I order these latter to give you such account, so that whenever the said articles shall be bartered in the said lands and islands, during the bartering, the things bartered shall be unloaded in presence of the said treasurer, and he shall note everything bartered for them, and he shall do this, setting down everything fully and specifically.

Furthermore, as you will see, I have ordered certain merchants to place on board the said fleet the merchandise and articles to be sent for ransoms. These are they whom the father bishop of Búrgos, very reverend in Christ and a member of our council, may appoint to furnish the same to the amount of four thousand ducats, which after subtracting the twentieth part of the profits which God shall give to said fleet, must be used for the redemption of captives. The remainder is to be divided between us and said merchants, each of whom draws profit according to the number of pounds he has placed on board. Also in all the expenses of the said fleet, the wages and costs, both in the merchandise and other things, you must see to it that our accountant takes note of what is placed on board, in our name and in the names of others, so that the amount of the shares will be known and what is due us. You shall deliver everything to our said treasurer in the presence of our accountant, who shall enter it on his books, their names and yours being signed at each entry, so that in everything there may be due caution and the requisite clearness.

You shall also see to it carefully that the bartering and trading of said fleet is done to the greatest possible advantage to our estates, and that everything is delivered to said treasurer, said accountant of said fleet taking note, in your presence, in order to bring it to us. The aforesaid portion which belongs to us you shall deliver to our officials at Sevilla; that which is due to said merchants and other persons you shall give and deliver to them after the return of the said fleet to these kingdoms, according to the order given you as hereinbefore stated. In everything, you must take care that the said treasurer records in his book and in that of said accountant, stating what is delivered to him, and the results of the bartering, it being entered in his book and in that of the said accountant—every one being present at the entries in said books, in order that each division of said entries may correspond with that of the other book, no more in one book than in the other. This will be signed by you and by said treasurer and accountant, as before stated, in the manner and according to the order prescribed in this our instructions. We command this so that everything may be stated clearly and that requisite caution be exercised in regard to our estate.

Moreover, you must watch and see to it that all the rents belonging to us [in (?)—blank space in *Alguns documentos*] whatever manner, in said lands and islands that are discovered by said fleet, [whether (?)—blank space in *Alguns documentos*] in trade or in any other way; also the rents of the salt marshes which in the said islands and lands have belonged up to the present and will hereafter belong to us.

Yten: You shall see to it that our treasurer of the said fleet collect the fifth and other rights whatsoever belonging to us, of all and whatsoever bartering that be made or shall be made in the future in said islands and lands; also the slaves, guanins,[217] pearls, and precious stones, drugs, or spices and other things whatsoever that must be delivered and which belong to us, fulfilling that which is commanded to and agreed upon with the said captains, merchants, and other persons. You will see that said accountant entrusts this to said treasurer, as aforesaid, in your presence, observing therein the order as before stated.

Moreover you must see to it that the said treasurer shall receive all the fines that have been imposed and shall be imposed by our said captains and by any justice and person whatever, and that said accountant shall enter them in a separate book, in your presence.

Moreover, you must exercise much care and vigilance to see that our service is complied with and to effect what is proper for the colonization and pacification of the lands that are found. You will advise us fully and specifically of the manner in which our instructions and mandates are complied with in said islands and lands; of our justice; of the treatment of the natives of said lands, with whom you must be careful to use good faith and fulfil all that is promised—they must be treated most affectionately, both in order that they may be influenced to become good Christians, which is our principal desire, and that they may with good will serve us and be under our government, subjection, and friendship; how said captains and officers observe our instructions, and other matters of our service; and of everything else of which you think I should be informed, as I state and declare herein.

When, with the blessing of Our Lord, the fleet shall set sail, you together with our other said captains, inspector general, and officers shall write me of the departure and of the caution you are employing. [Blank space in *Alguns documentos*]. In the future whenever you write me of the events of the said voyage and of those matters concerning which you must inform me, you will all together write me in one letter, but if you think that I should be advised privately of anything which relates to our service, you may do so.

Moreover, you must treat our said captains and officials well since they are those to whom we have entrusted duties, and they shall do the same to you. For I am sure that they will serve us on this voyage and in the future as good and loyal subjects as they have shown themselves to be heretofore; and it is my will to show them favor and grace. All that you see which may be suitable for our service you must guide and direct, aiding in all possible way to serve us to the best of your ability.

Yten: When in due time you have arrived in the regions where said fleet shall discover, you must investigate and ascertain what land it is. If it should be a land where you must barter, you must first effect the bartering of the merchandise of the said fleet before attending to any other private interest, following the decision and opinion of our said officials of the said fleet. After bartering the belongings of the fleet, the officers and people may barter the other merchandise of which, according to this mandate, they shall pay us the fifth part.

Yten: As one of the principal things required in such voyages is concord among the persons in charge, you must see to it carefully that there may be unity and harmony among you, and our said captains, and other officials. If there should be any misunderstanding among them, they must desist from all differences, and you and your companions shall settle all such and prevent them from taking place. Do the same yourselves and all being in harmony the interests of our service will be better guarded, which if the contrary is observed, would not be the case. This I order and charge you because therein you will serve me well.

Moreover, although the offices of our captains and inspector, treasurer, and accountant of said fleet are independent of each other, in that which relates to the trust of each, inasmuch as it is convenient for the good of our service and the increase of our royal income, for the colonization and pacification of our lands, each one must keep account of what pertains to the office of the other. Inasmuch as the office you hold as inspector general of the said fleet is an office of great trust, and it is necessary that there be exercised therein much diligence, care, and vigilance, I order you to charge and entrust yourself with this trust because it is the one office of said fleet on which all the others depend. Even should there be any negligence in the other offices and should there be no such good foresight and caution as is proper, if you fulfil your duty, it would be less inconvenient. You must labor and endeavor with all your strength to observe the care and thoroughness in everything relating to your said office and necessary for our service with that care and diligence which I expect from you, so that there may be a good record and the proper caution.

Although it has not been before stated, you are to have a separate book in which you shall enter all the aforesaid. Nevertheless you must be present at all entries and sign the books of our treasurer and accountant of the said fleet, because (though God forbid), should any accident befall any of the ships in which the said officials sail, it were well that in everything there should be due caution and a record of it; and that, besides being always present you have a separate book. Therefore I order and charge you that this book be similar to and contain the same account of the affairs of the said fleet as the one kept by the said accountant. You will keep a separate book, in which you will set down the accounts of the treasurer as herein stated. You will cause said treasurer and accountant to sign also in your book; but you shall not, on this account, neglect to be present in all matters, and observe diligence in the books of the others, as before mentioned.

Furthermore, that we may be informed of all, when at good time you will arrive at those lands and islands for which the said fleet is bound, you shall make a book and full relation of everything you see and find there. When you are about to return you shall have five copies made of this, placing one copy in each ship, so that in case of accident to any one of the said ships there may be a full account of everything. You must also place in each ship a list of everything which the said fleet brings in each one of the ships, each list being identical and in accordance with your books. You must take care that the goods brought by said fleet be divided among all the ships, placing in each one the amount deemed proper for our captains and officials.

I charge and order you to do all this and more which you may consider advantageous to our service and to the good interest of our estates and of said fleet, with that diligence and fidelity which I expect from you.

Barcelona, the sixth day of the month of April, one thousand, five hundred and nineteen. I, the King. By command of the King: Francisco de los Covos.

[*Endorsed*: "Instructions to Cartagena."]

Carta do Rei de Castella a Fernando de Magalhães e a Ruy Falero

+

El Rey

fernando de magallãins & Ruy falero caualleros de la orden de san tiago nros capitañs generales dell annada q mandamos haser para yr a descobrir & a los otros capitañs particulares de la dha armada & pilotos & maestres & contramaestres & marineros de las naos de la dha armada, porquanto yo tengo por çierto segund la mucha informaçiõ que he avido de personas que por esperiençia lo An visto q en las islas de maluco ay la espeçieria q prinçipalmente ys a buscar con esa dha armada & my voluntad es que derechamente sigais el viage a las dhas islas por la forma e maña que lo he dicho e mandado a vos el dcho fernando de magallãins, porende yo vos mando A todos & a cada uno de vos q en la navegaçion del dho viage sigais el pareçer & determinaçiõ del dho fernando de magallãins para que ants e primero que a otra parte alguna vais a las dhas islas de maluco sin que en ello Aya ninguna falta, porq asy cumple A nro seruiçio & despues De fecho esto se podra buscar lo demas que convenga conforme A lo q ileuais mãdado & los unos nj los otros non fagads njn fagan ende Al por alguna maña, so pena, de pdimy de biens e las psonas a la nra merced fecha en Barçelona a diez & nueve dias del mes de abril ano de mjll quinientos & diez e nueve años. Yo El Rey. Por mandado dEl Rey Fran_co_ de los covos.

pa q los del armada sigan el pareçer y determynaçiõ de magallanes pa q ants y prño q a otra p_te_ vayã a la espeçierja.

Letter from the King of Castile to
Fernando de Magalhães and Ruy Falero

+

The King.

Fernando de Magallãins and Ruy Falero, knights of the order of San Tiago, our captain-generals of the fleet which we are about to despatch on an expedition of discovery, and the other individual captains of the said fleet; the pilots, sailing masters, boatswains, and sailors in the ships of the said fleet: inasmuch as I am quite well assured by those who have actually been there, that the Maluco Islands are rich in spices—the chief article sought by the said fleet,—order you, the said Fernando de Magallãins, to pursue a direct course to the above-mentioned islands, exactly as I have told and commanded you. And I order you all individually and collectively, that, in the said voyage you heed strictly the counsels and decisions of the said Fernando de Magallãins; and that, first and foremost, before sailing elsewhere, you proceed without fail to the said Maluco Islands, for in this wise do you perform our service. Afterwards you may seek other suitable things, in accordance with your orders. And none of you shall act contrary to this our will, in any manner, under penalty of loss of property and life. Barcelona, April nineteen one thousand five hundred and nineteen: I, the King. By command of the King: Francisco de los Covos.

> [*Endorsed:* "In order that those sailing in the fleet may heed the counsels and decisions of magallanes, and that first and foremost, before proceeding elsewhere, they may sail to the spice islands."]

Extracto de Una Carta de Las Indias

Despues de esto escrito a V.S. llego ynigo lopez a los xviij de malaca el q_l_ truxo por nuevas q los castellanos estavan en maluco, q ptierõ tres naos de castilla y en ellas fernando magallaes por principal y fuerõ a [symbol] vista del cabo de san Agustin y de allj corrierõ obra de dozientas o trezientas leguas al luengo de la costa del brasil y fuerõ a dar en un rrio q atravessava toda la trra del brasil y era de agua dulce, anduvierõ por el seys o siete dias hasta q se vierõ de la otra parte del sul y por allj comencaron de yr a buscar a maluco anduvierõ cinco messes por vn golfo sin nunca [symbol] tierra nj hallar yslas y sienpre con vientos en popa, eneste paraje fuyo vna nao al magallanes y se torno non se sabe pte della, y eneste tpõ vuo vna grande confusion entre los castellanos de dezir q_l_ magallanes los levana a entregar alos Portugueses y determjnarõ dese levantar con las naos. supolo magallaes y hizose doliente y enbyo allamar vno a vno delos culpados y davãle vn mallo rrodeyro en la cabeça, mato los de qujen se temja y dio las capitanjas y cargos a otros aqujen el qujso, yendo porsu derrora adelante con poco mantenjmjento y agua, vuo vysta de vna ysia laqual era burneo qujsierõ salir en ella contra voluntad delos dela *trra* vuo entre vnos y otros gran pelea en la qual murio el magallanes y otros muchos hoh bres de fayçion q qdo el armada muy desaparejada de gente y estuvierõ en condiçion de se entregar ala gente dela *trra* levantose vn piloto portugues q yva con magallaes y tomo el leme en la mano y partio camjno de maluco alqual llego y hallo vn hombre de don tristan de meneses q dios aya, vujeronle ala mano y supieron todo lo q qujsieron del fizieron sus contratos bien largamete y a voluntad delos dela *trra* despendieron desus bonetes bermejos y paños q lebavan por los quales les fiziero carga destas dos naos, las quales partierõ de maluco cargadas de clavo y mal aparejadas de aparejos y costados dexaron en *trra* dos o tres honbres con barcos y talãqras y vnos tiros fechos por señal, estas naos trayan hecho fundamento de se venjr por las islas de maldiva porq por el camino q fuerõ tenjante por peligroso po el tpo los hizo arribar a burneo de donde se partio vna nao la mejor aderecçada pa essos rreynos la qual dios alla nos lieve, la otra con sesenta personas se tornava pa maluco por no estar pa acometer el camjno y fazer mucha agua, y fazia fundamento de hazer estançias en maluco con su artilleria y esperar

allj rrespuesta dela nao q partio pa castilla le q_l_ plazera a nro
s_or_ q no yra alla su el lo vujere por su serviçio. todas estas nuevas
supierõ por dos grumetes delas mismas naos q se qdarõ en burneo
por a[symbol] mjedo de yr las naos tan mal aderecadas, y de allj los
levo don juã* a timor adonde estava pedro merino—cargando de
soldados (?) y de allj se partio con estos dos grumetes y los truxo
a malaca a donde hallo a yñigo lopez q estana pa partir y se metio
con el y llegarõ a cochin a salvamento con los castellanos grumetes
de gujen se supo todo esto.

[*Addressed:* "S. Cel. & Cath.*ca* M.*tī*"]

[*Endorsed:* "A su mag xxjx de agosto de cochin a 23 de
Dies de 1522.

Avises del viage [sic] de Magallanes y su muerte y
noticias dela India portuguesa."]

Extract of a Letter from the Indies

After I had written the above to your lordship, Yñigo Lopez
arrived on the eighteenth from Malaca with the news that the
Castilians were in Maluco; that three vessels had left Castilla under
command of Fernando Magallaes. They had been sighted off the
cape of San Agustin, from which point they had run about two
hundred or three hundred leagues along the coast of Brasil. There
they anchored in a river[218] which flows across the whole of Brasil,
and was of fresh water. They sailed for six or seven days on this river
until they came to the other part of the south, whence they started
in quest of Maluco, sailing for five months in a wide expanse of
waters without ever seeing land or finding islands, and with a steady
stern wind. In this region one of the ships fled from Magallanes
and started to return, but nothing more has been heard of it At
this time a great uneasiness became manifest among the Castilians,
and it was rumored that Magallanes was going to deliver them over
to the Portuguese; and they resolved to mutiny and seize the ships.
Magallanes upon obtaining information of this was sorely grieved.
He summoned the guilty ones before him one by one, but they
flatly refused to come.[219] He killed those of whom he stood in fear,
and gave their captaincies and duties to those whom he thought
proper. He continued his forward course although he had but little

food and water, and finally came in sight of an island which was the island of Burneo. They tried to land there against the will of the inhabitants. A great fight ensued, in which Magallanes and many of his fighting men were killed, and when the fleet, deprived of many men, was in such straits that it could easily have fallen into the hands of the inhabitants of that land, a Portuguese pilot, who had come with Magallanes, came to the rescue, took the tiller, and turned the course of the vessel toward Maluco. He reached that place and found there one of the followers of Don Tristan de Meneses (may he rest in peace). They took him prisoner and obtained from him all the information that they desired. Then they made their bargains in detail and at the wish of those on land disposed of their red caps and clothes which they had carried with them, in return for which those on shore loaded their vessels; these left Maluco laden with cloves, but in very poor condition as to their rigging and hulls. They left two or three men with small boats and defenses, and some shot to use for signals. It was their intention to go with their ships through the islands of Maldiva because they considered the course that they were taking dangerous. The weather, however, compelled them to land at Burneo from which place one of the vessels which was in the better condition started for those kingdoms, and may God grant her safe arrival. The other vessel returned with sixty hands to Maluco for it was leaking badly and not in a condition to undertake the voyage. They resolved to make a stay at Maluco with the artillery and wait there for news of the vessel which had left for Castilla which may it please Our Lord not to bring to that place unless it be for his service. All this news was had from two deck-hands of the same vessels, who had remained at Burneo for fear of embarking in them while in so poor condition. From this place Don Juan brought them to Timor where Pedro Merino was in command of the soldiers,[220] and from there he departed with these two deck-hands and brought them to Malaca where he found Yñigo Lopez, who was about to leave. Joining with him they both arrived in safety at Cochin with the Castilian deck-hands from whom they obtained all the above information.

[*Addressed:* "Sacred Caesarean and Catholic Majesty."]
[*Endorsed:* "To his majesty, xxjx of August from Cochin, December 23, 1522.

De Molvccis Insulis

Most Reverend and Illustrious Lord: my only Lord, to you I most humbly commend myself. Not long ago one of those five ships returned which the emperor, while he was at Saragossa some years ago, had sent into a strange and hitherto unknown part of the world, to search for the islands in which spices grow. For although the Portuguese bring us a great quantity of them from the Golden Chersonesus, which we now call Malacca, nevertheless their own Indian possessions produce none but pepper. For it is well known that the other spices, as cinnamon, cloves, and the nutmeg, which we call muscat, and its covering [mace], which we call muscat-flower, are brought to their Indian possessions from distant islands hitherto only known by name, in ships held together not by iron fastenings, but merely by palm-leaves, and having round sails also woven out of palm-fibres. Ships of this sort they call "junks," and they are impelled by the wind only when it blows directly fore or aft.

Nor is it wonderful, that these islands have not been known to any mortal, almost up to our time. For whatever statements of ancient authors we have hitherto read with respect to the native soil of these spices, are partly entirely fabulous, and partly so far from truth, that the very regions, in which they asserted that these spices were produced, are scarcely less distant from the countries in which it is now ascertained that they grow, than we are ourselves.

For, not to mention others, Herodotus, in other respects a very good authority, states that cinnamon was found in birds' nests, into which the birds had brought it from very distant regions, among which birds he mentions especially the Phoenix—and I know not who has ever seen the nest of a Phoenix. But Pliny, who might have been thought to have had better means of knowing the facts, since long before his time many discoveries had been made by the fleets of Alexander the Great, and by other expeditions, states that cinnamon was produced in Ethiopia, on the borders of the land of the Troglodytes. Whereas we know now that cinnamon is produced at a very great distance from any part of Ethiopia, and especially from the country of the Troglodytes, *i.e.* dwellers in subterraneous caves.

Now it was necessary for our sailors, who have recently returned, who knew more about Ethiopia than about other countries, to sail round the whole world and that in a very wide circuit, before they discovered these islands and returned to Europe; and, since this voyage was a very remarkable one, and neither in our own time, nor in any former age, has such a voyage been accomplished, or even attempted, I have determined to send your Lordship a full and accurate account of the expedition.

I have taken much care in obtaining an account of the facts from the commanding officer of the squadron,[221] and from the individual sailors who have returned with him. They also made a statement to the emperor, and to several other persons, with such good faith and sincerity, that they appeared in their narrative, not merely to have abstained from fabulous statements, but also to contradict and refute the fabulous statements made by ancient authors.

For who ever believed that the Monosceli, or Sciapodes [one-legged men], the Scyrites, the Spithamæi [persons a span—seven and one-half inches—high], the Pigmies [height thirteen and one-half inches], and such-like were rather monsters than men? Yet, although the Castilians in their voyages westwards, and the Portuguese sailing eastwards, have sought out, discovered, and surveyed so many places even beyond the Tropic of Capricorn, and now these countrymen of ours have sailed completely round the world, none of them have found any trustworthy evidence in favor of the existence of such monsters; and therefore all such accounts ought to be regarded as fabulous, and as old wives' tales, handed down from one writer to another without any basis of truth. But, as I have to make a voyage round the world, I will not extend my prefatory remarks, but will come at once to the point.

Some thirty years ago, when the Castilians in the West, and the Portuguese in the East, had begun to search after new and unknown lands, in order to avoid any interference of one with the other, the kings of these countries divided the whole world between them, by the authority probably of Pope Alexander VI, on this plan, that a line should be drawn from the north to the south pole through a point three hundred and sixty leagues west of the Hesperides which they now call Cape Verde Islands, which would divide the earth's surface into two equal portions. All unknown lands hereafter discovered to the east of this line were assigned to the Portuguese; all on the west to the Castilians. Hence it came to pass that the Castilians always sailed southwest, and there discovered a very extensive continent, besides numerous large islands, abounding in gold, pearls, and other valuable commodities; and have quite recently discovered a large inland city named Tenoxtica [Mexico] situated in a lake like Venice. Peter Martyr,[222] an author who is more careful as to the accuracy of his statements than of the elegance of his style, has given a full but truthful description of this city. But the Portuguese sailing southward past the Hesperides [Cape Verde Islands] and the Fish-eating Ethiopians [West Coast of Africa], crossed the Equator and the Tropic of Capricorn, and sailing eastward discovered several, very large islands heretofore unknown, and also the sources of the Nile and the Troglodytes. Thence, by way of the Arabian and Persian Gulfs, they arrived at the shores of India within the Ganges, where now there is the very great trading station and the kingdom of Calicut. Hence they sailed to Taprobane which is now called Zamatara [Sumatra]. For where Ptolemy, Pliny, and other geographers placed Taprobane, there is now no island which can possibly be identified with it. Thence they came to the Golden Chersonesus, where now stands the well-peopled city of Malacca, the principal place of business of the East. After this they penetrated into a great gulf, as far as the nation of the Sinæ, who are now called Schinæ [Chinese], where they found a fair-complexioned and tolerably-civilized people, like our folks in Germany. They believe that the Seres and Asiatic Scythians extend as far as these parts.

And although there was a somewhat doubtful rumour afloat, that the Portuguese had advanced so far to the east, that they had come to the end of their own limits, and had passed over into the territory appointed for the Castilians, and that Malacca and the Great Gulf were within our limits, all this was more said than believed, until, four years ago, Ferdinand Magellan, a distinguished Portuguese, who had for many years sailed about the Eastern Seas as admiral of the Portuguese fleet, having quarreled with his king, who he considered had acted ungratefully towards him, and Christopher Haro, brother of my father-in-law, of Lisbon, who had, through his agents for many years carried on trade with those eastern countries, and more recently with the Chinese, so that he was well acquainted with these matters (he also, having been ill-used by the King of Portugal, had returned to his native country, Castille), pointed out to the emperor, that it was not yet clearly ascertained, whether Malacca was within the boundaries of the Portuguese or of the Castillians, because hitherto its longitude had not been definitely known; but that it was an undoubted fact that the Great Gulf and the Chinese nations were within the Castilian limits They asserted also that it was absolutely certain, that the islands called the Moluccas, in which all sorts of spices grow, and from which they were brought to Malacca, were contained in the western, or Castilian division, and that it would be possible to sail to them, and to bring the spices at less trouble and expense from their native soil to Castille. The plan of the voyage was to sail west, and then coasting the Southern Hemisphere round the south of America to the east. Yet it appeared to be a difficult undertaking, and one of which the practicability was doubtful. Not that it was impossible, *prima facie*, to sail from the west round the Southern Hemisphere to the east; but that it was uncertain, whether ingenious Nature, all whose works are wisely conceived, had so arranged the sea and the land that it might be possible to arrive by this course at the Eastern Seas. For it had not been ascertained whether that extensive region, which is called Terra Firma, separated the Western Ocean [the Atlantic] from the Eastern [the Pacific]; but it was plain that that continent extended in a southerly direction, and afterwards inclined to the west. Moreover two regions had been discovered in the north, one called Baccalearum from a new kind of fish,[223] the other called Florida; and if these were connected with Terra Firma, it would not be possible to pass from the Western Ocean to the Eastern; since although much trouble had been taken to discover any strait which might exist connecting the two oceans, none had yet been found. At the same time it was considered that to attempt to sail through the Portuguese concessions and the Eastern Seas would be a hazardous enterprise, and dangerous in the highest degree.

The emperor and his council considered that the plan proposed by Magellan and Haro, though holding out considerable advantages, was one of very considerable difficulty as to execution. After some delay, Magellan offered to go out himself, but Haro undertook to fit out a squadron at the expense of himself and his friends, provided that they were allowed to sail under the authority and patronage of his majesty. As each resolutely upheld his own scheme, the emperor himself fitted out a squadron of five ships, and appointed Magellan to the command. It was ordered that they should sail southwards by the coast of Terra Firma, until they found either the end of that country or some strait, by which they might arrive at the spice-bearing Moluccas.

Accordingly on the tenth of August, 1519, Ferdinand Magellan with his five ships sailed from Seville. In a few days they arrived at the Fortunate Islands, now called the Canaries. Thence they sailed to the islands of the Hesperides [Cape Verde]; and thence sailed in a southwesterly direction towards that continent which I have already mentioned [Terra Firma or South America], and after a favorable voyage of a few days discovered a promontory, which they called St. Mary's. Here admiral John Ruy Dias Solis, while exploring the shores of this continent by command of King Ferdinand the Catholic, was, with some of his companions, eaten by the Anthropophagi, whom the Indians call Cannibals. Hence they coasted along this continent, which extends far on southwards, and which I now think should be called the Southern Polar land, then gradually slopes off in a westerly direction, and so sailed several degrees south of the Tropic of Capricorn. But it was not so easy for them to do it, as for me to relate it. For not till the end of March in the following year, [1520] did they arrive at a bay, which they called St. Julian's Bay. Here the Antarctic polestar was forty-nine and one-third degrees above the horizon, this result being deduced from the sun's declination and altitude, and this star is principally used by our navigators for observations. They stated that the longitude was fifty-six degrees west of the Canaries.[224] For since the ancient geographers, and especially Ptolemy reckoned the distance easterly from the Fortunate Islands [Canaries] as far as Cattigara to be one hundred and eighty degrees, and our sailors have sailed as far as possible in a westerly direction, they reckoned the distance from the Canaries westward to Cattigara to be also one hundred and eighty degrees. Yet even though our sailors in so long a voyage and in one so distant from the land lay down and mark certain signs and limits of the longitude; they appear to me rather to have made some error in their method of reckoning of the longitude than to have attained any trustworthy result.

Meanwhile, however this may be, until more certain results are arrived at, I do not think that their statements should be absolutely rejected, but merely accepted provisionally. This bay appeared to be of great extent, and had rather the appearance of a strait. Therefore admiral Magellan directed two ships to survey the bay; and himself remained with the rest at anchor. After two days, they returned, and reported that the bay was shallow, and did not extend far inland. Our men on their return saw some Indians gathering shell-fish on the sea-shore, for the natives of all unknown countries are commonly called Indians. These Indians were very tall, ten spans high [seven feet six inches], clad in skins of wild beasts, darker-complexioned than would have been expected in that part of the world; and when some of our men went on shore and showed them bells and pictures, they began to dance round our men with a hoarse noise and unintelligible chant, and to excite our admiration they took arrows a cubit and a half long, and put them down their own throats to the bottom of their stomachs without seeming any the worse for it. Then they drew them up again, and seemed much pleased at having shown their bravery. At length three men came up as a deputation, and by means of signs requested our men to come with them further inland, as though they would receive them hospitably. Magellan sent with them seven men well equipped, to find out as much as possible about the country and its inhabitants. These seven went with the Indians some seven miles up the country, and came to a desolate and pathless wood. Here was a very low-built cottage roofed with skins of beasts. In it were two rooms, in one of which dwelt the women and children, and in the other the men. The women and children were thirteen in number, and the men five. These received their guests with a barbarous entertainment, but which they considered to be quite a royal one. For they slaughtered an animal much resembling a wild ass, and set before our men half-roasted steaks of it, but no other food or drink. Our men had to cover themselves at night with skins, on account of the severity of the wind and snow.

Before they went to sleep they arranged for a watch to be kept; the Indians did the same and lay near our men by the fire, snoring horribly. When day dawned, our men requested them to return with them, accompanied by their families to our ships. When the Indians persisted in refusing to do so, and our men had also persisted somewhat imperiously in their demands, the men went into the women's chamber. The Spaniards supposed that they had gone to consult their wives about this expedition. But they came out again as if to battle, wrapped up from head to foot in hideous skins, with their faces painted in various colours, and with bows and arrows, all ready for fighting, and appearing taller than ever. The Spaniards, thinking a skirmish was likely to take place, fired a gun. Although nobody was hit, yet these enormous giants, who just before seemed as though they were ready to fight and conquer Jove himself, were so alarmed at the sound, that they began to sue for peace. It was arranged that three men, leaving the rest behind, should return with our men to the ships, and so they started. But as our men not only could not run as fast as the giants, but could not even run as fast as the giants could walk, two of the three, seeing a wild ass grazing on a mountain at some distance, as they were going along, ran off after it and so escaped. The third was brought to the ships, but in a few days he died, having starved himself after the Indian fashion through homesickness. And although the admiral returned to that cottage, in order to make another of the giants prisoner, and bring him to the emperor, as a novelty, no one was found there, as all of them had removed elsewhere, and the cottage had disappeared. Hence it is plain that this nation is a nomad race, and although our men remained some time in that bay, as we shall presently mention, they never again saw an Indian on that coast; nor did they think that there was anything in that country that would make it worth while to explore the inland districts any further. And though Magellan was convinced that a longer stay there would be of no use, yet since for some days the sea was very rough and the weather tempestuous, and the land extended still further southward, so that the farther they advanced, the colder they would find the country, their departure was unavoidably put off from day to day, till the month of May arrived, at which time the winter sets in with great severity in those parts, so much so, that, though it was our summer-time, they had to make preparations for wintering there. Magellan, perceiving that the voyage would be a long one, in order that the provisions might last longer, ordered the rations to be diminished. The Spaniards endured this with patience for some days, but alarmed at the length of the winter and the barrenness of the land, at last petitioned their admiral Magellan, saying that it was evident that this continent extended an indefinite distance south-wards, and that there was no hope of discovering the end of it, or of discovering a strait; that a hard winter was setting in, and that several men had already died through scanty food and the hardships of the voyage; that they would not long be able to endure that restriction of provisions which he had enacted; that the emperor never intended that they should obstinately persevere in attempting to do what the natural circumstances of the case rendered it impossible to accomplish; that the toils they had already endured would be acknowledged and approved, since they had already advanced further than the boldest and most adventurous navigators had dared to do; that, if a south wind should spring up in a few days, they might easily sail to the north, and arrive at a milder climate. In reply, Magellan, who had already made up his mind either to carry out his design, or to die in the attempt, said that the emperor had ordered him to sail according to a certain plan, from which he could not and would not depart on any consideration whatever, and that therefore he should continue this voyage till he found either the end of this continent, or a strait. That though he could not do this at present, as the winter prevented him, yet it would be easy enough in the summer of this region; that if they would only sail along the coast to the south, the summer would be all one perpetual day; that they had means of providing against want of food and the inclemency of the weather, inasmuch as there was a great quantity of wood, that the sea produced shellfish, and numerous sorts of excellent fish; that there were springs of good water, and they could also help their stores by hunting and by shooting wild fowl; that bread and wine had not yet run short, and would not run short in future, provided that they used them for necessity and for the preservation of health, and not for pleasure and luxury: that nothing had yet been done worthy of much admiration, nor such as could give them a reasonable ground for returning; that the Portuguese not only yearly, but almost daily, in their voyages to the east, made no difficulty about sailing twelve degrees south of the tropic of Capricorn: what had they then to boast of, when they had only advanced some four degrees south of it; that he, for his part, had made up his mind to suffer anything that might happen, rather than to return to Spain with disgrace;

that he believed that his companions, or at any rate, those in whom the generous spirit of Spaniards was not totally extinct, were of the same way of thinking: that he had only to exhort them fearlessly to face the remainder of winter; that the greater their hardships and dangers were, the richer their reward would be for having opened up for the emperor a new world rich in spices and gold.

Magellan thought that by this address he had soothed and encouraged the minds of his men, but within a few days he was troubled by a wicked and disgraceful mutiny. For the sailors began to talk to one another of the long-standing ill-feeling existing between the Portuguese and the Castilians, and of Magellan's being a Portuguese; that there was nothing that he could do more to the credit of his own country than to lose this fleet with so many men on board: that it was not to be believed that he wished to find the Moluccas, even if he could, but that he would think it enough if he could delude the emperor for some years by holding out vain hopes, and that in the meanwhile something new would turn up, whereby the Castilians might be completely put out of the way of looking for spices: nor indeed was the direction of the voyage really towards the fertile Molucca islands, but towards snow and ice and everlasting bad weather. Magellan was exceedingly irritated by these conversations, and punished some of the men, but with somewhat more severity than was becoming to a foreigner, especially to one holding command in a distant part of the world. So they mutinied and took possession of one of the ships, and began to make preparations to return to Spain, but Magellan, with the rest of his men who had remained faithful to him, boarded that ship, and executed the ringleader and other leading mutineers, even some who could not legally be so treated: for they were royal officials, who were only liable to capital punishment by the emperor and his council. However under the circumstances no one ventured to resist. Yet there were some, who whispered to one another, that Magellan would go on exercising the same severity amongst the Castilians, as long as one was left, until having got rid of everyone of them, he could sail home to his own country again with the few Portuguese he had with him. The Castilians therefore remained still more hostile to the admiral. As soon as Magellan observed that the weather was less stormy and that winter began to break up, he sailed out of St. Julian's Bay on the twenty-fourth of August, 1520, as before. For some days he coasted along to the southward and at last sighted a cape, which they called Cape Santa Cruz. Here a storm from the east caught them, and one of the five ships was driven on shore and wrecked, but the crew and all goods on board were saved, except an African slave, who was drowned. After this the coast seemed to stretch a little south eastwards, and as they continued to explore it, on the twenty-sixth of November [1520] an opening was observed having the appearance of a strait; Magellan at once sailed in with his whole fleet, and seeing several bays in various directions, directed three of the ships to cruise about to ascertain whether there was any way through, undertaking to wait for them five days at the entrance of the strait, so that they might report what success they had. One of these ships was commanded by Alvaro de Mezquita, son of Magellan's brother, and this by the windings of the channel came out again into the ocean whence it had set out. When the Spaniards[225] saw that they were at a considerable distance from the other ships, they plotted among themselves to return home, and having put Alvaro their captain in irons, they sailed northwards, and at last reached the coast of Africa, and there took in provisions, and eight months after leaving the other ships they arrived in Spain, where they brought Alvaro to trial on the charge that it had chiefly been through his advice and persuasion that his uncle Magellan had adopted such severe measures against the Castilians. Magellan waited some days over the appointed time for this ship, and meanwhile one ship had returned, and reported that they had found nothing but a shallow bay, and the shores stony and with high cliffs; but the other reported that the greatest bay had the appearance of a strait, as they had sailed on for three days and had found no way out, but that the further they went the narrower the passage became, and it was so deep, that in many places they sounded without finding the bottom; they also noticed from the tide of the sea, that the flow was somewhat stronger than the ebb, and thence they conjectured that there was a passage that way into some other sea. On hearing this Magellan determined to sail along this channel. This strait, though not then known to be such, was of the breadth in some places of three, in others of two, in others of five or ten Italian miles,[226] and inclined slightly to the west. The latitude south was found to be fifty-two degrees, the longitude they estimated as the same as that of St. Julian's Bay. It being now hard upon the month of November, the length of the night was not much more than five hours; they saw no one on the shore. One night however a great number of fires was seen, especially on the left side, whence they conjectured that they had been seen by the inhabitants of those regions. But Magellan, seeing that the land was craggy, and bleak with perpetual winter, did not think it worth while to spend his time in exploring it, and so with his three ships continued, his voyage along the channel, until on the twenty-second day after he had set sail, he came out into another vast and open sea: the length of the strait they reckoned at about one hundred Spanish miles. The land which they had to the right was no doubt the continent we have before mentioned [South America]. On the left hand they thought that there was no continent, but only islands, as they occasionally heard on that side the reverberation and roar of the sea at a more distant part of the coast. Magellan saw that the main land extended due north, and therefore gave orders to turn away from that great continent, leaving it on the right hand, and to sail over that vast and extensive ocean, which had probably never been traversed by our ships or by those of any other nation, in a northwesterly direction, so that they might arrive at last at the Eastern Ocean, coming at it from the west, and again enter the torrid zone, for he was satisfied that the Moluccas were in the extreme east, and could not be far off the equator. They continued in this course, never deviating from it, except when compelled to do so now and then by the force of the wind; and when they had sailed on this course for forty days across the ocean with a strong wind, mostly favourable, and had seen nothing all around them but sea, and had now almost reached again the Tropic of Capricorn, they came in sight of two islands,[227] small and barren, and on directing their course to them found that they were uninhabited; but they stayed there two days for repose and refreshment, as plenty of fish was to be caught there. However they unanimously agreed to call these islands the Unfortunate Islands. Then they set sail again, and continued on the same course as before. After sailing for three months and twenty days with good fortune over this ocean, and having traversed a distance almost too long to estimate, having had a strong wind aft almost the whole of the time, and having again crossed the equator, they saw an island, which they afterwards learnt from the neighboring people was called Inuagana.[228] When they came nearer to it, they found the latitude to be eleven degrees north; the longitude they reckoned to be one hundred and fifty-eight degrees west of Cadiz. From this point they saw more and more islands, so that they found themselves in an extensive archipelago, but on arriving at Inuagana, they found it was uninhabited. Then they sailed towards another small island, where they saw two Indian canoes, for such is the Indian name of these strange boats; these canoes are scooped out of the single trunk of a tree, and hold one or at most two persons; and they are used to talk with each other by signs, like dumb people. They asked the Indians what the names of the islands were, and whence provisions could be procured, of which they were very deficient; they were given to understand that the first island they had seen was called Inuagana, that near which they then were, Acacan,[229] but that both were uninhabited; but that there was another island almost in sight, in the direction of which they pointed, called Selani,[230] and that abundance of provisions of all sorts was to be had there. Our men took in water at Acacan, and then sailed towards Selani, but a storm caught them so that they could not land there, but they were driven to another island called Massana,[231] where the king of three islands resides. From this island they sailed to Subuth [Zebu], a very large island, and well supplied, where having come to a friendly arrangement with the chief they immediately landed to celebrate divine worship according to Christian usage—for the festival of the resurrection of Him who has saved us was at hand. Accordingly with some of the sails of the ships and branches of trees they erected a chapel, and in it constructed an altar in the Christian fashion, and divine service was duly performed. The chief and a large crowd of Indians came up, and seemed much pleased with these religious rites They brought the admiral and some of the officers into the chief's cabin, and set before them what food they had. The bread was made of sago, which is obtained from the trunk of a tree not much unlike the palm. This is chopped up small, and fried in oil, and used as bread, a specimen of which I send to your lordship; their drink was a liquor which flows from the branches of palm-trees when cut, some birds also were served up at this meal; and also some of the fruit of the country. Magellan having noticed in the chief's house a sick person in a very wasted condition, asked who he was and from what disease he was suffering. He was told that it was the chief's grandson, and that he had been suffering for two years from a violent fever. Magellan exhorted him to be of good courage, that if he would devote himself to Christ, he would immediately recover his former health and strength. The Indian consented and adored the cross, and received baptism, and the next day declared that he was well again, rose from his bed, and walked about, and took his meals like the others. What visions he may have told to his friends I cannot say; but the chief and over twenty-two hundred Indians were baptized and professed the name and faith of Christ. Magellan seeing that this island was rich in gold and ginger, and that it was so conveniently situated with respect to the neighboring islands, that it would be easy, making this his headquarters, to explore their resources and natural productions, he therefore went to the chief of Subuth and suggested to him, that since he had turned away from the foolish and impious worship of false gods to the Christian religion, it would be proper that the chiefs of the neighboring islands should obey his rule; that he had determined to send envoys for this purpose, and if any of the chiefs should refuse to obey this summons, to compel them to do so by force of arms. The proposal pleased the savage, and the envoys were sent: the chiefs came in one by one and did homage to the chief of Subuth in the manner adopted in those countries. But the nearest island to Subuth is called Mauthan [Matan], and its king was superior in military force to the other chiefs; and he declined to do homage to one whom he had been accustomed to command for so long. Magellan, anxious to carry out his plan, ordered forty of his men, whom he could rely on for valor and military skill, to arm themselves, and passed over to the island Mauthan in boats, for it was very near. The chief of Subuth furnished him with some of his own people, to guide him as to the topography of the island and the character of the country, and, if it should be necessary, to help him in the battle. The king of Mauthan, seeing the arrival of our men, led into the field some three thousand of his people. Magellan drew up his own men and what artillery he had, though his force was somewhat small, on the shore, and although he saw that his own force was much inferior in numbers, and that his opponents were a warlike race, and were equipped with lances and other weapons, nevertheless thought it more advisable to face the enemy with them, than to retreat, or to avail himself of the aid of the

Subuth islanders. Accordingly he exhorted his men to take courage, and not to be alarmed at the superior force of the enemy; since it had often been the case, as had recently happened in the island [peninsula] of Yucatan, that two hundred Spaniards had routed two or even three hundred thousand Indians. He said to the Subuth islanders, that he had not brought them with him to fight, but to see the valour and military prowess of his men. Then he attacked the Mauthan islanders, and both sides fought boldly; but as the enemy surpassed our men in number, and used longer lances, to the great damage of our men, at last Magellan himself was thrust through and slain.[232] Although the survivors did not consider themselves fairly beaten, yet, as they had lost their leader, they retreated; but, as they retreated in good order, the enemy did not venture to pursue them. The Spaniards then, having lost their admiral, Magellan, and seven of their comrades, returned to Subuth, where they chose as their new admiral John Serrano, a man of no contemptible ability. He renewed the alliance with the chief of Subuth, by making him additional presents, and undertook to conquer the king of Mauthan. Magellan had been the owner of a slave, a native of the Moluccas, whom he had formerly bought in Malacca; and by means of this slave, who was able to speak Spanish fluently, and of an interpreter of Subuth, who could speak the Moluccan language, our men carried on their negotiations. This slave had taken part in the fight with the Mauthan islanders, and had been slightly wounded, for which reason he lay by all day intending to nurse himself. Serrano, who could do no business without his help, rated him soundly, and told him that though his master Magellan was dead, he was still a slave, and that he would find that such was the case, and would get a good flogging into the bargain, if he did not exert himself and do what was required of him more zealously. This speech much incensed the slave against our people: but he concealed his anger and in a few days he went to the chief of Subuth, and told him that the avarice of the Spaniards was insatiable: that they had determined, as soon as they should have defeated the king of Mauthan, to turn round upon him, and take him away as a prisoner; and that the only course for him [the chief of Subuth] to adopt was to anticipate treachery by treachery. The savage believed this, and secretly came to an understanding with the king of Mauthan, and made arrangements with him for common action against our people.

Admiral Serrano, and twenty-seven of the principal officers and men, were invited to a solemn banquet. These, quite unsuspectingly, for the natives had carefully dissembled their intentions, went on shore without any precautions, to take their dinner with the chief. While they were at table, some armed men, who had been concealed close by, ran in and slew them. A great outcry was made: it was reported in our ships that our men were killed, and that the whole island was hostile to us; our men saw, from on board the ships, that the handsome cross, which they had set up in a tree, was torn down by the natives and cut up into fragments. When the Spaniards, who had remained on board, heard of the slaughter of our men, they feared further treachery: so they weighed anchor and began to set sail without delay. Soon afterwards Serrano was brought to the coast a prisoner; he entreated them to deliver him from so miserable a captivity, saying that he had got leave to be ransomed, if his men would agree to it. Although our men thought it was disgraceful to leave their commander behind in this way, their fear of the treachery of the islanders was so great, that they put out to sea, leaving Serrano on the shore in vain lamenting and beseeching his comrades to rescue him. The Spaniards, having lost their commander and several of their comrades, sailed on sad and anxious, not merely on account of the loss they had suffered, but also because their numbers had been so diminished, that it was no longer possible to work the three remaining ships.

On this question they consulted together, and unanimously came to the conclusion, that the best plan would be to burn one of the ships, and to sail home in the two remaining. They therefore sailed to a neighboring island, called Cohol [Bohol], and having put the rigging and stores of one of the ships on board the two others, set it on fire. Hence they proceeded to the island of Gibeth.[233] Although they found that this island was well supplied with gold and ginger and many other things, they did not think it desirable to stay there any length of time, as they could not establish friendly relations with the natives; and they were too few in number to venture to use force. From Gibeth they proceeded to the island of Porne [Borneo]. In this archipelago there are two large islands: one of which is called Siloli [Gilolo], whose king had six hundred children. Siloli is larger than Porne, for Siloli can hardly be circumnavigated in six months, but Porne in three months. Although

Siloli is larger than Porne, yet the latter is more fertile, and distinguished as containing a large city of the same name as the island. And since Porne must be considered to be more important than the other islands, which they had hitherto visited, and it was from it that the other islanders had learnt the arts of civilized life, I have determined to describe briefly the manners and customs of these nations. All these islanders are Caphrae or Kafirs, *i.e.,* heathens, they worship the sun and moon as gods; they assign the government of the day to the sun, and that of the night to the moon; the sun they consider to be male, and the moon female, and that they are the parents of the other stars, all of which they consider to be gods, though little ones. They salute, rather than adore, the rising sun, with certain hymns. Also they salute the bright moon at night, from whom they ask for children, for the increase of their flocks and herds, for an abundant supply of the fruits of the earth, and for other things of that sort. But they practice piety and justice: and especially love peace and quiet, and have great aversion to war. As long as their king maintains peace, they show him divine honours: but if he is anxious for war, they never rest till he is slain by the enemy in battle. When the king has determined on war, which very seldom happens, his men set him in the front rank, where he has to stand the whole brunt of the combat; and they do not exert themselves vigorously against the enemy, till they know that the king has fallen: then they begin to fight for liberty and for their new king: nor has any king of theirs entered on a war without being slain in battle. For this reason they seldom engage in war, and they think it unjust to extend their frontiers. Their chief care is to avoid giving offence to the neighboring nations or to strangers. But if at any time they are attacked, they retaliate; and yet, lest further ill should arise, they at once endeavor to come to terms. They think that party acts most creditably, which is the first to propose terms of peace; that it is disgraceful to be anticipated in so doing; and that it is scandalous and detestable to refuse peace to those who ask for it, even though the latter should have been the aggressors: all the neighboring people unite in destroying such refusers of peace as impious and abominable. Hence they mostly pass their lives in peace and leisure. Robberies and murders are quite unknown among them. No one may speak to the king but his wives and children, except at a distance by hollow canes, which they apply to his ear, and through which they whisper what they have to say. They think that at death men have no perception as they had none before they were born. Their houses are small, built of wood and earth, covered partly with rubble and partly with palm-leaves. It is ascertained that there are twenty thousand houses in the city of Porne. They marry as many wives as they can afford to keep; they eat birds and fish; make bread of rice; and drink a liquor drawn from the palm tree— of which we have spoken before. Some carry on trade with the neighbouring islands, to which they sail in junks, some are employed in hunting and shooting, some in fishing, some in agriculture: their clothes are made of cotton. Their animals are nearly the same as ours, excepting sheep, oxen, and asses: their horses are very slight and small. They have a great supply of camphor, ginger, and cinnamon. On leaving this island our men, having paid their respects to the king, and propitiated him by presents, sailed to the Moluccas, their way to which had been pointed out to them by the king. Then they came to the coast of the island of Solo,[234] where they heard that pearls were to be found as large as doves' eggs, or even hens' eggs, but that they were only to be had in very deep water. Our men did not bring home any single large pearl, as they were not there at the season of the year for pearl-fishing. They said however that they found an oyster there the flesh of which weighed forty-seven pounds. Hence I should be disposed to believe that pearls of the size mentioned would be found there; for it is certain that large pearls are found in oysters. And, not to forget it, I will add that our men reported that the islanders of Porne asserted that the king wore two pearls in his crown as large as goose eggs. After this they came to the island of Gilona, where they saw some men with such long ears, that they reached down to their shoulders; and when they expressed their astonishment, the natives told them, that in an island not far off, there were men, who had such long and wide ears, that one ear could, when they liked, cover the whole of their heads. But as our men were not in search of monsters but of spices, they did not trouble themselves about such rubbish, but sailed direct for the Moluccas, where they arrived in the eighth month after their admiral Magellan had been slain in the island of Mauthan. The islands are five in number, and are called, Tarante, Muthil, Thedori, Mare, and Matthien,[235] situated partly to the north, partly to the south, and partly on the equator; the productions are cloves, nutmegs, and cinnamon: they are all close together, but of small extent. A few years ago the kings [of] Marmin began to believe that the soul is immortal. They were induced to believe this solely from the following reason, that they observed that a certain very beautiful small bird never settled on the earth, or on anything that was on the earth; but that these birds sometimes fell dead from the sky to the earth. And when the Mohammedans, who visited them for trading purposes, declared that these birds came from Paradise, the place of abode of departed souls, these princes adopted the Mohammedan faith, which makes wonderful promises respecting this same paradise. They call this bird Mamuco Diata; and they venerate it so highly, that the kings think themselves safe in battle under their protection, even when, according to their custom, they are placed in the front line of the army in battle. The common people are Kafirs, and have much the same manners and customs as the islanders of Porne, already spoken of; they are much in need of supplies from abroad, inasmuch as their country only produces spices, which they willingly exchange for the poisonous articles arsenic and sublimated mercury, and for the linen which they generally wear; but what use they make of these poisons has not yet been ascertained. They live on sago-bread, fish, and sometimes parrots; they live in very low-built cabins: in short, all they esteem and value is peace, leisure, and spices. The former, the greatest of blessings, the wickedness of mankind seems to have banished from our part of the world to theirs: but our avarice and insatiable desire of the luxuries of the table has urged us to seek for spices even in those distant lands. To such a degree has the perversity of human nature persisted in driving away as far as possible that which is conducive to happiness, and in seeking for articles of luxury in the remotest parts of the world. Our men having carefully examined the position of the Moluccas, and of each separate island, and also into the characters of the chiefs, sailed to Thedori, because they understood that this island produced a greater abundance of cloves than the others, and also that the king excelled the other kings in prudence and humanity. Providing themselves with presents they went on shore, and paid their respect to the king, and handed him the presents as the gift of the emperor. He accepted the presents graciously, and looking up to heaven said, "It is now two years since I learnt from observation of the stars that you were sent by the great King of kings to seek for these lands. Wherefore your arrival is the more agreeable to me, inasmuch as it has already been foreseen from the signification of the stars. And since I know that nothing happens to man, which has not long since been ordained by the decree of Fate and of the stars, I will not be the man to resist the determinations of Fate and the stars, but will spontaneously abdicate my royal power, and consider myself for the future, as carrying on the government of this island as your king's viceroy. So bring your ships into the harbour, and order the rest of your companions to land in safety, so that now after so much tossing about on the sea, and so many dangers, you may securely enjoy the comforts of life on shore, and recruit your strength; and consider yourselves to be coming into your own king's dominions." Having thus spoken, the king laid aside his diadem, and embraced each of our men, and directed such refreshments as the country produced to be set on table. Our men, delighted at this, returned to their companions, and told them what had taken place. They were much delighted by the graciousness and benevolence of the king, and took up their quarters in the island. When they had been entertained for some days by the king's munificence, they sent envoys thence to the other kings, to investigate the resources of the islands, and to secure the good will of the chiefs. Tarante was the nearest; it is a very small island, its circumference being a little over six Italian miles. The next is Matthien, and that also is small. These three produce a great quantity of cloves, but every fourth year the crop is far larger than at other times. These trees only grow on precipitous rocks, and they grow so close together as to form groves. The tree resembles the laurel as regards its leaves, its closeness of growth, and its height; the clove, so called from its resemblance to a nail [Latin, *clavus*] grows at the very tip of each twig; first a bud appears, and then a blossom much like that of the orange; the point of the clove first shows itself at the end of the twig, until it attains its full growth; at first it is reddish, but the heat of the sun soon turns it black. The natives share groves of this tree among themselves, just as we do vineyards: they keep the cloves in pits, till the merchants fetch them away. The fourth island, Muthil, is no larger than the rest. This island produces cinnamon; the tree is full of shoots, and in other respects fruitless, it thrives best in a dry soil, and is very much like the pomegranate tree. When the bark cracks through the heat of the sun, it is pulled off the tree, and being dried in the sun a short time becomes cinnamon. Near Muthil is another island, called Bada [Badjan or Batchian], more extensive than the Moluccas; in it the nutmeg grows. The tree is tall and wide-spreading, a good deal like a walnut tree; the fruit too is produced just in the same way as a walnut, being protected by a double covering, first a soft envelope, and under this a thin reticulated membrane which encloses the nut. This membrane we call Muskatblüthe, the Spaniards call it mace, it is an excellent and wholesome spice. Within this is a hard shell, like that of a filbert, inside which is the nutmeg properly so called. Ginger also is produced in all the islands of this archipelago: some is sown, some grows spontaneously; but the sown ginger is the best. The plant is like the saffron-plant, and its root, which resembles the root of saffron, is what we call ginger. Our men were kindly received by the various chiefs, who all, after the example of the King of Thedori, spontaneously submitted themselves to the imperial government. But the Spaniards, having now only two ships, determined to bring with them specimens of all sorts of spices, etc., but to load the ships mainly with cloves, because there had been a very abundant crop of it this season, and the ships could contain a great quantity of this kind of spice. Having laden their ships with cloves, and received letters and presents from the chiefs to the emperor, they prepared to sail away. The letters were filled with assurances of fidelity and respect: the gifts were Indian swords, etc. The most remarkable curiosities were some of the birds, called Mamuco Diata, that is the Bird of God, with which they think themselves safe and invincible in battle. Five of these were sent, one of which I procured from the captain of the ship, and now send it to your lordship—not that you will think it a defence against treachery and violence, but because you will be pleased with its rarity and beauty. I also send some cinnamon, nutmegs, and cloves, that you may see that our spices are not only not inferior to those imported by the Venetians and Portuguese, but of superior quality, because they are fresher. Soon after our men had sailed from Thedori, the larger of the two ships [the Trinidad] sprang a leak, which let in so much water, that they were obliged to return to Thedori. The Spaniards seeing that this defect could not be put right except with much labor and loss of time, agreed that the other ship [the Victoria] should sail to the Cape of

Cattigara, thence across the ocean as far as possible from the Indian coast, lest they should be seen by the Portuguese, until they came in sight of the southern point of Africa, beyond the tropic of Capricorn, which the Portuguese call the Cape of Good Hope, for thence the voyage to Spain would be easy. It was also arranged that, when the repairs of the other ship were completed, it should sail back through the archipelago and the Vast [Pacific] Ocean to the coast of the continent which we have already mentioned [South America], until they came to the Isthmus of Darien, where only a narrow neck of land divides the South Sea from the Western Sea, in which are the islands belonging to Spain. The smaller ship accordingly set sail again from Thedori, and though they went as far as twelve degrees south, they did not find Cattigara,[236] which Ptolemy considered to lie considerably south of the equator; however after a long voyage, they arrived in sight of the Cape of Good Hope, and thence sailed to the Cape Verde Islands. Here this ship also, after having been so long at sea, began to be leaky, and the men, who had lost several of their companions through hardships in the course of their adventures, were unable to keep the water pumped out. They therefore landed at one of the islands called Santiago, to buy slaves. As our men, sailor-like, had no money, they offered cloves in exchange for slaves. When the Portuguese officials heard of this, they committed thirteen of our men to prison. The rest, eighteen in number, being alarmed at the position in which they found themselves, left their companions behind, and sailed direct to Spain. Sixteen months after they had sailed from Thedori, on the sixth of September 1522 they arrived safe and sound at a port [San Lucar] near Seville. These sailors are certainly more worthy of perpetual fame, than the Argonauts who sailed with Jason to Colchis; and the ship itself deserves to be placed among the constellations more than the ship Argo. For the Argo only sailed from Greece through the Black Sea; but our ship setting put from Seville sailed first southwards, then through the whole of the West, into the Eastern Seas, then back again into the Western.

I humbly commend myself to your
Most Reverend Lordship.
Written at Valladolid twenty-fourth of October 1522.
Your Most Reverend and Most Illustrious Lordship's

Most humble and perpetual servant,
Maximilianus Transylvanus.

Cologne—[printed] at the house of Eucharius Cervicornus. A.D. 1523—in the month of January.

BIBLIOGRAPHICAL DATA

The Line of Demarcation

Papal Bulls of 1493.—The originals of the bulls of May 3 and 4 exist in the archives of the Vatican; and authenticated copies are in the Archivo general de Indias at Seville, their pressmark being "Patronato, Simancas—Bulas; Est. 1, caj. 1, leg. 1." The Archivo Nacional of Lisbon (which is housed in the Torre do Tombo) has one of the originals of the Bull of May 4—pressmark, "Gaveta 10, maco 11, n°. 16." The *Inter cætera* of May 3 was not known to be in existence until 1797, when it was discovered by Muñoz in the Simancas archives (from which many documents have since been transferred to the archives at Seville); in recent years it has been found in those of the Vatican also. There is in the British Museum a MS. copy (in Spanish translation) of the Bull of May 4—its pressmark being "Papeles varias de Indias, 13,977." The Bull of September 25 is known only through the Spanish translation made (August 30, 1554) by Grecian de Aldrete, secretary of Felipe II of Spain; this is at Seville, with pressmark as above. Harrisse could not find the Latin original of this document at Simancas Seville, or Rome. For the bulls of May 3 and 4 our translation is made from the Latin text given in Heywood's *Documenta selecta et tabulario secreto Vaticano* (Roma, 1893), pp.14-26; that contains also photographic facsimiles of the original bulls. Certain formal ecclesiastical phrases which Heywood only indicates by "etc." have been, for the sake of completeness, translated in full in the first bull. The bulls are also published in Raynaldi's *Annales ecclesiastici* (Lucæ, Typis Leonardi Venturini, MDCCLIV), xi, pp. 213-215; Hernaez's *Coleción de bulas, breves,* etc. (Bruselas, 1879), i, pp. 12-16; *Doc. inéd. Amér. y Oceania,* xxxiv, pp. 14-21; and in *Fonti Italiani* (Roma, 1892), part iii. The bull

Inter cætera of May 3 may also be found in Navarrete's *Col. de viages*, ii, pp. 23-27 (ed. 1825; or pp. 29-33, ed. 1859); *Eximiæ* of same date, in Solorzano's *De jure Indiarum* (Madrid, 1629), i, pp. 612, 613. *Inter cætera* of May 4 is also given in Solorzano, p. 610; *Alguns documentos,* (Lisboa, MDCCCXCII), pp. 65-68; and Calvo's *Recueil complet de traités de l'Amérique latine* (Paris, 1862), i (premiere période), pp. 1-15, in both Latin and Spanish versions. For the Bull of September 25 we have used the Spanish text, which Navarrete gives *ut supra*, pp. 404-406 (449-451, 2d ed.)—Solorzano's Latin version, which has been followed by Hernaez and other editors, being probably only a retranslation from the Spanish. For good discussions of these bulls and of the Demarcation Line, with abundant citations of authorities, see Bourne's "Demarcation Line of Pope Alexander VI," in *Amer. Hist. Assn. Rep.*, 1891, pp. 101-130 (republished in *Yale Review*, May, 1892), and in his *Essays in Historical Criticism* (N. Y., 1901), pp. 193-217; S.E. Dawson's "Lines of Demarcation of Pope Alexander VI, and the Treaty of Tordesillas," in *Canad. Roy. Soc. Trans.*, 1899, sec. ii, pp. 467-546; and Harrisse's *Diplomatic History of America* (London, 1897).

Treaty of Tordesillas (June 7, 1494).—The original MS. of this document is in the Seville archives—pressmark, "Simancas—Bulas; est. 1, caj. 1, leg. 1." It is also found in the Torre do Tombo of Lisbon—its pressmark being "Gaveta 17, maço 2, n°. 24;" there is another copy—pressmark "Gaveta 18, maço 2, n°. 2"—apparently a duplicate of the former. The text of the treaty is published in G. Fa de Martens's *Traités de l'Europe, Supplément* (Gottingue, 1802), i, pp. 372-388; Navarrete's *Col. de viages*, ii, pp. 130-143 (147-162, 2nd ed.); *Alguns documentos,* pp. 69-80; Calvo's *Recueil de traités*, i, pp. 16-36; and *Doc. inéd. Amér. y Oceania*, xxxvi, pp. 54-74. Our translation is made from the version in *Alguns documentos*, as that most closely following the original; and in foot-notes are indicated some of the variations of Navarrete's text from that in *Alguns documentos*.

Compact between the monarchs of Spain and Portugal (April 15, 1495).—The original MS. of this document is in the Seville archives "Patronato Real." We translate from Navarrete, *ut supra*, ii, pp. 170-173 (192-195, 2d ed.). It is published also in *Doc. inéd. Amér. y Oceania*, xxxviii, pp. 336-341.

Papal Bull, Præcelsæ (Nov. 3, 1514).—The original of this bull exists in Torre do Tombo, Lisbon—pressmark, "Maço 20 de bullas, n°. 18;" it is written on parchment, and covers twenty folios. It is printed in full in *Corpo diplomatico portuguez* (Lisboa, 1862), i, pp. 275-298; and a brief synopsis is given (in Portuguese) in *Alguns documentos*, p. 366. We present a similar synopsis, with a short extract from the bull.

Letters of Cárlos I (1523).—The originals of these documents are in the Seville archives, in "Patronato Real." We translate from the text in Navarrete, *ut supra*, vol. iv (1837), as follows: instructions to the ambassadors, pp. 301-305; letter to Zúñiga, pp. 312-320.

Treaty of Vitoria (Feb. 19, 1524).—The original is in the Seville archives—pressmark, "Papeles del Maluco, de 1519 á 1547, leg°. 1°." The translation here published is made from Navarrete, *ut supra*, pp. 320-326.

Junta of Badajoz (April-May, 1524).—The originals of these documents are at Seville, in the "Patronato Real." The copies made therefrom by Juan Bautista Muñoz, in pursuance of orders given him by Cárlos IV to write a history of Spanish discovery and conquest, are in the library of the Real Academia de la Historia, Madrid. Our translations and synopses are made from Navarrete's text, *ut supra*, as follows: extract from the records of possession and ownership, pp. 355-368; opinions of Spanish astronomers and pilots, pp. 333-355; letters to Spanish deputies, pp. 326-333.

Treaty of Zaragoza (April 22, 1529).—The original of this document is in Torre do Tombo, Lisbon—pressmark, "Gaveta 18, maco 8, n°. 29." Our translation is made from the text in *Alguns documentos*, pp. 495-512. This treaty has been published also in Navarrete, *ut supra*, pp. 389-406; and in Martens's *Supp. Traités de l'Europe*, i, pp. 398-421. It was appended to the treaty of 1750 between Spain and Portugal.

Papal Bull, Eximiæ (Nov. 16, 1501)

Our translation is made from Navarrete, *ut supra*, ii, pp. 408, 409 (454, 455, 2d ed.). The bull is published also in Hernaez's *Col. de bulas*, i, pp. 20-25; and in *Doc. inéd. Amér. y Oceania* xxxiv, pp. 22-29.

Life and Voyage of Fernao de Magalhaes

Our résumé of various contemporary documents is made from Navarrete, *ut supra*, iv (1837), pp. 110-406. The MS. of the letter of authorization to Falero and Magallánes is in Torre do Tombo, Lisbon—pressmark, "Gaveta 18, maço 8, n°. 39." It is published in *Alguns documentos*, pp. 418, 419, from which our translation is made. The originals of the letters of 1519 (from copies of which we translate except instructions to Cartagena, from *Alguns documentos*) are in Torre do Tombo—their respective pressmarks as follows: letter of Cárlos I to Manuel, "Gaveta 18, maço 5, n°. 26;" instructions to Cartagena, "Corpo chron., parte *3a*, maço 7, n°. 18;" letter of Cárlos I to Magallánes and Falero, "Corpo chron., parte *1a*, maço 24, n°. 64." These letters are published in *Alguns documentos*, pp. 422-430. The letter of 1522 is translated from a copy of the original MS. in the Simancas archives—pressmark, "Secretaria de Estada, leg. 367, fol. 94."

De Molvccis Insulis. The first edition of this book was printed in January, 1523, at Cologne, by Hirzhorn (Latinized as Cervicornus). In November, 1523, it was published at Rome by Minitius Calvus, also second edition February, 1524. There has been much controversy regarding the priority of the Cologne edition, some writers claiming that it was really issued in 1524; but the question is apparently settled by the fact that Johann Schöner cites the book in his letter (written in 1523) to Reimer von Stréitberg (Streytpergk); see Stevens's *Johann Schoner* (London, MDCCCLXXXVIII), pp. 99, 153. We reproduce here the translation made by the late Henry Stevens *(ut supra*, pp. 103-146); it is accompanied therein (pp. 57-90) by a phototypographic facsimile of the original print. Fuller details regarding this work will appear in the volume devoted to bibliography, which will be published at the end of this series.

CHRONOLOGICAL TABLES

1493-1803

List of Roman Pontiffs

Alexander VI (Rodrigo Borgia, or Lenzuoli).—Born Jan. 1, 1431; became pontiff, Aug. 11, 1492; died Aug. 18, 1503.

Pius III (Francesco Todischini Piccolomini).—Born May 9, 1439; became pontiff, Sept. 22, 1503; died Oct. 18, 1503.

Julius II (Guiliano della Rovere).—Born Dec. 15, 1443; became pontiff, Oct. 31 or Nov. 1, 1503; died Feb. 2, 1513.

Leo X (Giovanni de' Medici).—Born Dec. 11, 1475; became pontiff, March 11, 1513; died Dec. 1, 1521.

Hadrianus VI (Florian Boyers).—Born Mar. 2, 1459; became pontiff, Jan. 9, 1522; died Sept. 14, 1523.

Clemens VII (Giulio de' Medici).—Born 1475 (?); became pontiff, Nov. 19, 1523; died Sept. 26, 1534.

Paulus III (Alessandro Farnese).—Born Feb. 28, 1468; became pontiff, Oct. 13, 1534; died Nov. 10, 1549.

Julius III (Giovanni Maria de Ciocchi del Monte).—Born Sept. 10, 1487; became pontiff, Feb. 8, 1550; died Mar. 23, 1555.

Marcellus II (Marcello Cervini).—Born May 6, 1501; became pontiff, Apr. 9, 1555; died May 1, 1555.

Paulus IV (Giovanni Pietro Caraffa).—Born June 28, 1476; became pontiff, May 23, 1555; died Aug. 18, 1559.

Pius IV (Giovanni Angelo de' Medici).—Born Mar. 31, 1499; became pontiff, Dec. 26, 1559; died Dec. 9, 1565.

Pius V (Michele Ghisleri).—Born Jan. 17, 1504; became pontiff, Jan. 7, 1566; died May 1, 1572.

Gregorius XIII (Ugo Buoncompagno).—Born Feb. 7, 1502; became pontiff, May 13, 1572; died Apr. 10, 1585.

Sixtus V (Felice Peretto).—Born Dec. 13, 1521; became pontiff, Apr. 24, 1585; died Aug. 27, 1590.

Urbanus VII (Giovanni Battista Castagna).—Born Aug. 4, 1521; became pontiff, Sept. 15, 1590; died Sept. 27, 1590.

Gregorius XIV (Nicola Sfondrati).—Born Feb. 11, 1535; became pontiff, Dec. 5, 1590; died Oct. 15, 1591.

Innocentius IX (Giovanni Antonio Facchinetti).—Born July 20, 1519; became pontiff, Oct. 29, 1591; died Dec. 30, 1591.

Clemens VIII (Ippolito Aldobrandini).—Born Feb. 24, 1536; became pontiff, Jan. 30, 1592; died Mar. 3, 1605.

Leo XI (Alessandro Ottaviano de' Medici).—Born 1535; became pontiff, Apr. 1, 1605; died Apr. 27, 1605.

Paulus V (Camillo Borghese).—Born Sept. 17, 1552; became pontiff, May 16, 1605; died Jan. 28, 1621.

Gregorius XV (Alessandro Ludovisio).—Born Jan. 9, 1554; became pontiff, Feb. 9, 1621; died July 8, 1623.

Urbanus VIII (Maffeo Barberini).—Born Mar. 26, 1568; became pontiff, Aug. 6, 1623; died July 29, 1644.

Innocentius X (Giovanni Battista Pamfilio).—Born Mar. 7, 1572 (or 1573); became pontiff, Sept. 15, 1644; died Jan. 7, 1655.

Alexander VII (Fabio Chigi).—Born Feb. 13, 1599; became pontiff, Apr. 7, 1655; died May 22, 1667.

Clemens IX (Giulio Rospigliosi).—Born Jan. 28, 1600; became pontiff, June 20, 1667; died Dec. 9, 1669.

Clemens X (Giovanni Battista Emilio Altieri).—Born July 15, 1590; became pontiff, Apr. 29, 1670; died July 22, 1676.

Innocentius XI (Benedetto Odescalchi).—Born May 16, 1611; became pontiff, Sept. 21, 1676; died Aug. 12, 1689.

Alexander VIII (Pietro Ottoboni).—Born Apr. 10, 1610; became pontiff, Oct. 6, 1689; died Feb. 1, 1691.

Innocentius XII (Antonio Pignatelli).—Born Mar. 13, 1615; became pontiff, July 12, 1691; died Sept. 27, 1700.

Clemens XI (Giovanni Francesco Albani).—Born July 23, 1649; became pontiff, Nov. 23, 1700; died Mar. 19, 1721.

Innocentius XIII (Michel Angelo Conti).—Born May 15, 1655; became pontiff, May 8, 1722; died Mar. 7, 1724.

Benedictus XIII (Vicenzo Marco Orsino).—* Born Feb. 2, 1649; became pontiff, May 29, 1724; died Feb. 21, 1730.

Clemens XII (Lorenzo Corsini).—Born Apr. 11 (?), 1652; became pontiff, July 12, 1730; died Feb. 6, 1740.

Benedictus XIV (Prospero Lambertini).—Born Mar. 31, 1675; became pontiff, Aug. 17, 1740; died May 3, 1758.

Clemens XIII (Carlo Rezzonico).—Born Mar. 17, 1693; became pontiff, July 6, 1758; died Feb. 2, 1769.

Clemens XIV (Giovanni Vincenzo Antonio Ganganelli).—Born Oct. 31, 1705; became pontiff, May 19, 1769; died Sept. 22, 1774.

Pius VI (Giovanni Angelo Braschi).—Born Dec. 27, 1717; became pontiff, Feb. 15, 1775; died Aug. 29, 1799.

Pius VII (Gregorio Barnaba Luigi Chiaramonti).—Born Aug. 14, 1742; became pontiff, Mar. 14, 1800; died Aug. 20, 1823.

List of the Rulers of Spain

House of Castilla and Aragon

Isabel I of Castilla.—Born at Madrigal de las Altas Torres (Avila), April 22, 1451; daughter of Juan II of Castilla and Isabel of Portugal. Married Fernando II of Aragón, Oct. 18 or 19, 1469. Succeeded her brother Enrique IV on the throne of Castilla and Leon; proclaimed queen Dec. 13, 1474. Died at Medina del Campo (Valladolid), Nov. 26, 1504. Named as her heirs her daughter Juana and the latter's husband, Philip of Austria; and appointed Fernando (now V of Castilla) regent of Castilla and León during the minority of Juana's son Cárlos. Fernando and Isabel were styled "the Catholic Sovereigns."

Fernando V of Castilla (II of Aragón and Navarra).—Born at Sos (Zaragoza), May 10, 1452; son of Juan II and Juana Enriquez of Aragón and Navarra. Died at Madrigalejo, Jan. 23, 1516. During Isabel's life, was king-consort, and governed her dominions only by virtue of this relation; after her death, was regent only of Castilla, which dignity he held until his death, except from June 27, 1506, to Aug. 21, 1507, during which period he retired to Aragón, in favor of Juana's husband Philip. Inheriting the throne of Aragón and Navarra (Jan. 20, 1479), his marriage with Isabel (1469) and their conquest of Granada (1492) united under one monarchy the provinces now comprised in the country of Spain.

Juana.—Born at Toledo, in 1479; second daughter of Isabel and Fernando. Married Philip of Austria, Oct. 20 or 21, 1496. Died at Tordesillas, April 11, 1555. Reigned from Nov. 26, 1504, until her death—jointly with her husband, during his life; and with her son thereafter—but under her father's regency until 1516; during her reign she was more or less subject to insanity, and was but nominally queen, seldom exercising royal powers, and living in strict seclusion. Known as "la Loca," "the Mad."

House of Austria

Felipe I (Philip of Austria).—Born at Bruges, July 22, 1478; son of Maximilian I, emperor of Germany, and Maria de Borgoña. By his marriage to Juana, was king-consort of Castilla from Nov. 26, 1504, until his death. Died at Búrgos, Sept. 25, 1506. Styled "el Hermoso," "the Beautiful."

Cárlos I (Charles V, emperor of Germany).—Born at Ghent, Feb. 25, 1500; son of Felipe I and Juana. Landed in Spain in 1517. Married Isabel of Portugal (daughter of Manoel), March 11, 1526. Abdicated in favor of his son Felipe II, Jan. 16, 1556; died at monastery of Yuste, Aug. 30, 1558. Elected Emperor of Germany in June, 1519. Reigned over Spain jointly with Juana. During his minority, Fernando was regent until his death (1516); thereafter Cardinal Jiminez (Ximenes) de Cisneros acted in that capacity until the latter's death (Nov. 8, 1517); with the cardinal was associated, nominally, Adrian, dean of Louvain.

Felipe II.—Born at Vallodolid, May 21, 1527; son of Cárlos I and Isabel. Married Maria, daughter of João III of Portugal, Nov. 15, 1543; Mary Tudor of England, July 25, 1554; Marie Elisabeth of Valois, Feb. 2, 1560; Anna of Austria, in 1570. Acted as regent for his father from June 23, 1551 until March 28, 1556, when he was proclaimed king. Died at the Escorial, Sept. 13, 1598. Became king of Portugal in April, 1581, taking the oath at Lisbon.

Felipe III.—Born at Madrid, April 14, 1578; son of Felipe II and Anna of Austria. Married Margaret of Austria, Nov. 13, 1598, two months after his accession to the throne. Died at Madrid, March 31, 1621. Surnamed "el Piadoso," "the Pious."

Felipe IV.—Born at Valladolid, April 8, 1605; son of Felipe III and Margaret. Married Isabel of Bourbon, in 1615; Mariana of Austria, in 1649. Succeeded his father as king, and died at Madrid, Sept. 17, 1665. The sovereignty of Spain over Portugal ceased Dec. 1, 1640.

Cárlos II.—Born Nov. 6, 1661; son of Felipe IV and Mariana. Married Marie Louise of Orleans, in 1679; Mariana of Bavaria, in 1690. Died Nov. 1, 1700, the last Spanish ruler of the house of Austria. During his minority his mother was regent (Sept. 17, 1665 to Nov. 16, 1675). Surnamed "el Hechizado," "the Bewitched."

House of Bourbon

Felipe V (Philip of Anjou).—Born at Versailles, Dec. 19, 1683; son of Louis, dauphin of France, and Mariana of Bavaria. Proclaimed king Nov. 24, 1700. Married Maria Louisa of Savoy, Sept. 11, 1701; Isabel Farnese, Sept. 16, 1714. Abdicated in favor of his son Luis I, Jan. 10, 1724; but resumed the government on Sept. 6 following, in consequence of Luis's death. Died at Madrid, July 9, 1746. The Spanish crown was bequeathed to him by Cárlos II.

Luis I.—Born Aug. 5, 1707; son of Felipe V and Maria Louisa. Married Louise Elisabeth of Orleans, Nov. 16, 1721. By his father's abdication of the throne Luis was nominally king from Jan. 19, 1724 until his death, Aug. 31 following.

Fernando VI.—Born Sept. 23, 1713; son of Felipe V and Maria Louisa. Married Maria Teresa Barbara of Braganza, Jan. 19, 1729. Died at Villaviciosa de Odon (Madrid), Aug. 10, 1759.

Cárlos III.—Born at Madrid, Jan. 20, 1716; son of Felipe V and Isabel Farnese. Married Maria Amalia of Saxony. Died at Madrid, Dec. 14, 1788.

Cárlos IV.—Born Nov. 11, 1748; son of Cárlos III. Married Maria Louisa of Parma. Proclaimed king, Jan. 17, 1789; abdicated the throne March 18, 1808; died at Naples, Jan. 19, 1819.

List of the Rulers of Portugal

House of Aviz

João II.—Born at Lisbon, May 3, 1455; son of Affonso V. Married Leonor de Lancaster, Jan. 22, 1471. Reigned from Aug. 31, 1481 until his death. Died at Villa de Alvor, Oct. 25, 1495. Styled "the Perfect Prince," also "the Great," and "the Severe."

Manoel.—Born May 31, 1469; cousin of João II. Married Isabel of Castilla (eldest daughter of Fernando and Isabel), in 1497; Maria, her sister, Oct. 30, 1500; Leonora, sister of Charles V of Germany in 1518. Died Dec. 13, 1521. Styled "the Fortunate."

João III.—Born at Lisbon, June 6, 1502; son of Manoel and Maria. Reigned from Dec. 19, 1521, until his death, June 11, 1557. Married Catarina sister of Charles V of Germany.

Sebastião.—Born Jan. 20, 1554; grandson of João III. Slain in battle, Aug. 4, 1578. His grandmother Catarina acted as regent during his minority (1557-68).

Henrique.—Born at Lisbon, Jan. 31, 1512; son of Manoel; became a cardinal in the Roman church. Reigned from Aug. 29, 1578 until Jan. 31, 1580; had been associated with Catarina in the regency.

Antonio.—Born in 1531; grandson (but regarded by most writers as illegitimate) of Manoel. Reigned from June 19 to Sept. 2, 1580.

House of Austria (Spain)

Filippe I.—Reigned from Sept. 2, 1580 (taking oath at Lisbon in April, 1581), to Sept. 13, 1598. See Felipe II of Spain.

Filippe II.—Reigned from Sept. 13, 1598 to Mar 31, 1621. See Felipe III of Spain.

Filippe III.—Reigned from Mar. 31, 1621 to Nov. 31, 1640. See Felipe IV of Spain.

House of Braganza

João IV.—Born March 19, 1604; son of Theodosio II, duke of Braganza, and Ana de Velasco. Married Luiza de Guzmán, Jan.

13, 1633. Reigned from Dec. 1, 1640 until his death, Nov. 6, 1656. Styled "the Fortunate."

Affonso VI.—Born Aug. 21, 1643; son of João IV and Luiza. Married Maria Francesca Isabel of Savoy, in 1666. Compelled to renounce the throne, as incompetent, Nov. 23, 1667. Died at Cintra, Sept. 12, 1683. During his minority, his mother acted as regent (Nov. 6, 1656 to June 22, 1662); during the latter part of his reign, his brother Pedro.

Pedro II.—Born April 26, 1648; son of João IV. Married Maria Francesca Isabel of Savoy, March 27, 1668; Maria Sophia Elizabeth of Bavaria, in 1687. Died Dec. 9, 1706. Regent for Affonso, from Nov. 23, 1667 until the latter's death; king, from Sept. 12, 1683 to Dec. 9, 1706.

João V.—Born at Lisbon, Oct. 22, 1689; son of Pedro II. Married Maria Anna of Austria, July 9, 1708. Reigned from Jan. 1, 1707 until his death, July 31, 1750.

José I.—Born June 6, 1714; son of João V. Married Mariana Victoria, Dec. 27, 1727. Reigned from his father's death until his own, Feb. 24, 1777.

María I.—Born in 1734; daughter of José I. Married Pedro, younger brother of José (and her uncle), in 1760. Died at Rio de Janeiro, Brazil, in 1816. Reigned jointly with her husband, Feb. 24, 1777 until his death (1786); but as she became insane, her son João VI acted as regent until her death.

Pedro III.—Reigned jointly with his wife, María I, until his death (1786).

João VI.—Born at Lisbon, May 13, 1769; son of María I and Pedro III. Married Carlotta of Spain. Reigned from Mar. 16, 1816 to March 10, 1826; but had been regent for Maria since 1799, and had been in charge of the government from March 10, 1792.

NOTES

1   Documents marked with an asterisk are printed in both the original language and English translation.

2   *The Philippine Islands, Moluccas, Siam, Cambodia, Japan, and China at the close of the Sixteenth Century*, by Antonio de Morga, Hakluyt Society, London, 1868, p. 265. This will be cited usually as Morga.

3   "The crown and sceptre of Spain has come to extend itself over all that the sun looks on, from its rising to its setting." Morga, p 6. Down to the end of the year 1844 the Manilan calendar was reckoned after that of Spain, that is, Manila time was about sixteen hours slower than Madrid time. Finally, with the approval of the Archbishop in 1844, the thirty-first of December was dropped and the Philippines transferred, so to speak, into the Eastern Hemisphere. Thenceforward Manila time was about eight hours ahead of Madrid time. Jagor: *Reisen in den Philippinen,* pp. 1-2.

4   For a fuller account of the negotiations relating to these bulls and the Treaty of Tordesillas see Harrisse: *Diplomatic History of America*, 1452-1494, S.E. Dawson: *The Lines of Demarcation of Pope Alexander VI and the Treaty of Tordesillas*, or E.G. Bourne: *Essays in Historical Criticism.* The texts are printed in this volume.

5   The names used by Columbus in his interview with the King of Portugal. Ruy de Pina: *Chronica d'el rey Joaõ II, Collecaõ de Livros Ineditos de Historia Portugueze*, ii, p. 177.

6   This is also Harrisse's view, *Diplomatic History of America*, p. 74.

7   "Sábese la concession del Papa Alexandro; la division del mundo como una naranja." Letter of Alonso de Zuazo to Charles V, January 22, 1518. *Docs. Inéd. de Indias*, i, p. 296 (From Harrisse, p. 174). Cf. also Maximilianus Transylvanus in *First Voyage Round the World by Magellan.* Hakluyt Society, p. 185.

8   The question is fully discussed in Guillemard's *Life of Ferdinand Magellan,* pp. 68-69.

9   Guillemard, *Magellan*, p. 71.

10   *First Voyage Round the World by Magellan*, p. 187.

11   Navarrete, *Coleccion de los Viages y Descubrimientos*, etc., iv, p. 117.

12   Las Casas: *Historia de las Indias. Col. de Docs. Inéd. para la Historia de España*, lxv, pp. 376-377. This account by Las Casas apparently has been overlooked by English writers on Magellan. It is noticed by Peschel, *Geschichte des Zeitalters der Entdeckungen,* p. 488.

13   See Guillemard's comparison between the voyages of Columbus and Magellan in *Life of Magellan*, p. 258.

14   See Pigafetta's account in *The First Voyage Round the World by Magellan*, p. 74.

15   Pigafetta, *ibid.*, p. 76.

16   The description of the Philippines and their inhabitants which we owe to the Italian Pigafetta who accompanied Magellan is especially noteworthy not only as the first European account of them, but also as affording a gauge by which to estimate the changes wrought by the Spanish conquest and the missions.

17   See E. G. Bourne: *Essays in Historical Criticism*, pp. 209-211 for an account of the Badajos Junta which attempted to settle the question of the rights to the Moluccas. The documents are in Navarrete, iv, pp. 333-370, a somewhat abridged translation of which is presented in this volume. Sandoval attributes the sale of the Moluccas to Charles's financial straits. Navarrete, iv, xx. The treaty of sale is in Navarrete, iv, pp. 389-406.

18   Navarrete, iv, p. 394.

19   Navarrete, iv, p. 396.

20   See the correspondence in *Col. de Doc. Inéditos de Ultramar*, vol. ii (vol. i of subdivision *de las Islas Filipinas*), p. 66.

21   *Relacion del Viaje que hizo desde la Nueva-España à las Islas del Poniente Ruy Gomez de Villalobos*, written by García Descalante Alvarado. *Coleccion de Docs. Inéd. del Archivo de Indias* v, p. 127. The name was first given in July or August 1543 to some of the smaller islands in the group. On page 122, Alvarado writes "chinos que vienen a Mindanao y à las Philipinas." Montero y Vidal says that the island first to receive the name was Leyte. *Hist. Gen. de Filipinas*, i, p. 27, In 1561, Urdaneta uses "las islas

Filipinas" in the ordinary way; see his "Derrotero" prepared for the expedition. *Col. Docs. Inéd.* vol. i, p. 130 ff.

22   *Col. de Docs. Inéd. de Ultramar*, vol. ii, pp. 95-96.

23   *Ibid.,* pp. 109-111.

24   In September, 1568, a Portuguese squadron despatched by the Governor of the Moluccas appeared off Cebu to drive the Spaniards out of the Visayan Islands. The commander satisfied himself with diplomatic protests. Montero y Vidal: *Hist. Gen. de Filipinas*, i, p. 34.

25   Montero y Vidal, i, pp. 41-42.

26   Juan de Grijalva. From W.E. Retana's extracts from his *Cronica de la Orden de N.P.S. Augustin en las provincias de la Nueva España, etc.* (1533-1592) in Retana's edition of Zúñiga's *Estadismo de las Islas Filipinas*, ii. p. 219 ff. Juan de Salcedo after being promoted to the high rank of *Maestre de Campo* (an independent command) died suddenly in 1576 at the age of twenty-seven. Far from amassing wealth in his career he died poor. In his will he provided that after the payment of his debts the residue of his property should be given to certain Indians of his *encomienda*. *Ibid.,* p. 615.

27   This account of the conversion is based on Grijalva's contemporary narrative; see Retana's *Zúñiga*, ii, pp. 219-220.

28   Montero y Vidal, i, p. 59.

29   Retana's *Zúñiga*, ii, p. 222; Morga, Hakluyt Society edition, pp. 307-308; Montero y Vidal, i, p. 60.

30   He was lieutenant to the Governor and the first justice to be appointed to the supreme court (Audiencia) on its reorganization. His *Sucesos de la islas Philipinas—Mexici ad Indos, anno 1609*, is a work of great rarity. It was reprinted in Paris in 1890 with annotations by the Filipino author and patriot, Dr. José Rizal and with an Introduction by Blumentritt. Rizal tries to show that the Filipinos have retrograded in civilization under Spanish rule; cf. Retana's comments in his Zúñiga, ii, p. 277. The references to Morga to follow are to the Hakluyt Society edition.

31   A natural transference of the familiar name in Spain for Mohammedans.

32   Morga, pp. 296-297.

33   Footnote 32: Morga. p. 323.

34   *Relacion de las Encomiendas existentes en Filipinas el dia 31 de Mayo de 1591.* in Retana: *Archivo del Bibliofilo Filipino*, iv, pp. 39-112.

35 Mendoza, *The History of the Great and Mighty Kingdom of China*. Hakluyt Society edition, ii, p. 263.

36 Printed in Retana's *Archivo*, iii, pp. 3-45.

37 "Of little avail would have been the valor and constancy with which Legaspi and his worthy companions overcame the natives of the islands, if the apostolic zeal of the missionaries had not seconded their exertions, and aided to consolidate the enterprise. The latter were the real conquerors; they who without any other arms than their virtues, gained over the good will of the islanders, caused the Spanish name to be beloved, and gave the king, as it were by a miracle, two millions more of submissive and Christian subjects." Tomas de Comyn, *State of the Philippine Islands, etc.,* translated by William Walton, London, 1821, p. 209. Comyn was the general manager of the Royal Philippine Company for eight years in Manila and is described by his latest editor, Senor del Pan, editor of the *Revista de Filipinas*, as a man of "extensive knowledge especially in the social sciences." Retana characterizes his book as "un libro de merito extraordinario," Zúñiga, ii, pp. 175-76. Mallat says: "C'est par la seule influence de la religion que l'on a conquis les Philippines, et cette influence pourra seule les conserver." *Les Philippines, histoire, geographie, moeurs, agriculture, industrie et commerce des Colonies espagnoles dans l'oceanie.* Par J. Mallat, Paris, 1846, i, p. 40. I may say that this work seems to me the best of all the modern works on the Philippines. The author was a man of scientific training who went to the islands to study them after a preparatory residence in Spain for two years.

38 Morga, p. 325.

39 Mallat, i, p. 389.

40 Morga, p. 320.

41 Mallat, i, pp. 382-385.

42 Morga, p. 312. Mallat, ii, p. 240.

43 Morga, p. 313. Mallat, ii, p. 244.

44 The first regular hospital in the thirteen colonies was the Pennsylvania Hospital, incorporated in 1751. Patients were first admitted in 1752. Cornell, *History of Pennsylvania*, pp. 409-411. There are references to a hospital in New Amsterdam in 1658, but the New York hospital was the first institution of the kind of any importance. It was founded in 1771, but patients were not admitted till 1791. *Memorial History of New York*, iv, p. 407.

There was no hospital for the treatment of general diseases in Boston until the nineteenth century. The Massachusetts General Hospital was chartered in 1811. *Memorial History of Boston*, iv, p. 548.

45 Morga, p. 350.

46 Morga, p. 314.

47 Friar Juan Francisco de San Antonio who went to the Philippines in 1724, says that "up to the present time there has not been found a scrap of writing relating to religion, ceremonial, or the ancient political institutions." *Chronicás de la Apostolica Provincia de San Gregorio, etc.* (Sampoloc, near Manila, 1735), i, pp. 149-150 (cited from Retana's *Zúñiga*, ii, p. 294.

48 They used palm leaves for paper and an iron stylus for a pen. "L'escriture ne leur sert que pour s'escrire les uns aux autres, car ils n'ont point d'histoires ny de Livres d'aucune Science; nos Religieux ont imprime des livres en la langue des Isles des choses de nostre Religion." *Relation des Isles Philippines, Faite par un Religieux qui y a demeure 18 ans*, in Thévenot's *Voyages Curieux.* Paris 1663, ii (p. 5, of the "Relation"). This narrative is one of the earliest to contain a reproduction of the old Tagal alphabet. Retana ascribes it to a Jesuit and dates it about 1640: p. 13 of the catalogue of his library appended to *Archivo del Bibliofilo Filipino*, i. The earliest printed data on the Tagal language according to Retana are those given in Chirino's *Relacion de las Islas Filipinas*, Rome, 1604.

49 Mendoza's *Historie of the Kingdome of China*, volume ii, p. 263.

50 *Ibid.*, p. 264.

51 Morga, p. 319.

52 *Relation d'un Religieux*, Thévenot, volume ii, (p. 7 of the Relation).

53 On the powers of the Governor, see Morga, pp. 344-345.

54 Throughout this Introduction the Spanish "peso" is rendered by "dollar." The reader will bear in mind the varying purchasing power of the dollar. To arrive at an approximate equivalent ten may be used as a multiplier for the sixteenth and early seventeenth centuries, and five for the middle of the eighteenth century.

55 It may be remembered that the official conscience in the seventeenth and eighteenth centuries was not so sensitive in regard to "tips" as it is expected to be today. Le Gentil writes:

"Les Gouverneurs de Manille corrompent journellement leurs grâces, et les Manillois ne les abordent guère pour leur en demander, sans se précautioner auparavant du rameau d'or; seul et unique moyen de se les rendre favorables. Un soir étant allé voir le Gouverneur, in 1767, à peine m'eût-il demandé des nouvelles de ma senté qu'il alla me chercher une bouteille de verre de chopine, mesure de Paris, (half-pint) pleine de paillettes d'or, il me la fit voir en me disant que c'étoit un présént dont on l'avoit *régalé* ce jour-là même; *Oi,* me dit-il, *me regalaron de este."* *Voyage dans Les Mers de L'Inde,* Paris, 1781, ii, pp. 152-153. Le Gentil was in the Philippines about eighteen months in 1766-67 on a scientific mission. His account of conditions there is one of the most thorough and valuable that we have for the eighteenth century. As a layman and man of science his views are a useful offset against those of the clerical historians.

56   *Voyage,* ii, p. 153. "The Royal Audience was established to restrain the despotism of the Governors, which it has never prevented; for the gentlemen of the gown are always weak-kneed and the Governor can send them under guard to Spain, pack them oft to the provinces to take a census of the Indians or imprison them, which has been done several times without any serious consequences." Zúñiga: *Estadismo de las Islas Filipinos o mis Viages por este Pais,* ed. Retana, i, p. 244.

57   "Cuando se pusieren edictos, publicaren, y pregonaren las residencias, sea de forma que vengan á noticia de los Indios, para que puedan pedir justicia de sus agravios con entera libertad." *Law of 1556,* lib. v, tit. xv, ley xxviii of the *Recopilacion de Leyes de los Reinos de las Indias.*

58   *Recopilacion,* lib. v, tit. xv, ley vii.

59   Churchill's *Voyages,* iv, pp. 427-428.

60   "I request the reader not to infer from my opinion of the tribunals of residence, my confidence in their efficacy. My homage is immediately and solely addressed to the wisdom of the law. I resign all criticism on its operation, to those who know the seductive influence of Plutus over the feeble and pliant Themis." De Pons: *Voyage to the Eastern Part of Terra Firma or the Spanish Main in South America during the years 1801, 1802, 1803, and 1804.* New York, 1806, ii, p. 25.

61   "Une loi très-sage, mais malheureusement sans effet, qui devrait modérer cette autorité excessive, est celle qui permet à

chaque citoyen de poursuivre le gouverneur vétéran devant son successeur; mais celui-ci est intéressé à excuser tout ce qu'on reproche à son prédécesseur; et le citoyen assez téméraire pour se plaindre, est exposé à de nouvelles et à de plus fortes vexations." *Voyage de La Pérouse autour du Monde.* Paris, 1797, ii, p. 350.

62   His comments on the kind of officials needed are not without interest today: "A governor must understand war but he must not be over confident of his abilities. Let him give ear to the advice of those who know the country where things are managed very differently from what they are in Europe. Those who have tried to carry on war in the islands as it is carried on in Flanders and elsewhere in Europe have fallen into irreparable mistakes. The main thing, however, is to aim at the welfare of the people, to treat them kindly, to be friendly toward foreigners, to take pains to have the ships for New Spain sail promptly and in good order, to promote trade with neighboring people and to encourage ship-building. In a word, to live with the Indians rather like a father than like a governor." *Relation et Memorial de l'etat des Isles Philippines, et des Isles Moluques* by Ferdinand de los Rios Coronel, Prestre et Procureur General des Isles Philippines, etc. *Thevenot,* ii (p. 23 of the Relation).

63   Morga, p. 345. *Recopilacion,* lib. ii, tit. xv, ley xi.

64   *Ibid.,* ley lviii. Le Gentil, ii, pp. 159, 161.

65   *Recopilacion,* lib. ii, tit. xv, ley xi.

66   Mallat, i, pp. 349-50. For a historical summary of the variations in the names of the provinces see Retana's Zúñiga's *Estadismo,* ii, p. 376 ff.

67   They received the tribute in kind in fixed amounts and made money out of the fluctuations of the market prices. At times of scarcity and consequent high prices this procedure doubled or trebled the burden of the tribute. See *State of the Philippine Islands,* by Tomas de Comyn, translated by William Walton, p. 197. Mallat says: "Rien n'est plus funeste au pays que la permission qui est accordée aux alcaldes de faire le commerce pour leur compte." i, p. 351. See also Retana's note, Zúñiga, *Estadismo,* ii, p. 530. This right to trade was abolished in 1844.

68   "It is a fact common enough to see a hair-dresser or a lackey converted into a governor; a sailor or a deserter, transformed

into a district magistrate, collector, or military commander of a populous province, without other counsellor than his own crude understanding, or any other guide than his passions. Such a metamorphosis would excite laughter in a comedy or farce; but, realized in the theatre of human life, it must give rise to sensations of a very different nature. Who is there that does not feel horror-struck, and tremble for the innocent, when he sees a being of this kind transferred from the yard-arm to the seat of justice, deciding in the first instance on the honor, lives, and property of a hundred thousand persons, and haughtily exacting the homage and incense of the spiritual ministers of the towns under his jurisdiction, as well as of the parish curates, respectable for their acquirements and benevolence, and who in their own native places, would possibly have rejected as a servant the very man whom in the Philippines they are compelled to court, and obey as a sovereign." *State of the Philippine Islands*, London, 1821, p. 194.

69   Morga, p. 323.

70   Jagor describes an election which he saw in the town of Lauane, of four thousand five hundred inhabitants, in the little island of the same name which lies just off the north shore of Samar. As it is the only description of such a local election that I recall I quote it in full. "It took place in the town house. At the table sits the Governor or his proxy, on his right the pastor and on his left the secretary who is the interpreter. All the Cabezas de Barangay, the Gobernadorcillo and those who have formerly been such have taken their places on the benches. In the first place six of the Cabezas, and six of the ex-Gobernadorcillos respectively are chosen by lot to serve as electors. The Gobernadorcillo in office makes the thirteenth. The rest now leave the room. After the chairman has read the rules and exhorted the electors to fulfil their duty conscientiously, they go one by one to the table and write three names on a ballot. Whoever receives the largest number of votes is forthwith nominated for Gobernadorcillo for the ensuing year, if the pastor or the electors make no well-founded objections subject to the confirmation of the superior court in Manila, which is a matter of course since the influence of the pastor would prevent an unsuitable choice. The same process was followed in the election of the other

local officials except that the new Gobernadorcillo was called in that he might make any objections to the selections. The whole transaction was very quiet and dignified." *Reisen in den Philippinen*, Berlin, 1873, pp. 189-190.

Sir John Bowring's account of this system of local administration is the clearest of those I have found in English books. *A Visit to the Philippine Islands*, London, 1859, pp. 89-93.

71   The Gobernadorcillo in council with the other Cabezas presented a name to the superior authority for appointment Bowring, p. 90.

72   Zúñiga, *Estadismo de las Islas Filipinas*, i, p. 245. Cf. Mallat, i, p. 358.

73   Comyn: *State of the Philippine Islands*, ch. vii.

74   Mallat, i, pp. 40, 386. Jagor, pp. 95-97.

75   Mallat, i, p. 380 ff. Comyn, p. 212 ff.

76   Mallat, i, p. 365.

77   Morga, p. 333.

78   Delgado: *Historia de Filipinas*, Biblioteca Histories Filipina, Manila, 1892, pp. 155-156. Delgado wrote in 1750-51. Somewhat different figures are given by Le Gentil on the basis of the official records in 1735, ii, p. 182. His total is 705,903 persons.

79   Le Gentil, i, p. 186.

80   *Recopilacion*, lib. vi, tit iii, ley xxi. Morga, p. 330.

"Avec toutes les recommandations possible, il arrive encore que le moine chargé de la peuplade par où vous voyagez, vous laisse rarement parler seul aux Indiens. Lorsque vous parlez en sa présence à quelque Indien qui entend un peu le Castillan, si ce Religieux trouve mauvais que vous conversiez trop long-temps avec ce Naturel, il lui fait entendre dans la langue du pays, de ne vous point répondre en Castillan, mais dans sa langue: l'Indien obéit." Le Gentil, ii, p. 185.

81   *State of the Philippine Islands*, pp. 216-217. These responsibilities and the isolation from Europeans together with the climate frequently brought on insanity. Le Gentil, ii, p. 129. Mallat, i, p. 388.

82   *Ibid.*, p. 214.

83   In 1637 the military force maintained in the islands consisted of one thousand seven hundred and two Spaniards and one

hundred and forty Indians. *Memorial de D. Juan Grau y Monfalcon, Procurador General de las Islas Filipinas, Docs. Inéditos del Archivo de Indias*, vi, p. 425. In 1787 the garrison at Manila consisted of one regiment of Mexicans comprising one thousand three hundred men, two artillery companies of eighty men each, three cavalry companies of fifty men each. La Pérouse, ii, p. 368.

84 *Apuntes Interesantes sobre Las Islas Filipinas, etc., escritos por un Español de larga esperiencia en el pais y amante del progresso*, Madrid, 1869, p. 13. This very interesting and valuable work was written in the main by Vicente Barrantes, who was a member of the Governor's council and his secretary. On the authorship see Retana's *Archivo ii, Biblioteca Gen.*, p. 25, which corrects his conjecture published in his Zúñiga, ii, p. 135.

85 *Apuntes Interesantes*, pp. 42-43.

86 Zúñiga, *Estadismo*, i, p. 246; Le Gentil, ii, p. 172.

87 Le Gentil, ii, p. 172.

88 Morga, p. 336.

89 Morga, *ibid*.

90 *Memorial dado al Rey por D. Juan Grau y Monfalcon, Procurado General de las Islas Filipinas. Docs. Inéditos del Archivo de Indias*, vi, p. 444.

91 *Recopilacion*, lib. ix, tit. xxxv, ley vi and ley xv. As will be seen there was usually only one ship.

92 *Ibid.*, ley xxxiv.

93 *Ibid.*, ley lxviii.

94 *Ibid.*, ley lxxviii.

95 *Ibid.*, ley xlv.

96 Morga, p. 344. Zúñiga, i, pp. 271-274. "El barco de Acapulco ha sido la causa de que los espanoles hayan abandonado las riquezas naturales e industriales de las Islas." *Ibid.*, p. 443.

97 Le Gentil, ii, pp. 203-230; Zúñiga, i, p. 266 ff.

98 Le Gentil, ii, p. 205; Careri, *Voyage Round the World*, Churchill's *Voyages*, iv, p. 477.

99 Zúñiga, i, p. 267.

100 Le Gentil, ii, p. 205.

101 Le Gentil, ii, p. 207.

102 Zúñiga, i, p. 268.

103 Churchill's *Voyages*, iv, p. 491. I am aware that grave doubts as to the reality of Gemelli Careri's travels existed in the eighteenth

century. Robertson says "it seems now to be a received opinion (founded as far as I know, on no good evidence) that Careri was never out of Italy, and that his famous *Giro del Mondo* is an account of a fictitious voyage." Note 150, *History of America*. The most specific charges against Careri relate to his account of his experiences in China. See Prévost's *Histoire des Voyages*, v, pp. 469-70. His description of the Philippines and of the voyage to Acapulco is full of details that have every appearance of being the result of personal observation. In fact, I do not see how it is possible that this part of his book is not authentic. The only book of travels which contains a detailed account of the voyage from Manila to Acapulco written before Careri published that is described in Medina's *Bibliografía Española de Filipinas* is the *Peregrinacion del Mundo del Doctor D. Pedro Cubero Sebastian*, of which an edition was published in 1682 in Naples, Careri's own home; but Careri's account is no more like Cubero's than any two descriptions of the same voyage are bound to be; nor is it clear that Careri ever saw Cubero Sebastian's narrative.

104   Zúñiga, i, p. 268. Careri mentions the case of a Dominican who paid five hundred dollars for the eastern passage. *Op. cit.* p. 478; on page 423 he says the usual fare for cabin and diet was five hundred to six hundred dollars.

105   Churchill's *Voyages*, iv, p. 499.

106   *Op. cit.* p. 491. Yet Careri had no such experience as befell Cubero Sebastian in his voyage. When they were nearing the end of the voyage a very fatal disease, "el berben, o mal de Loanda" (probably the same as beri-beri), broke out, as well as dysentery, from which few escaped who were attacked. There were ninety-two deaths in fifteen days. Out of four hundred persons on board, two hundred and eight died before Acapulco was reached. *Peregrination del Mundo de D. Pedro Cubero Sebastian*, Zaragoza, 1688, p. 268.

107   Careri: *Op. cit.* p. 503.

108   Montero y Vidal: *Hist. Gen. de Filipinas*, i, pp. 458, 463. On page 461 is a brief bibliography of the history of Philippine commerce. According to Montero y Vidal, the best modern history of Philippine commerce is *La Libertad de comercio en las islas Filipinas,* by D. Manuel de Azcarraga y Palmero, Madrid, 1872.

109   Montero y Vidal, ii, p. 122.

110   *Ibid.*, ii, p. 297.

111   Comyn: *State of the Philippine Islands*, pp. 83-97.

112   *Estadismo*, i, p. 272.

113   Zúñiga, i, p. 274.

Le Gentil remarked that as the Spaniards in Manila had no landed estates to give them an assured and permanent income, they were dependent upon the Acapulco trade, and had no resources to fall back upon if the galleon were lost. Money left in trust was often lost or embezzled by executors or guardians, and it was rare that wealth was retained three generations in the same family. *Voyage*, ii, pp. 110-112.

114   Of the commerce with China it is not necessary to speak at length, as a full account of it is given in Morga. It was entirely in the hands of the Chinese and Mestizos and brought to Manila oriental textiles of all kinds, objects of art, jewelry, metal work and metals, nails, grain, preserves, fruit, pork, fowls, domestic animals, pets, "and a thousand other gewgaws and ornaments of little cost and price which are valued among the Spaniards." (Morga, p. 339.) Besides the Chinese, that with Japan, Borneo, the Moluccas, Siam, and India was so considerable that in spite of the obstructions upon the commerce with America, Manila seemed to the traveler Careri (p. 444) "one of the greatest places of trade in the world."

115   *Documentos Inéditos del Archivo de Indias*, v, pp. 475-77.

116   It would be vain to guess how many hundred people there are who are familiar with the denunciations of Las Casas to one who knows anything of the more than six hundred laws defining the status and aiming, at the protection of the Indians in the *Recopilacion*.

117   Cf. Jagor: *Reisen in den Philippinen*, p. 31.

118   *Voyage de La Pérouse autour du Monde*, Paris, 1797, ii, p. 347.

119   *History of the Indian Archipelago, etc.*, by John Crawfurd, F. R. S. Edinburgh, 1820, vol. ii, pp. 447-48.

120   That I take to be his meaning. His words are: "Ces institutions (i. e., the local administration) si sages et si paternelles ont valu à l'Espagne la conservation d'une colonie dont les habitants jouissent, à notre avis, de plus de liberté, de bonheur et de tranquilleté que-ceux d'aucune autre nation." i, p. 357. Cf. also his final chapter: "L'idigène des Philippines est l'homme plus

heureux du monde. Malgré son tribut, il n'est pas d'être vivant en société qui paye moins d'impôt que lui. Il est libre, il est heureux et ne pense nullement à se soulever." ii, p. 369.

121   *A Visit to the Philippine Islands*, London, 1859, p. 18. Cf. the recent opinion of the English engineer, Frederic H. Sawyer, who lived in Luzon for fourteen years. "The islands were badly governed by Spain, yet Spaniards and natives lived together in great harmony, and I do not know where I could find a colony in which Europeans mixed as much socially with the natives. Not in Java, where a native of position must dismount to salute the humblest Dutchman. Not in British India, where the Englishwoman has now made the gulf between British and native into a bottomless pit." *The Inhabitants of the Philippines*, New York, 1900. p. 125.

122   *Reisen in den Philippinen*, p. 287.

123   *Cornhill Magazine*, 1878, pp. 161, 167. This article is reprinted in Palgrave's *Ulysses, or Scenes in Many Lands*.

124   *The Inhabitants of the Philippines*, pp. vi, viii.

125   "Ils font voir beaucoup d'inclination et d'empressement pour aller á l'église lesjours de Fêtes et Solemnités; mais pour ouir la Messe les jours de preceptes, pour se confesser et communier lorsque la Sainte Église l'ordonne, il faut employer le fouet, et les traiter comme des enfans à l'école." Quoted by Le Gentil, ii, p. 61, from Friar Juan Francisco de San Antonio's *Chronicas de la Apostolica Provincia de San Gregorio, etc.*, commonly known as the *Franciscan History*. It will be remembered that in our own country in the eighteenth century college discipline was still enforced by corporal punishment; and that attendance upon church was compulsory, where there was an established church, as in New England.

126   *Voyage*, ii, p. 62.

127   *Voyage*, ii, p. 350.

128   *Voyage*, ii, pp. 95, 97.

129   Le Gentil says the lassitude of the body reacts upon the mind. "In this scorching region one can only vegetate. Insanity is commonly the result of hard study and excessive application." *Voyage*, ii, p. 94.

130   *La Imprenta en Manila desde sus origenes hasta 1810*, Santiago de Chile, 1896.

131   *Adiciones y Observaciones à La Imprenta en Manila*, Madrid, 1899.

132   For representative lists of these, see Blumentritt's privately printed *Bibliotheca Philippina*, Theile i and ii.

133   It is, all things considered, a singular fact that in all that list there is no translation of parts of the Bible, except of course the fragmentary paraphrases in the catechism and doctrinals. The only item indicating first-hand Biblical study in the Philippines under the old regime that has come to my notice in the bibliographies of Medina and Retana is this, that Juan de la Concepcion the historian left in manuscript a translation of the Holy Bible into Spanish. *La Imprenta en Manila*, p. 221. This failure to translate the Bible into the native languages was not peculiar to Spanish rule in the Philippines. Protestant Holland, far behind Spain in providing for native education, was equally opposed to the circulation of the Bible. "Even as late as the second or third decade of this century the New Testament was considered a revolutionary work, and Herr Bruckner, who translated it, had his edition destroyed by Government." Guillemard, *Malaysia and the Pacific Archipelagoes*, p. 129.

134   Mallat says that the elements were more generally taught than in most of the country districts of Europe (i, p. 386) and quotes the assertion of the Archbishop of Manila: "There are many villages such as Argas, Dalaguete, Bolohon, Cebu, and several in the province of Iloilo, where not a single boy or girl can be found who cannot read and write, an advantage of which few places in Europe can boast." *Ibid.*, p. 388.

135   *Estadismo*, i, p. 300.

136   *Estadismo*, i, p. 63.

137   Zúñiga, i, pp. 73-75

138   *Voyage*, ii, p. 131.

139   *Ibid.*, p. 132, and Zúñiga, i, p. 76. A modern work on this drama is *El Teatro tagalo* by Vicente Barrantes, Madrid, 1889.

140   Number 877 in Retana's *Biblioteca Filipina*. This novel was published in Manila in 1885. Friar Bustamente was a Franciscan.

141   *Estadismo*, i, pp. 60-61. Commodore Alava was on his way to make scientific observations of the volcano of Taal.

     Le Gentil writes: "Selon une Ordonnance du Roi, renouvelée peut-être cent fois, il est ordonné aux Religieux d'enseigner le castillan aux jeunes Indiens; mais Sa Majesté, m'ont unanimement assuré les Espagnoles à Manille, n'a point encore été obéie jusqu'a ce jour." *Voyage*, ii, p. 184. Cf. Zúñiga. *Estadismo*, i, pp. 299-300.

For some of these ordinances see Retana's notes to Zúñiga, ii, p. 57 ff.

142   Cf. Retana's views expressed ten years ago upon the impracticability of supplanting to any extent the Tagal language by the Spanish. The same considerations apply equally well to English. *Estadismo*, ii, p. 59 ff.

143   *Estadismo*, i, pp. 12-13.

144   Retana's *Zúñiga*, ii, p. 527.

145   *Estadismo*, i, p. 174. I cannot take leave of Zúñiga's book without recording my opinion that it is the finest flower of the Philippine literature. Zúñiga did for the island of Luzon what Arthur Young did for France a few years earlier, or to take an apter parallel, what President Dwight did for New England. His careful observations, relieved of tedium by a rare charm of style, his sweetness of temper, quiet humor, his love of nature and of man all combine to make his "Travels" a work that would be accorded a conspicuous place in the literature of any country. An English translation will appear in the present series.

146   Referring to the fort built by Columbus (December, 1492) at La Navidad, a port on the northern coast of Hispaniola (Hayti). Upon the admiral's return, a year later, he found that the garrison whom he had left in this fort had been destroyed by hostile Indians.

147   That is, by some act so clear or manifest that no formal sentence of excommunication is requisite.

148   The Gold Coast of Africa, named by its Portuguese discoverers (about 1471) *Oro de la Mina* (this is the *Minere Auri* of our text).

149   Our text reads "commissario mayor;" Navarrete reads "Comendador mayor."

150   Our text reads "vos damos todo nuestro poder conplido en aquella mas abta forma que podemos;" Navarrete reads "vos damosnuestro poder cumplido en aquella manera é forma que podemos."

151   In Navarrete the words "& subcessores & de todos nuestros reynos & señorios" are omitted.

152 Our text reads "qualqujer conçierto, asiento, limjtaçion, demarcaçion, & concordia sobre lo que dicho es, por los vientos & grados de norte & del sol, & por aquellas partes divivisiones [sic   & lugares del caelo & de la mar & de la tierra;" Navarrete reads "cualquier concierto é limitacion del mar Océano, ó concordia sobre lo que dicho es, pór los vientos y grados de Norte y Sur, y por aquellas partes, divisiones y lugares de seco y mar y de la tierra."

153 Our text reads "& asi vos damos el dicho poder pera que podays dexar al dicho Rey de Portugal & a sus reynos & subcesores todos los mares, yslas, & tieras que fueren & estovieren dentro de qualqujer limitaçion & demarcacion, que con el fincaren & quedaren;" Navarrete reads the same (with allowances for modem typography) up to "demarcaçion," and then adds "de costas, mares, islas y tierras que fincaren y quedaren."

154 Our text reads "que todos los mares, yslas & tierras, que fueren & escovjeren dentrode la limjtaçion & demarcaçion de costas, mares & yslas & tierras, que quedaren & fincaren con nos, & con nuestros subçesores, para que sean nuestros, & de nuestro señorio & conqujsta, & asi de nuestros reynos & subçesores dellos, con aquellas limjtaçjones & exebciones;" Navarrete reads "que todos las mares, islas y tierras que fueren ó estuvieren dentro el límite y demarcation de las costas, mares y islas y tierras que quedaren por Nos y por nuestros subcesores, y de nuestro Señorio y conquista, sean de nuestros Reinos y subcesores de ellos, con aquellas limitaciones y exenciones."

155 Our text reads "contrato de las pases;" Navarrete reads "contrato de las partes."

156 Navarrete reads "Sagres"

157 Our text reads "& constituymos a todos juntamente & a dos de vos, & a uno yn soljdun;" Navarrete reads "y constituimos a todos juntamente y á cada uno de vos *in solidum*."

158 See p. 116 and note 149.

159 See p. 117, and note 151, where the language is almost identical.

160 Our text reads "la qual raya olinea se aya;" Navarrete reads "la cual reya o lineo é señal se haya."

161 This paragraph reads differently in Navarrete, but its sense is the same.

162 Our text reads "grados del sol e norte;" Navarrete reads "grados de Sur y Norte."

163 Navarrete is very faulty in this section. He omits entirely the following: "& por sus gentes, o in otra qualqujer manera dentro de las otras ciento y veynte leguas, que quedan para cunplimjento de las trezientas & setenta leguas, en que ha de acabar la dicha raya que se ha de faser de polo a polo, como dicho es, en qualqujer parte de las dichas ciento & veyte *[sic]* leguas para los dichos polos, que sean alladas fasta el dicho dia, queden, & finquen para los dichos señores Rey & Reyna de Castilla, & de Aragon, etc., &." This omission quite obscures the sense.

164 This confirmation was given by Pope Julius II in a bull promulgated January 24, 1506. See *Alguns documentos*, pp. 142-143; and Bourne's *Essays in Historical Criticism*, p. 203.

165 Another dispatch of like tenor was issued in Madrid on May 7 of the same year.—*Navarrete*.

166 The original of this bull is in Torre do Tombo, Lisbon, bearing pressmark "Col. de Bullas, maço 29, n_o_. 6." It occupies pp. 276-279 of *Corpo diplomatico Portuguez*. The synopsis from which the above is translated is in *Alguns documentos*, p. 14., but the date as there given is wrong, "Quarto Decimo Kalendae Julii," being June 18 and not 17. See also Bourne, *Essays in Historical Criticism*, pp. 194, 195.

167 See Bourne, *ut supra*, p. 195, from which this synopsis is taken. The original of this bull exists in Torre do Tombo, its pressmark being "Coll. de Bullas, maço 7°, n°. 29." It occupies pp. 279-286 of *Corpo diplomatico Portuguez*, and is printed also in *Alguns documentus*, pp. 14-20.

168 This military order was founded (August 14, 1318) by the Portuguese king Dionisio; its knights served against the Moors, also in Africa and India. Pope Calixtus III invested its grand prior with the spiritual powers conferred on a bishop. In 1522, João III became grand-master of the order; and in 1551 this dignity passed to the crown *in perpetuo*. In 1789, this order had four hundred and thirty-four commanderies, and twenty-six villages and estates. It is now only a civil and honorary order.

169 See Bourne *ut supra*, p. 195. The original is in Torre do Tombo, bearing pressmark "Coll. de Bullas, maco 29, n°. 6. Inserta." This bull occupies pp. 286-296 of *Corpo diplomatico Portuguez*. It is printed also in *Alguns documentos*, pp. 47-55.

170 See *Corpo diplomatico Portuguez*, p. 296.

171 Cape Noon (Naon, Non, Nun) is situated near the south-west extremity of the coast of Morocco; Cape Bojador (Bogiador) projects into the Atlantic at a point two degrees thirty-eight minutes farther south than Noon.

172 See *Corpo diplomatico Portuguez*, p. 297, and *Alguns documentos*, p. 366.

173 One of the great military orders of Spain, named for its patron St. James, and founded to protect his shrine at Compostella from incursions by the Moors. It received papal sanction in 1175; in 1476 Ferdinand of Castile became its grand master; thus uniting the order to the crown of Spain.

174 The letter here mentioned (see Navarrete's *Col. de viages*, iv, p. 312) expresses Cárlos's regret that his negotiations with the Portuguese ambassadors regarding the ownership of the Malucos have been fruitless, and his desire that the difficulties should be amicably adjusted; he refers João to Zúñiga for full details.

175 Navarrete omits this section. It will be found in the Treaty of Tordesillas.

176 The Spanish monarch was at this time engaged in his quarrels with François I of France.

177 In another letter of the same date the Emperor complains to the King of Portugal that the latter's ambassadors have not been willing to abide by the treaty of Tordesillas in their conferences with the Castilian plenipotentiaries, "although our right to those regions discovered and taken possession of by our fleet is fully apparent from the treaties and compacts negotiated over the division of lands and the line of demarcation, and confirmed in the name of each one of us." Neither would they discuss the new propositions submitted to them—"although with some prejudice to our right;" nor would they themselves submit new propositions; consequently they are returning to Portugal without reaching any decision. The letter closes by saying that the Emperor is about to write about the whole affair to his representative, "Juan de Zúñiga, knight of the order of Santiago, residing there [at Lisbon] in our behalf;" and King João is earnestly requested to rest assured of the love and affection of the Spanish monarch.

178 This was an ancient office in the royal house of Castile.

179 Bartulo was an Italian jurisconsult, born (1313) at Sasso-Ferrato, in Umbria; he died at Perusa in 1356. He was entrusted

with several important political commissions and wrote upon various points of civil law; some of his works were used as text books in the most famous universities. He has been styled "the first and most thorough of the interpreters of law."

Baldo is evidently one of the two brothers Pietro and Angelo Baldo de Ubaldis, both eminent Italian jurisconsults. The former was born at Perusa, in 1324, and died at Pavia, April 28, 1406. He was a man of vast erudition, and held many important posts—his influence extending so far that Charles VI of France implored his aid at the Roman court for convening a general council. He was the author of a number of commentaries and other works. Angelo was born in 1328, and died in 1407; he was (at the same time with his brother) professor of civil law at Perusa, and wrote several commentaries and monographs.

180   Original in folio bound in parchment. It has forty-three good sheets.—Note by Muñoz. (Cited by Navarrete).

181   The matter in brackets in these proceedings is evidently notes made by Muñoz, although they may have been made by the Castilian secretary.

182   The number acting for Portugal was not greater than for Spain, as Gomara points out and whom Herrera copies, but the same on either side, only while Portugal had two attorneys, Spain had one attorney and one advocate.—*Navarrete.*

183   This date should be June 7, 1494. The Spanish letter of authorization was dated June 5.

184   Original in handwriting of Don Hernando Colon. (Navarrete, tomo iv, no. xxvii, pp. 343-355.

185   Of these navigators, Aloysius (Luigi) da Ca da Mosto made a voyage to Cape Verde and Senegal, in 1454-55; Antonio de Noly, to the Cape Verde Islands, in 1462; Pedro de Cintra (Italianized as Piero d'Sinzia), to Senegal, in 1462; Diego Cano, to the Congo River and inland, in 1484; Bartolomé Diaz discovered the Cape of Good Hope in 1486; and Vasco da Gama made several voyages to India, the first in 1497.

186   This is a Latin translation of *Paesi nouamente retronati* (Vicenza, 1507)—the earliest known collection of voyages. It is supposed to have been compiled by Alessandro Zorzi, a Venetian cosmographer (according to Bartlett); but Fracanzio di Montalboddo, according to Quaritch *(Catalogue* No. 362, 1885). Facsimiles of the titles of both books are given in Bartlett's *Bibliotheca Americana*, part i, p. 40.

187   This is the book called today "the first book of the Kings."

188   The original is in folio bound in parchment, with ninety-five good sheets.—Note by Muñoz (cited by Navarrete).

189   The original is "Ambrosio y Teodosio y Macrobio." The same error was made by Jaime Ferrer, who likewise gives these names as those of three distinct men instead of one, his true name being "Aurelius Theodosius Macrobius." See Dawson's *Lines of Demarcation*, 1899, p. 510.

190   Referring to the *Ymago Mundi* (1483?) of Pierre d'Ailly, archbishop of Cambray, and cardinal; regarding this book, see Bartlett's *Bibl. Americana*, part i, pp. 3-5.

191   This was the title conferred on Christopher Columbus by the Catholic sovereigns.

192   The individuals of the municipal governing body upon whom devolves the economic government of a city.—*Novisimo diccionario de la lengua castellana* (Paris and Mexico, 1899). See also *Diccionario enciclopedico hispano-americano* (Barcelona, 1887-1899), tomo xvii, pp. 302-303.

193   The Consejo de las Ordenes [Council of the Military Orders] was created by Charles V, from the separate councils of the various military orders. This council consisted of a president and six or eight knights, and both temporal and ecclesiastical powers were conferred upon it. Clement VI approved it, extending its jurisdiction to tithes, benefices, marriages, and other matters of ordinary authority, and both Paul III and Saint Pius V confirmed it. Two important tribunals were created, one called the Tribunal of the Churches, and the other the Apostolic Tribunal. The first was created by Charles V, and was under the charge of a Judge protector, and had charge of the repairs, building, and adornment of the churches of the military orders. The second was created by Philip II, in virtue of the bull of Gregory XIII, of October 20, 1584,—this bull having as its object the amicable adjustment of the disputes between the military orders and the prelates in regard to jurisdiction, tithes, etc. In 1714 the jurisdiction of the council was limited by Felipe IV, to the ecclesiastical and temporal affairs of their own institution. In 1836 the council was reorganized under the name of tribunal. The tribunal of the churches was suppressed, as were also the offices of comptroller and the remaining fiscal officials, and the funds

diverted into the national treasury. Jurisdiction in ecclesiastical matters was limited to the four military orders of Santiago, Calatrava, Alcántara, and Montesa. See *Dic.-encic. hisp-amer.,* tomo v, pp. 821, 822.

194   Casa de Contratación de las Indias (House of Commerce of the Indies). A tribunal, having as its object the investigation and determination of matters pertaining to the commerce and trade of the Indies. It consisted of a president and several executive officials,—both professional and unprofessional men—and a togated fiscal agent. It was formerly in Seville, but removed later to Cadiz.—*Dic. encic. hisp.-amer.,* iv, p. 844. The documents relating to the affairs of this house were kept formerly in a special archives, but are housed at present in the Archivo general de Indias in Seville.

195   The *corregidor* was the representative of the royal person, and combined both judicial and executive functions; in some large cities he was made president of the city council, with administrative functions—an office nearly equivalent to that of mayor in American cities.

196   See this document at p. 139, *ante.*

197   García de Loaisa, a noted Spanish prelate, was born at Talavera (Toledo) in 1479; at the age of sixteen, he entered the Dominican order, of which he became provincial for Spain (1518), and finally general of the order. He was greatly esteemed by the emperor Charles V, who chose Loasia as his confessor; and he soon afterward became bishop of Osma, and president of the Council of the Indies. Later, he was made a cardinal, and elevated to the archbishopric of Seville. He acted as Charles's representative at the court of Rome, and was, less than a year before his death, appointed general of the Inquisition; even in that short time one hundred and twenty persons were burned at the stake, and six hundred more punished in various ways. Loaisa died April 21, 1546.

198   The military order of Calatrava was formed to hold the town of that name against the Moors, and was organized in 1164; it was annexed to the Castilian crown during the reign of Cárlos I.

199   It is said that this fair at Medina del Campo is still held (in May and October of each year); and that money was lent by the crown to persons who desired loans—hence the allusion in the text.

200   Ordinarily the tithes in each diocese were divided into four equal parts—of which one was set aside for the bishop, and one for the chapter. Then the other two were divided into nine portions *(novenii)*, whereof one and one-half were for the *fabrica* of the church (the corporate body who administered its temporalities, consisting of the *cura* and churchwardens), four for the *parrocos* (parish priests) and lower clergy, one and one-half for the hospitals, and two for the King—all but this last being variable. See Baluffi's *America en tempo Spagnuola* (Ancona, 1844) ii, p. 41.—*Rev.* T. C. *Middleton*, O. S. A.

201   The documents published by Navarrete in full, or in copious extracts, are the most valuable; and they are usually such as are otherwise comparatively or wholly unknown. It is to be regretted that Navarrete has modernized the spelling, and otherwise "improved" the text; but the originals are presented in all essential features, and form a valuable collection of early documentary material.

202   An extract from Magalhães's first will (December 17, 1504) and the whole of his second (August 24, 1519) are given in English translation in Guillemard's *Life of Magellan*, London, 1890, appendix ii, pp. 316-326.

203   He therein petitions that the sum of twelve thousand five hundred maravedis, allowed him for his services, be paid to the convent of Vitoria at Triana.

204   Fernão de Magalhães was a native of Oporto, and of noble lineage. In early life he entered the Portuguese army, in which he rendered distinguished service; from 1505 until probably 1511 he was in India. Finding no opportunity for promotion in Portugal, he transferred his allegiance (1518) to the King of Castile, and promised the latter that he would discover a new route to Moluccas. Magalhães set out on this expedition September 20, 1519, with five ships, and discovered the strait which bears his name; he also discovered and explored partially the Philippine Archipelago. He was slain in a fight with the natives in the island of Matan, April 27, 1521.

205   Navarrete presents only an analysis of this letter.

206   An itemized account (condensed) of the expenses involved in the preparation and equipment of the fleet is given by Navarrete, no. xvii, pp. 162-182. An English translation is presented in Guillemard's *Life of Magellan*, appendix iv, pp. 329-336. From a

comparison of the two, it appears that the latter had access to the original documents at Seville. Few slight differences occur between them. The figures as given by Navarrete show several errors. The student will do well to examine both of these lists. No. xviii in Navarrete, pp. 182-188, shows the amounts and distribution of the food and other stores carried.

207   Navarrete says, *ut supra*, p. xiii, that the officials of the House of Trade were always hostile to Magallánes. The Portuguese machinations to cause the defeat and ruin of the expedition and the efforts put forth to induce Magallánes to return to his allegiance are well shown in two documents. The first is a letter written the Portuguese king by Alvaro da Costa, September 28, 1518. Navarrete, no. vi, pp. 123, 124, gives a Spanish extract made by Muñoz from the original in Portugal, and Guillemard, *ut supra*, pp. 114-116 (see also note, p. 116), gives in part an English translation. The second document is a letter written from Seville, July 18, 1519, by the Portuguese factor Sebastian Alvarez to the King of Portugal. Navarrete, no. xv, pp. 153-155, gives a Spanish extract made by Muñoz. The Portuguese of the entire letter is published in *Alguns Documentos*, pp. 431-435. Guillemard, *ut supra*, pp. 130-134, gives an English translation of its essential portions, which is borrowed, in part, by Butterworth in *Story of Magellan*, pp. 46-48, New York, 1899.

208   All these are synopses of the documents.

209   *Ibid.*

210   More than this number actually sailed; see Guillemard, *Life of Magellan*, p. 336.

211   The matter in brackets is evidently by Navarrete.

212   This document opens with a list of the various dignities of the King and Queen of Spain, which is omitted here, as being similar to that already given in the Treaty of Tordesillas.

213   Reference is here made to Juana, Cárlos I's mother, the daughter and nominally the successor of Isabella, and later of Ferdinand. Juana being inflicted with insanity from 1503 until her death in 1555, Ferdinand acted as regent until his death (1516), when Cardinal Ximenes succeeded him in that capacity, acting until Cárlos I attained his majority. (1518)—Juana still being queen of Castile and Aragon.

214   The original is defective here, and these readings are conjectural.

215   The title given formerly to the governor of a province.

216   The Portuguese transcriber was unable to decipher the original of the bracketed words. Navarrete, who prints these instructions to Magalhães and Falero, *(Col. de Viages*, tomo iv, pp. 116-121) reads this passage thus "quien se pase" and continues "é se asiente." *Alguns Documentos* reads "que . . ." and continues "& se entregue." The MS. in Torre do Tombo from which the Portuguese transcript was made read "q enpase," continuing as does the Portuguese version. It must be remembered that Navarrete took his copy from the original document (existing in Seville) of the agreement made with Magalhães and Falero, made March 22, 1518; this was included in the instructions given to Juan de Cartagena, the recipient of the present letter, and was doubtless copied from the original in Seville.

217   A metal found by Columbus in the Isla Española. It is composed of 18 parts gold, 6 of silver, and 8 of copper.—*Dic. de la Lengua Castellano*.

218   This must have been the Strait of Magellan.

219   The Spanish reads literally, "They gave him a blow on the head with a mallet."

220   The original is defective here, and this reading is only conjectural.

221   Juan Sebastian del Cano.—*Stevens*.

222   Pietro Martire d'Anghiera (commonly known as Peter Martyr) was an Italian priest and historian, who was born in 1455. At the age of thirty-two years he went to the Castilian court; at various times, he served in the army (during two campaigns), maintained a school for boys, was sent as an ambassador to other courts, and in many ways occupied a prominent place in the affairs of the Spanish Kingdom. He died in 1526. His most noted work was *De orbe nouo Decades* (Alcala, 1516); it had numerous editions, and was translated into several other languages. An English translation of the first three Decades was made by Richard Eden (London, 1555); this was reprinted in Arber's *First Three English Books on America* (Birmingham, 1885).

223   The name Bacallaos (according to early French writers a Basque appellation of the codfish) was also applied, by a natural extension, to the region afterward known as Canada.

According to Peter Martyr, the name Bacallaos was given to those lands by Sebastian Cabot, "because of the great multitudes of fishes found in the seas thereabout." See *Jesuit Relations* (Cleveland reissue), i, p. 308, and ii, p. 295.

224 Fifty-six degrees west of the Canaries would be about seventy-four degrees west of Greenwich—Magellan was some ten or twelve degrees out.—*Stevens.*

225 Among whom was Esteven Gomez; this ship was the "San Antonio."—*Steven's.*

226 The measure of length known as a mile varies greatly in different countries. The geographical or nautical mile (one-sixtieth of a degree of the equator, and equal to 1.153 English statute miles) is used by mariners of all nations. The *milha* of Portugal is equivalent to 1.2786 English miles; the Italian *miglio* varies from O.6214 to 1.3835 English miles; the *legua* (league) of Spain amounts to 4.2151 English miles.

227 San Pablo and Tiburones. Cf. Droysen and Andree's *Historischer Hand Atlas*, 1884, Karte 83; also Admiralty Chart, Sec. xv, 767.—*Stevens.*

228 Inarajan, now confined to the port on the southeast coast of Guajan, the southermost of the Ladrones.—*Stevens.*

229 Acacan,*i.e. Sosan*-jaya, the watering place at the west end of Rota Island, north of Guajan.—*Stevens.*

230 The Caylon of Magellan, now confined to the port on the southwest side of the island of Leyte, Philippines.—*Stevens.*

231 The Maasin of Coello, or Masin of Admiralty Chart, Sec. xiii, 943; at south end of island of Leyte, the Selani of text.—*Stevens.*

232 In the museum of the Colegio de Agustinos Filipinos at Valladolid, Spain, is a tablet bearing the following inscription (in English translation): "On the twenty-sixth of April, 1521, died on this spot, while fighting valiantly, Don Hernando Magallánes, general of the Spanish fleet, whose name alone is his greatest eulogy. Desiring that the memory of the place where so famous and fatal an event took place should not perish, and circumstances not permitting us at this time to erect a monument worthy of the heroic discoverer, this present inscription is religiously and humbly consecrated, as a memorial, by the parochial priest of the island, the reverend father Fray Benito Perez, on the twenty-ninth of February, 1843." This tablet is about three feet by one and one-half feet in size, and

is made of molave wood; the letters (capitals) are neatly carved in the wood—the work being done, in all probability, by some native under the priest's supervision. Attached to the tablet is a card, bearing the following inscription: "This inscription, cut in molave wood, was accidentally found by the very reverend father Fray Jorge Romanillos, the present parish priest of Opong, in the island of Mactang, where it stood beside a cross, before the erection of the monument. He sends it as a memento to the royal college of the Augustinian Fathers of the Filipinas, at Valladolid, in the year 1887."

233   Or Quipit, the port of this name on the northwest part of Mindanao, applied in error to the whole island.—*Stevens*.

234   Probably Yolo, certainly one of the Sulu islands.—*Stevens*.

235   *I.e.* Ternate, Moter, Tidore, Maru, Mutjan.—*Stevens*.

236   "They did not find Cattigara" is as true today as when Maximilian wrote in 1522. For various conflicting authorities upon its site *north* of the equator, cf. ante p.312, and McCrindle's *Ancient India*, 1885, p.10. Ptolemy however places it (Asia Tab. xi) nine degrees *south* of the equator. For a curious chapter upon this point see Manoel Godinho de Eredia's *Malacca*, edited by Janssen, Brussels, 1883. 4to, part 3. Why not Kota-Radja at the north end of Sumatra?—*Stevens*.

BIBLIOBAZAAR

The essential book market!

Did you know that you can get any of our titles in large print?

Did you know that we have an ever-growing collection of books in many languages?

**Order online:
www.bibliobazaar.com**

Find all of your favorite classic books!

Stay up to date with the latest government reports!

At BiblioBazaar, we aim to make knowledge more accessible by making thousands of titles available to you- *quickly and affordably*.

Contact us:
BiblioBazaar
PO Box 21206
Charleston, SC 29413

LaVergne, TN USA
17 March 2011
220596LV00001B/38/A